The First Arc of the Great Circle

How to Do 1001 Stupid Things
And Still Be Covered By Grace

A Life Cycle

By

Peter B. Cannon

[handwritten] Enjoy!

[handwritten] www.Firstarc.com

D1279583

© 2003 by Peter B. Cannon. All rights reserved.

No part of this book may be reproduced, stored in a retrieval system,
or transmitted by any means, electronic, mechanical, photocopying,
recording, or otherwise, without written permission from the author.

ISBN: 1-4107-0173-5 (e-book)
ISBN: 1-4107-0174-3 (Paperback)

Library of Congress Control Number: 2002096419

This book is printed on acid free paper.

Printed in the United States of America
Bloomington, IN

1stBooks – rev. 12/26/02

This is my story, this is my song.

I dedicate this to you.

Brushes with Fame

General Douglas MacArthur

Albert Einstein

Dr. Scofield

Emmet Kelly

Grace Kelly's Family

Bobby Thompson

Wannamaker Family

Walter Scott

Mennen Family

Kimberly-Kleenex

Pancho Gonzalez

Fred Waring

Guy Lombardo

Louis Armstrong

Eddie Condon

Dizzy Gillispe

Talbot Brothers "Bermuda Buggy Ride"

Oleg Cassini

Bill Cosby

Dustin Hoffman

Perry Como

Arthur Ashe

Don Rickles

Frank Sinatra

Dean Martin

Shirley McLain

Jack Benny

Danny Thomas

Peter Faulk

Robert Culp

Huntington Hartford

Jacqueline B. Kennedy

Arnie Palmer et al

Miss Sweden – Ingrid

Linda Eastman – McCartney

Chevy Chase

Frank Borman

Dr. Oppenheimer

Kathy Hartford

Jimmy Buffet

Sammy Davis

Chris Everette

John John Kennedy

Cassius Clay

Syrian Terrorist Gang

More I'm sure.

Table of Contents

Prologue

This is a story which could be partly yours because of the common realities that we all share. It is also very possible that our paths have crossed either in time or place, and each of us had a different experience there, but still shared a mutual awareness. Hopefully then, this is not just a story of one person traveling through life, but chapters of each of us, of where we have been and where we are going. Hopefully it will be an encouragement to all to be able to tell their story of their searching, which I would love to hear. Maybe this story of mine will awaken yours.

To give you some background, during the 20 years before the *First Arc of the Great Circle*, I was born just before the outbreak of World War II. My parents were at a New York Giant football game the day when stunned fans heard that the Japanese had bombed Pearl Harbor. They listened on the car radio on their way home to the grim details, as sparse as they were at the time.

The great day of my birth was on February 5th of the year of 1939. My dad was still working as a clerk with a small investment-banking firm called First Boston Corporation, or FBC. He worked hard to become a salesman of underwriting bond and stock offerings, and by the beginning of the *First Arc* he was a senior vice president. I lived in two homes in Plainfield, New Jersey. A small two story home during the war in which I had started a fire imitating the tanks my uncle was fighting in over in Africa by using matches for artillery shells. I just remember the sirens and firemen stomping past me to tear out the walls in my bedroom where I had been locked in due to sleepwalking into dog poop the night before. My parents didn't hear my calls for help from under my bed, but my brother did and awoke them when he found my door locked and smoke pouring out under it. I'm sure that is not all the trouble I caused.

Then soon after playing my drum around the entire block to celebrate the end of the war and my uncle's return, we moved to 1210 Evergreen Avenue, which I thought was one of the biggest homes in the world. Obviously I had not much experience in this field, but I was very happy here in this four floor white colonial house. We had the tree swing and the hutch of rabbits out back by the tool shed and garage.

Below us was my school and up Evergreen Avenue was a steep hill on which we sledded when there was no school. Every weekday my mom would take my dad to the train station, kiss him goodbye and watch him get on the Jersey Central, as its steam engine would tug it away toward New York. Eventually the engines became diesels and there was air conditioning or heat which made the year round commuting easier. A few times dad would take me to work and I found that after the train ride to Jersey City, the ferry floated us across the Hudson where we walked to Wall Street.

On one such occasion there was a ticker tape parade for one of the world's heroes, General MacArthur. I had been to Princeton football games where one would throw long streamers of paper down toward the field. Well, while sitting on a twelfth story window ledge I was given a roll of ticker tape. How was one to know that you were supposed to punch out the middle plug in the spool and let the paper stream out from the center of the two-pound roll? I had always just held the outer end of the paper streamer and throw the roll. Imagine my surprise when it didn't stream out and I was just looking at a two inch piece of paper in my hand. The other two pounds of paper missile was plummeting down toward my hero the General. After it landed I don't know where, he looked up and waved at me and I started breathing again.

My brother Bill was four years older and I looked up to him when he was around, but he went away to school in his sixth grade. Why I do not know, but he was there struggling to stay in Lawrenceville Prep School, the launching pad for Princeton University. Our dad never went to college, and so it was a very high priority for us to go. Neither of us were what you would call students, let alone good students. I really have no idea what he learned from seven years of private school and the night school at Rutgers. But he, like my dad, started at the bottom at J&J in the mailroom. Eventually he too worked into sales like dad and then got married like dad.

I went to Evergreen School and then two years at Plainfield High School. The public school scene in the 50's was getting tense what with race relations and just the general hood mentality. A guy that later married my cousin was always in the fight mode. But one time he tried acting tough around the police at the high school football field. The cops took him into the ticket house and smacked him around until he settled down. I saw it all through the window. His story is that he became one of New Jersey's best State Policemen. I know that day had a major part in his life, because otherwise he was on his way to jail within a few years. Discipline brings respect for others and oneself.

I had a great fear while I was there at high school. Being about the smallest in the freshman class, I was daily teased by a group of kids and often cornered on the back stairs when I tried to avoid them. I started lifting weights, jumping rope and even boxing in spite of my braces. I also studied a book on Judo and practiced on my brother whenever he was around. It was at the football field when I was alone after a late practice and heading home when tough guy and his friends cut me off. They wanted a trophy and I was going to be it this day. I told them I would take them on but it had to be one at a time and got them to agree. And then pointing at the leader, mister tough guy, we went at it. I figured if I could take him while I was still fresh, the other punks would chicken out. I had him down and helpless in less that thirty seconds and thankfully I guessed right, none of the others would step forward and they never bothered me again. They were black, which never made any difference in grade school, but all of a sudden I was awoken to a new reality.

One of the highlights was going to the Princeton football games with my family. On one occasion my dad pointed out Professor Einstein. I didn't know too much about him except he was one of the other heroes that helped win the World War II. Needless to say, my meeting him as he shuffled across the campus has not left my fond memories.

I later left high school and did my sophomore year over at a prep school called Governor Dummer. No, I thought that also, but that was actually a man's name, not our objective. This was a very New England based school where everyone was out to go to Princeton or

Yale. The studies were light years past me, and I had a really tough time with it.

And hockey was not really my sport, but it was big up there. For warm ups we would have to shovel the snow off the ice. Not the best of conditions. Then in a game, a defenseman about 100 pounds thicker than I checked me into the waist high boards and I spun like a top along the top rail. I think I dislocated something in my back forever. The nurse taped me up across the lower back. This hindered the possibility of doing a daily function. After three days I went back to the nurse to confess my embarrassing plight. She asked me if I had a spoon in my room. Panicked, I said "Like Hell I will!" and went painfully running out of the dispensary. She finally caught up with me to give me medicine to try and aleve the problem, and a spoon to take it with. Talk about a rush to judgment. I was relieved.

My first year here was not really fun, but I do enjoy looking back on Newburyport, Massachusetts for what it is: A nice place to visit. On a recent trip to Prince Edward Island I took my family to see the campus. I didn't realize it but it is the oldest surviving private school in the country, started in the late 1600's. Very colonial, and co-ed now too.

The next year my folks decided to send me even further away and further north. They must have thought I loved ice and snow and −50 degree weather. It was a 14 hour train ride north from New York City to Lake Placid. One of my hometown friends, Cotty, somehow also got into Northwood School as well. Both of us were survivors. I actually enjoyed this school more than I thought. We not only had free use of the Lake Placid Club, but also great Olympic facilities such as hockey inside the Olympic arena, skiing, bob sled run and some of the guys used their jumps.

Our hockey team usually won the Nationals in Madison Square Garden and put out some really great players to the colleges of Dartmouth, Cornell and Colgate. One classmate, Lew, even went to Princeton. He was our Valedictorian. And was he surprised when I was called up after him at graduation as Cum Laude. So was I, but after getting caught with beer on my breath one night, I was restricted for the last six months to the school building and that left me nothing to do but study. So it was really an accident that I was cum laude.

Because my grades were so good I decided to see if I could get into Yale. I certainly didn't want to go there except for an interview during the Princeton – Yale football weekend. Lew and I were both awarded appointments for an interview on that weekend. The fifth bus we rode to the New Haven Campus had all the "Bull Dogs" dates on it and we were the only guys. That was fun. I stayed with Jerry Henry, a friend's brother and life long friend of my brother's. Actually 'half' of Plainfield was staying in his dorm room and it was a non-stop party. My appointment was early Saturday morning and I didn't want to go, but I owed them the decency of an appearance. When the dean of admissions asked me why I wanted to go to Yale, I told him I didn't, and saved him a lot of time by returning to the party. Everyone remembers that weekend, but nobody remembers who won.

I was also accepted at the University of Hawaii, where I had heard you went to classes in bare feet if so desired. Now that was my kind of studying. But my father had other plans and that was to send me where his best friend had gone, Lehigh University in Bethlehem, Pennsylvania. This friend of dad's was now quite wealthy and his son Pete was also one of my best friends. So that is where Pete and I went to further our education. Pete was a better student while I was easily distracted. My main interest was not in the field of academics. But that is the rest of the story.

I realized that there was more to life than what I had experienced. I never felt a satisfaction from anything so far, and I didn't know where I would find it. That was my quest, and this is my story and this is my song. I welcome you all to come along. But I warn you not to go half way, or you will be missing what I have to say!

Ask yourself, "What would you be doing right now if it didn't matter what people thought of you? Take one action today to move toward your goal, your dream. Don't worry about whether it is the right door for you to open. Just do something! If you have a righteous calling, answer it!

And now, on to the ***First Arc of the Great Circle***

Movin' On Down

I remember the expression on Dad's face as I backed my almost new `54 Ford out of the driveway to head for Florida. Mom had her face hidden in a Kleenex of sorts, as she tended to cry at most events in life. This occasion was to her probably the most excruciating of her 50+ years, because her baby was leaving the nest. But the expression of joy and happiness on Dad's face was really what I wanted to see. I wasn't leaving home for good. (I mean, I'd see them again, so why cry? We are so optimistic at this wonderful age, or was it that we just think we are indestructible?) Of course my survival was completely dependent on my own cunning and strength. I never gave any thought that I may have been watched over by a Guardian Angel. Wasn't that the some one who put money under your pillow when you lost another tooth? These and many other enlightening thoughts scrolled through my mind as I traveled down the road to Florida, ah yes, free to *BE* Florida.

This trip had been on my mind for a few years. But now, since I was 21 years old, I knew I could legally do just about anything I wanted that was not against the law. In fact, the main reason to go to Florida was that my best boyhood friend had moved there and was living the good life in Fort Lauderdale. So I was going there to buy him a beer. Everyone needs a reason to go somewhere, don't they? That was mine.

The first 'Port of Call' cruising south became the University of Virginia where another boyhood buddy, Cotty Barlow, was at College. He was expecting me and it was quite a reunion. We had been through a lot in life already, but the future wasn't finished with us. Our history included going to the same prep school at Northwood in Lake Placid, New York and spending every New Years Eve together at one of our 'mega' parties. But this visit was special.

Besides giving me the Jeffersonian tour and letting me see my first polo game, Cotty showed me his prowess with women by picking up a girl using sign language across a smoky room. She was a veritable beauty too. Unfortunately he passed out before he could put

1

a notch in his belt. The next morning at the crack of noon I barely made it to my shiny forest green car, and headed south before I got a full education.

The thirst was building up in me by the time I reached the Carolinas. It was nighttime and the only roads south meandered through moonlit swamps, which almost made me wish I did have a guardian angel, or a gun or something. Shadows seemed to dart behind trees and they were living in these swamps and out to 'git' me.

Now I knew it was my imagination, but after four or five hours of nothing but darkness, the vision of people in the middle of the road put my hair on end. Suddenly I could see they wanted me to stop, as they were not getting out of the road. Did they need help? I slowed some, but then I saw the faces of a gang with clubs. I put on my bright lights, lay on the horn and stomped my trusty Ford into passing gear. I saw the faces of killers turn to horror as they tried to get out of the road. I hoped I didn't hit anyone, but it was them or me at that moment. Their clubs were swung at the car and black faces tried to look into the windshield as chains were crashing and maybe bodies thumping just as I again saw nothing but the blackness of night in the swamp. It seemed even darker though, but I thought it was because my heart was beating up my chest trying to explode. I drove until almost dawn when I came to a small city with a motel where I could crash.

At the crack of noon again, on my way back from eating eggs and grits (my first experience with artificial potatoes), I saw the scratches on the sides of my car. Then I saw why the night had become darker than coal. The right headlight was busted. Now I was sure it hadn't been my imagination the previous night, rather a living nightmare. While almost losing my grits, I jumped into my car and headed for warm, sunny Florida, swearing never to return to the swamps of Carolina.[1]

I couldn't get over the feeling of warmth, and the humidity, causing plants to yield their original fragrances. Florida was a haven from northern winter, where cold was the way of life that never let a body stop shivering. Have you ever gotten excited over the smell of

---

[1] The Author of Life has since had the writer of this journey living in North Carolina for over twenty years as of this writing. Moral: One shouldn't swear.

ice? I never knew the difference. This was my age of discovery, my time of unearthing the wonders of life. Remember that? Ah, what joys those days of innocence beheld. If you have ever taken a midwinter excursion to Puerto Rico or points south during the annual ice age, then you know of what I wondered.

My destination was unknown unless I could find my friend Cliff. He and I had grown up spending our summers together since youth in Mantoloking, NJ. We had speedboats, sail boats, and girl friends that we have not seen since. We were survivors of the Last Great Polio Terror, which caused many of our friends to leave this earth. And there were many others who didn't stay in bed, even after feeling better, who became crippled for life. All this happened as a result of going to a movie, or some other innocent act, unlike some present-day killer diseases. We made it through this nightmare unscathed to live and see the new Saulk vaccine change life for us drastically, for which humankind should be eternally thankful.

Let me take this opportunity to say that as often the "I" pronoun is used in my story, it is not because of my preoccupation with myself, but rather as an example of the universality of us all. You are the "I" maybe not in every situation, but maybe in some of your realities or fantasies. Your ability to relate makes this trip through life yours as much as mine. So I welcome you, my traversing friend, and warn you, the journey is not all sugar and cream, or wine and roses, but certainly they will be encountered in abundance. I expect you may at times envy me or hate me or love me, but it is not about you or me. It is about Grace, which I could not explain at the time, but only recognize through the blessing of hindsight.

I had imagined that Cliff would be living the life of the rich and famous when I found him at his family home. He always had everything I was running away from in order to get to the basics of life. But he didn't let it affect him, and that we had in common also. His next-door neighbor had a name familiar to all, the young Kimberley of Kleenex fame and fortune, which liked his women from the prime cut department. I personally had never seen such beautiful women be so affectionate in such a mature manner, and on such a

3

luxury yacht. Though my father knew more Board of Directors than I knew people, this guy was my first experience of living adjacent to one of them. Although in Mantoloking, New Jersey, Cliff and I had neighbors between us from the list of *Who's Who in the World*. There was Mr. Scott who invented paper towels, Mr. Mennen who kept under arms dry, the Wanemakers, the head of J & J International, and General Johnson himself, just to name a few.

No one had more $$ than Cliff's dad, at least in my mind. His big Rolls Royce, Cadillac convertible and fat cigars reeked of wealth. He made his money originally during prohibition by pulling a truck up to the speakeasy and proclaiming he was with the Federal Alcohol Commission and that this was a raid! He coerced them into loading up his truck with almost but not all their booze so they'd still be in business to raid again. Then he'd take the booze and sell it to a speakeasy in another town where he was known as a very reliable supplier. He also donated generously to both Republican and Democratic Parties, for his own sort of politics. This was the background Clifford had to grow from, and he did it admirably, as hindsight now proves.

But here I was, headed for a grand time of scuba diving, cruising and buying my friend a beer. When I arrived at their family winter home in Pompano Beach I was royally welcomed to stay, but Clifford had joined the Navy and was in UDT Training in San Diego, on the other side of the world! For so it seemed California certainly must be. His gracious parents put up with me for two weeks while I found a job parking cars at an extravagant beach hotel/restaurant. I made more than I ever had as a grocery store bagger or even as a management trainee with a prestigious Wall Street firm. Within two weeks I even exceeded my life's earnings selling those soft shell crabs every summer of my youth. All of a sudden California did not seem an impossible journey. Route 66 was the *numero uno* TV show at the time and started me dreaming. I found a map of the country and eyeballed it every night until I pictured myself heading west to buy my buddy Clifford a beer.

Movin' On Out

A 1954 Ford was made to go out west, and I was meant to go with it. What a great duo we made as we left the beauty of Southern Florida for points unknown. We became the closest travelers, totally dependent on one another, as if life depended on it. It was nice to be so important for a change instead of just a kid. And that was my name for her, *Kid*. This made her kind of a peer, but I was the elder, and therefore had some sort of precedence.

In order to leave Florida, we headed north. I saw on the map in my mind's eye that we had to take a left to head out there, to get out West that is. It was in Tallahassee when my eyes were getting tired, that my body was saying "Let me stop and rest!" Wow, Tallahassee! The Capitol of the alligator state! And there was the Police Headquarters. Maybe they could tell me where I can find a safe place to lie down for a while and rest my weary body.

The cops here were very hospitable. They even let me use a jail cell to lie down in for a while rather than have to pay for a room somewhere, or worse yet, have an accident by falling asleep on the road. It was a brand new city hall and police station, with quite comfortable cells. The Sergeant showed me the open cell and said I could use it if I wanted to rest for a few hours. I said "Sure!" and went into a deep snooze mode.

I guess it was about three hours later, around 7pm, when I awoke and found to my shear panic that my cell door was locked. No one was around except a creep in cell # 6. He was no help, as he didn't speak *inglés*. I hollered to "Let me out!" But not a mouse was stirring. I screamed and rattled the bars with a metal cup. Nothing. Finally after some foul thoughts and equally foul language were expressed, a different cop came in and said that if I didn't shut up I'd be staying in there two more weeks. Freak out! I stuttered and stammered some foolishness, and then he started laughing and the cell door opened automatically. Out I strode, not too confidently. The cop then took me to the Chief's office where all was played back on tape much to my embarrassment and their great amusement. After they got me laughing too, they told me this was a dry town. But they also told me where I could get a nice dinner and beer and even fixed me up with a girl from the local state teachers college. What a night! It gave me a whole new respect for the men in blue.

To me Texas was a distant country yet to be traversed. I don't think I really knew anything about our great Country other than what I saw on TV, which was mostly Westerns, Wrestling, and test patterns by this time. Oh yes, there was also boxing by Gillette, and the Texaco Amateur Hour, but none of them, let alone school, prepared me for what I was about to learn.

All of a sudden, I was not only out of Florida, which seemed forever, but I was crossing a whole new world of swamps and approaching NEW ORLEANS! Wow! I'd even heard of that, and Mardi Gras, and all that wild stuff. Maybe if I spent a night here I could find what ever I'm looking for. And if not, well I'd just keep on heading for San Diego to see my friend Clifford and buy him that beer.

I had heard that the City was a dangerous place for a single guy to stay in, so I found a decent motel outside of town. The literature in the room told of a bus tour that would take in three or four jazz clubs and a French restaurant for $12. That was a lot but I sprang for a big night on the town. It was incredible how 37 people on a bus could be so different. But all I cared about was my night. So at each club I distanced myself from the tour so as to be 'cool.' At Pee Wee Hunt's, a famous jazz club, I was at the bar having a hurricane when the bus driver came over and slammed his flat hand over the top of my glass, and with a razor sharpness to his tone, told the bartender to serve me a straight drink and to never try that again to his tours. Well blow me down if I hadn't been served a "mickie". I would have been taken outside and rolled for everything on me, and maybe found dead by some alley bum. They must have thought by my clothes I was Mr. Rich tourist, and they would have wasted me when they found $7 in my wallet. The driver had a son my age and looked after me pretty well that night. Or could he be, I wondered then, a guardian angel?

Later that night at the *My Oh My Club* I was entertained by some of the biggest women I had ever seen. They could have made up the sexiest NFL team ever. The bus driver was the one who opened my eyes to this bizarre world when he told me the blonde one making eyes with me was a man, a guy in drag. They all were guys. I don't think I said 'my oh my.' I said "Get me the h--- out of here!" and made a scramble for the door.

Next stop was the Jazz Club on Bourbon Street. It was so cool, because this was the birthplace of the blues, and of jazz. I used to sneak into New York City when I was 15 and hit Basin Street and Eddie Condon's and see Satchmo and Dizzy Gillespie and Ella Fitzgerald and so many greats. But this was the ultimate, so when the band started playing *When the Saints*…I was right there with them as we all marched out of the club and through the streets of New Orleans singing *Oh When the Saints Go Marching In*. Oh how I loved to be in that number! Unforgettable, even with enough Hurricanes in me to fuel a torch. I slept well that night. Before being dropped off at the last motel, the bus driver told me his family story and how and why he had looked after me like a son. I appreciate that to this day. The next morning I was feeling rough, but I had to move on. I had spent a week's budget in one night, and I knew I'd have to make it up soon.

It wouldn't be long before the credit card that my Dad had loaned me to get to Florida would be sending bills to my home indicating that I was taking the long route home. But I figured that if anything ever happened to me, at least they would have a paper trail of my travels. It was an Esso card so it was good at most any station that was part of Standard Oil before the breakup by the anti trust bust. I had taken a road out of New Orleans that was back country and bayou bound. It went to nowhere, down dead ends of crayfish lane and jambalaya trail. This was special country, but a place I didn't belong. The smell of water, fish and swamp was haunting, as were the people who seemed to just be a part of the scene. I became lost and soon learned that not everyone in this country speaks the same language. This is hard to realize now in the days of TV, Bojangles and Cajun Rock. But back then, this was the Discovery Channel first hand, and I loved it!

My dark green '54 Ford blended in, not too subtly, with the horses and rowboats. But I found that a smile is universal and blends in anywhere. Well, almost anywhere. So I smiled and said Esso, because my "Green Hornet" was about to choke dry and I hadn't seen a gas station since I first smelled Gumbo. This new language barrier was just what I didn't need, but if I couldn't understand them, then they couldn't understand me. So I began speaking in my own dialect and jabbered, smiled, and flashed my Esso card. They nodded, shrugged and pointed, down another dead end. But there behind a shed was an old gas pump with a sign saying pay down "dere". So I pumped and am still looking for *"down dere"*. It was time to move on. No paper trail here!

This area was full of people living a lifestyle that I could only imagine. I would have loved to stay on somehow and become a part of it, but I felt pressed to buy my friend Clifford that beer, wherever he was. So on I continued to whatever and wherever, which soon became the huge State of Texas. Somewhere about half way across the country-sized state, I had to sleep for a few hours, which I had learned to do pretty comfortably in my car. So the "Kid" and I rested. When I awoke dawn was arising and close by were some cowpokes near some sheds. For some reason I got out of my car to stretch and meandered over to see what was happening. They nodded and waved, and I was offered coffee and they were joking about me riding herd. I had never herded anything, but I said "I done some riding" and could use some money for my trip. They hired me on right there and I was so excited to suddenly be doing something I had only seen on television in westerns!

So we wrangled cattle, all day. I have never been so sore in my life. Every part of my body was screaming at me to stop. Finally, as the sun set in the west, this little doggie crawled into his Ford and fell asleep, with the promise to do more of the same tomorrow. Well, all I remember was that as I went to sleep, the cattle were a mooing. But when I arose with the sun, all was silent. very silent. It hit me like a brick! All those four-legged critters had been turned into steaks as I slept! This was too much for a city boy, and feeling sick in the gut I didn't even go for my pay. It was all I could do to just move on.

I drove forever, planning to stop for nothing. Texas had to be bigger than most countries. It is true; this is where the deer and the antelope play. They were ready to jump out in front of Kid at any time. But by the time I got to San Antonio I was ready for some R&R. I had remembered that a salesman (whom I met at my brother's company meeting in Hollywood, Florida) lived in San Antonio and had said to look him up if I ever got near Texas. He had worked with J&J, (the band aid people) so I just gave him a call. And true to the Southern Hospitality I had anticipated, he said to come on over and spend a few nights with his family. This I did as I saw another way of life with my own eyes. We had cookouts, went horseback riding and watched tornados dance across the desert. We visited the Alamo and saw where Custer saw all those Indians. It was great and much appreciated, as I needed the rest after my ordeal the night before at my "Home Home on the Range."

I left their home for the unknown at dusk. I thought I'd cross some desert country at night and pull into Arizona somewhere the following day. If you ever need a spooky ride, one of the best is crossing the desert at night, alone. It is amazing what the naked eye perceives as truth out there. It's enough to put the pedal to the metal, which I did. About sunrise I came upon a small unidentifiable town with the cutest diner open for breakfast. I was starving! Inside there were two of the cutest waitresses just waiting for someone to walk into their web. I sat at the middle of their lair, at the counter. "Are you staying here or just passing through?" they cooed. Being as how I thought only of life, I said, "Just passing through." "Oh," one said, "Nobody that's anybody ever stays on here." Well, that's the first time anyone thought I was a somebody. That almost convinced me to make this fantasy town my new home. But, after I satisfied my stomach's desire, the urge to get to California continued to drive me on. So, fill em up and move em out! Whew!

Tuscan! I'd heard of it, but like every place else I had bumped into heading west, it was another unknown surprise. There was a road I came upon which sounded like one I would enjoy exploring: *Whiskey Speedway*. After sizing it up and down, the next need was a motel room. This I needed some help with. Stopping at a bar lounge I saw another New Jersey license plate. Two guys coming out were getting into that car next to mine, so I said something like, "Good to see another Jerseyite." Whoa, the guy freaked and started swearing and coming after me to kick the jersey out of me. His buddy kept trying to talk him out of it while I managed to keep out of range, until the buddy won. He was able to get him into that car, telling him I didn't mean anything. I waited till they had left before going inside. There I had a very cold one while looking one eye out the window for the return of "Jersey". Now, I thought, I remembered why I had left home, and promised I might never return. There had been many other incidents of my youth there in Plainfield, New Jersey when I had been jumped, mugged or stalked.

This reminded me that a friend from Plainfield had moved to Arizona somewhere. I killed some time by looking up his name in the local phone book and there it was. That was too big a coincidence for it to be anyone else. I called and found from his wife that he was a gun curator at the museum next to the University. Wow! He had always been interested in US history and majored in it at Princeton University. And here we meet again. Peter and Lois Chamberlain have raised a beautiful family there in the wonders of the desert, riding and camping up in the mountains in their free time. If I sound envious, I'm not. Time to move on after finding Whiskey Speedway was a bunch of strip joints and bars, which I didn't need after the afternoons adventures. Sorry Tuscan. I didn't give you the chance you surely think you deserve. But California calls. There's gold under those suds! Gotta have a Bud with my friend.

On the way out of town, I saw signs to a Country Club where a tennis tournament was scheduled. As I passed by the area I decided to check it out. Tennis was one of my favorite sports in school. As Captain of our team in Lake Placid, I was even ball boy for some of the greats of the 50's including Poncho Gonzales. I remember him smashing a ball at my head because I couldn't get his first serve out of the net where it was stuck. What a temper he had! But imagine my astonishment when I came upon the American Davis Cup Team here in Tucson for a practice session before taking on Mexico, and seeing a Negro on the court. I figured he had a temper maybe worse than Poncho. I watched and waited as this young cool dude, Arthur Ashe, hit every shot just right. He made a bet with his teammate for a beer.

After he won they found out he doesn't drink beer. I met him and most of the team. Their player coach was Tony Trabert who was very polite, but rather protective of his team. Then they found out I had crashed their club and gave me the cool shoulder, so off I went down the desert road ready to kick a scorpion in the butt. I couldn't believe what I had done. For me this was really ballsy.

You had to realize how insecure I was while I was at this point in my life. Here I was, 21 years old, all alone and coming from a rather protective family and school life. I knew the facts of life, but was very nervous about them. I felt I needed a couple drinks to let down some kind of barriers that inhibited me from being myself. A popper (beer) or two seemed to be able to take my focus off myself and onto the other person, which always makes for better conversation. And for a while that's what happened with those national heroes of tennis. Then when I mentioned that I had been Captain of our varsity tennis team, I got real insecure as the focus came on me instead of them. But at least I had talked with them, and told them how I had met them in Lake Placid, New York as a ball boy. They remembered because its not everywhere you play tennis on ice. Yep, they had stretched a canvas tennis court tarp over our ice hockey arena and played hard court tennis. No wonder Poncho was out of sorts up there.

All this and more flashed through my minds eye as I drove through the spectacular desert of the great southwest. There I was, just schussing this narrow winding blacktop road, meandering through sand for no apparent reason except to have a beer in San Diego. But like life, the winds came a blowing, and suddenly the road disappeared in a sand storm. It was like a whiteout while skiing when everything looks the same, or driving in a very dense fog and navigating out the driver's side window on the yellow line. What a helpless feeling it was, but again, my hindsight showed me how our guardian angels can get us from here to the impossible "there". I had a feeling that if I stopped and waited out the storm, I would just be another sand dune in the desert forever. Fortunately, the wind was behind me, or I think Kiddo would have needed a new paint job or to travel naked from then on. So onward Kid and I pushed until we'd made it to the other side. To my surprise the road started to lift out of the sand and Kid was traveling upwards. Was she in a launch mode or were there mountains lifting us out of a death-by-sand valley? The last time I looked at a map was in Florida, so everything had been a surprise when I arrived somewhere. But this was the biggest surprise so far because I was just about to yield myself to a sandy grave, not part of my original dream at all! And now I was being lifted upward out of the storm and soaring into the sun. Up up and away! And then from a mountain peak it seemed the sun was setting out over the invisible ocean. Could it be I smelled a beer down below in San Diego? "Yahoo!" I screamed to Kid. We had made it! I spent this beautiful night wrapped up on the hood of my `54 Ford under the stars. I felt that maybe Jimmy Dean must still be alive!

California Dreamer

It was as exciting as the Gold Rush of '49, only the gold was going to have a bubbly white head as it raced to quench my thirst. But first I needed to find my buddy Cliff. Looked like Navy ships over there on the harbor. I head Kid in that direction and we weave through guards and buildings until I get to someone who is able to tell me that Clifford is on a training mission in the arctic and will be here on leave in two weeks. On leave means he can leave I hope. So I ensconced myself in some fancy digs at the YMCA and got me a high paying job as a movie usher at a scuzzy theater not too far away. So for two weeks I am surviving for "the moment".

One day before work I was wandering down sailor alley to get a color photo I had made for my Mom, and as I passed the tattoo parlors and a sleazy bar, who do I see walking directly toward me but Clifford. Or is it a mirage? Two guys scream and run and hug and laugh! Maybe we could have gotten arrested in those days for such an outburst. But we didn't care what others thought. He exclaimed, "What are you doing here? Whatever you tell me I won't believe it! This is incredible!" I told him I had driven all the way out here to buy him a beer, and he said he was just given leave and was looking to get a beer! So right there we just walked into scuzzy bar and had us an unforgettable suds. Or two. Finally he said, "Lets go to Vegas for the weekend." I said, "Where's that?" "We'll find it" he assured me, and off we went to see the Wizard of Oz.

We left Kid behind and took Clifford's older car and headed for the desert. On the long ride we got to catch up on the several years we had not seen each other since growing up together every summer from 1949 thru about 1958. We had been boat racing, girl watching, bar hopping, beach combing and doing very well at each for several years. But then as life would have it we got separate interests, our fathers interests to be exact. That included college for me and a girl for Cliff. But when his relationship didn't work out he decided to join the Navy rather than put up with his very domineering father.

He told me about his last trip as a UDT seaman. Frogman as some would have it. How one stormy night they had awakened him to take an acetylene torch overboard to cut loose the cable of a depth charge, which had wound around the ship's propeller shaft. While the ship was tossing in the high seas, Cliff had to burn the cable loose before the depth charge hit the hull of the boat and sent everyone to the deep dark yonder. If it were just a story it would have been awesome, but this is the way Clifford's life had always been. Never dull.

With all the excitement of catching up, we almost didn't notice the big white line across the desert road in the middle of nowhere. But as we whizzed over it at 100 mph, we hoped it was the first line. And so it was, as we saw a few miles further another line and a posse of police with dozens of cars pulled over. Fortunately we had slowed down to look up and there was the spotter plane, timing people from white line to white line. I guess if you made the three-mile distance in less than two minutes, they had ya. We had stopped and relieved ourselves and continued our pace, whizzing by the crowd of no-gooders.

It wasn't too long before the desert deposited us in the middle of a mirage, maybe a paradise. There were a gad zillion lights burning the night sky white as 30-foot cowboys beckoned travelers into the casino hotels along a strip of hotels like I've never seen. What the blazes was all this!

Well, of course, you all know now. But at that time the Strip had only been a paved road for a few years. The lighted way had been a dirt road until just recently. But to Cliff and I everything was a total surprise. We decided to check into a non-classy motel so as to save our big bankroll for the casinos. I think our joint bankroll was almost, well two to three hundred buckaroos. We had to do some heavy acting, so as not to be thrown out of town as beggars. A tourist in Vegas has to carry a few grand or he is taking up space that the mob can use better by getting rid of the trash.

We, therefore, put on our best duds, a coat and tie type of preppy look, and sauntered into the casino of the Tropicana. Whoa, this was it, the living end, and the ultimate scene! There's money and booze and women everywhere. Cliff eyeballs it all and comes up with a plan. We were sure we were the first to come up with this system in Vegas. We saw that gamblers were getting their drinks free from these gorgeous babes with almost nothing on those bodies that had been gifted in puberty. But we decided over in a corner huddle that we had blown our cover here in the Tropicana.

We decided to go downtown where there were more casual casinos. We had heard of the Golden Nugget, and found it right on the corner of the Strip and some main street. We strutted through the 'air curtain' to the inside where we were now cool. Cliff went right up to a dice table and put down a dollar on the *Pass line* as per the plan. I acted like I never knew him and went to the other end of the busy table and put a dollar on the *Don't Pass line* and immediately ordered an adult beverage from a nearby "adulteress". He had ten dollars, and I had ten. Our system was to drink as much as we could until either he had won my ten or I had won his stash. It was working so well that I had even gotten the name of my adult waitress, who had to be a perfect 36. She even brought me a free pack of cigarettes when I ran out with my third or fourth complementary drink. This was heaven. I could handle this forever.

But the mob had had just about enough of our game. We noticed some agitation amongst the heavyweights, and picked up our chips. I gave Cliff his three chips back so we had our ten chips again and wandered to another pasture so as to keep our system pure. As we drift into the Fremont Hotel we decided to up our bets to five chips at a time and play with $50 bucks each. That way we look like "big" spenders from the east and get a little more respect. I see Cliff head for a craps table and I head for the other end of it. He places his bet, as do I. Quickly he is up $30 and I'm up another drink and down $30. No sweat. The system works! The croupier's cries of "Coming out," are familiar now. The women are looking even better. But how come they took Cliff's bet up and didn't pay me? Then it happened again. And again. Whoa, they've got our $15! We pick up our bankroll and start our saunter again as we lick our wounds. Cliff decided to try some actual gambling, and won $200! We're in fat city again!

Hunger sets in and we see "All you can Eat" at the Silver Slipper for $.99. We gorged ourselves on roast beef and all the fixings. Then we had breakfast with all the fixings before our 99 cents ran out. The sun was just rising and so were we. Out to the pool we headed, at the Desert Inn. And the showgirls were just arriving for a dip before they go home and sleep all day. And these two guys were ready for some of the same. And when we woke up around the pool, we were surrounded by ugly Americans, also known as tourists. So off we went to shower and change into something a little less outstanding than last night's outfits.

This was our last day before we'd have to leave to get Cliff back on ship by 0600 hours. Otherwise AWOL would be his end of a career in the US Navy. Now, that didn't seem such a bad choice at the time. Las Vegas was something we could handle a lot easier than anything else we had seen out there. But we didn't want to purchase the 'good life' in exchange for a stockade. So in order to be civil, after partying all day and night again, we started driving out the Strip for the desert crossing back to San Diego. But Clifford's car had other ideas and dropped its transmission right on the stroke of midnight. It was then that we realized what a 24-hour town means. Even the Auto transmission shop was open, towed us in, fixed the problem, and we were on our way to the sailing ships departure with just enough time to make it.

If we had been late, Cliff would have spent some time in the brig, a sailor's jail, for being AWOL. Not a pleasant prospect, so we broke all speed records. It reminded us of when we used to slip into New York City in his Thunderbird and drive over 100 mph on our way home to make our parent's curfew. One time we ended up approaching Washington D.C., having missed our Jersey shore exit by over 80 miles. Well, this trip was just as hairy, but we finally pulled out on the docks. I took his car as he ran for his Ship, the *USS Sioux*. (Pronounced Sue, which is the name of the girl that broke up with him and caused him to join the Navy. Poor guy, every time he heard the name he still thought of her.)

I heard later that he was flown out to his ship and that they somehow hadn't missed him yet and he squeaked by again. This was not a major voyage, and so I decided to stay in town until he returned in about 10 days. I returned back to the YMCA and to my job as a movie usher, where I met all kinds of single girls. I found California girls to be very outgoing and vivacious, and they loved to show me around. So I would spend my days going out with them to Mission Beach, Coronado Beach, and Balboa Beach and just fell in love with San Diego. This was the age before the surfboard rage, (if that can be imagined today). So we body surfed those huge waves that you see on TV and in the movies. What a rush. Another natural high to be enjoyed now as well as then. One cute little girl took me to the San Diego Zoo, which was also an unforgettable event in my life. This Zoo is a must visit if you ever get in that area. The Zoo is right in the middle of the city, and goes all the way to the ocean, with every animal in its native environment. I was impressed.

And suddenly the 10th day arrived, and Clifford had a weekend leave before his next three-month tour onboard 'Sue'. We decided to just stay around San Diego and have some fun before we split company again for an unknown length of time. We hit the beach and rode some of those dream waves that seem to love Southern California and Hawaii. We had ridden those little Jersey waves all our lives together, but this was our ultimate surfing day. At night we decided to go to Tijuana and see what all the fuss was about.

As we decided not to take the car into Mexico, we walked across the bridge. You can smell the border. The difference between the US and Mexico was like the gap between Heaven and Hell. We had heard not to drink the water, or Montezuma would have his revenge. So we decided to have a Corona Beer. In the bar we strolled into, there was a greasy looking punk shouting obscenities over the loud speakers, while one ugly hooker after another abused themselves in front of everyone. Then Maria showed up. Now she was a looker, not a hooker. I mean she was easy on the eyes. She invited us into a "private" back room. We weren't allowed to bring our beers, so we were basically unarmed and unprepared for what the back room beheld. The stench from raw drugs and sex and filth permeated the air and my breathing shut down. I was about to throw up from the steamy scene of coupling couples, and we headed for the exit. This little slimy guy blocked our way and convinced us to stay with his switchblade. We turned to stay when Clifford returned to his face with a fast fist. As he sank to the floor we walked to the nearest exit and once we hit the street we ran all the way back to good ole US soil.

This was my first time outside of the US borders, and I was ready to never leave again if that was what existed out there. *Fortunately, in future years I ventured outside again, and again. The many trips outside our borders, however, have always ended in my joy at returning home.*

The weekend flew by and I had to say goodbye to my buddy and move on. This was not easy, as we had really had a good time, and we didn't know if we'd ever see each other again. I thought about that possibility as Kid and I drove back across the desert to Las Vegas. I had been offered several job opportunities during my last recent visit there, and decided I better go where opportunity knocks.

Of course opportunity was knocking back on "Wall Street" where I had worked for a couple summers. I was receiving mail in San Diego at General Delivery wondering when I might soon return to work there again. Actually, I was quite sure my father had inspired the partners of the firm to write me so as to encourage my return home. But I knew that if I took up their offer, it would be for life, and it would be my father's life I'd be living, not my own. And what was my life to be now that I had been recently terminated by my sweet academias at college. I had no idea, but I was willing to search for this and other truths so my life could be full and peaceful. My father always had admonished, "Just be Happy!" But being happy was not enough. There was something else I needed to fill my nervous and insecure feelings, but what? So my search went on.

Alone again, crossing the desert, I was oblivious of the dangers surrounding me. What were those bags in front of car radiators other people were sporting? Could it be cold water to keep their cars from over heating? Nah. Maybe spare water to put in their radiators in case they boiled over in this 100 degree heat. Nah, Kid had never boiled over. "Kid, you feeling cool?" I started talking again to my car. Not much else to do in the middle of the desert. Is that a buzzard up in the sky? No it's super cops, with their aerial speed trap. I slowed down to around 80mph and soon came upon a crowd at the blue light special. Right here in desert city. I cruised on by because I stopped between the lines on the highway to admire a cactus. So my timing crossing the painted speed lines on Route probably came out to 40mph. Good thing I watch out for buzzards out here. They have all kinds savaging the desert, especially in the casinos, as I was about to find out.

Lost In Las Vegas

Never in my wildest dreams would I picture myself riding onto the strip in Las Vegas by myself. But, here I was. Ready to take on the --Mafia? A limo passed me with Don Rickles giving me the brush-off look from his baaack seat. I was now officially low life.

Kid and I rode down through the big hotels toward downtown. There were all kinds of excitement in town, especially when I heard gunshots coming from the alley across from the Mint Casino. Three ugly cowboys came staggering onto the main street laughing and shooting. I was about to ignore them when they saw me and did a "My my my" about me. With two guns drawn they surround me up against the building wall. They're talking nonsense about how they caught them one, and he needs to spend some time doing time. No one else seems to care, and I realize I don't know a soul in this town. They walk me across the street where a makeshift jail is there with a couple others in the cage. It took me a few minutes of total fear when I found out from my fellow jail bird (and she was a cute one too) that we had been caught not wearing a $1 Hellderado Button. The weeklong Helldorado week had just started. And I began it in jail.

Some Dude walked up and bought my bird a button and bailed her out. I am left caged alone, but now I just know someone will bail me out. Just before this faith disappeared, an ugly bird bailed me out too. I got out of there a bit wiser. The week was fantastic what with World Class rodeos every day. To save money I tried sneaking in through the animal shoots and sitting up on the railing just like the cowboys. Except they didn't fall down into the bull pen like I did Some how those bulls just about ignored me while I tried to get my scared butt out of there. One of the riders said I should sit on the rail with them so if I fall it's not into the bullpen. Of course I did.

But after getting out of jail I figured I better find myself a home. I started asking prices for an apartment or a motel room. I thought things were cheap out here, but that was for the tourists. You want to live here you got to pay. That's why I ended up finding a room at the far end of town, out by Ellis Air Force Base. A 'nice' little motel with an old lady managing it who charged me to work for her. I emptied trash, cleaned her pool and whatever to lower my rent. I finally got a real job that I saw in the paper: "Wanted: Salesman. Must be good. Too many leads." I had never sold before, but my new boss didn't know that. Hank Nanni was a drummer on the Strip, but had started this new business. It was going so well, he needed me. So off I went with my demo vacuum machine with a hot lead.

I went through three weeks and a hundred "hot leads" without a sale. I was down to selling my cherished old coin collection to get a hamburger. By this time I'm getting good with the presentation, but not the close. I listened to Hank everyday so I could learn to really sell. Finally I'm in a house with a lady who had just bought some crummy vacuum the week before. When she saw mine she definitely wanted it. Then her three daughters woke up. They were Showgirls from the Tropicana on the Strip. They started stepping over my hoses and stuff in the living room, with no clothes on their gorgeous…never mind. Let's just say I made the sale. But the contract was so screwed up, I had to go back there the next day and rewrite the whole deal. Fortunately, those dancers were still asleep, so I got it right and had My First Sale!!

I celebrated by going out to dinner at the *All You Can Eat $.99* buffet at the Silver Slipper. My boss was buying it for me because I had to wait for her check to clear before I got my commission.

It was while I was in the long buffet line that the girl behind me, that I let get in front of me, happened to pop two nickels in the double slot machine next to us. She had just gotten off the plane, and it was her first bet. Just as she pulled the lever the lights started flashing indicating double jackpot time. And when the wheels stopped she had 6 bars going straight across, and MONEY just pouring out of the machines. She won $2,500, and another $2,500 for double. She was so happy she almost forgot to ask me to go with her when she decided the $.99 dinner was unnecessary. We went to the Dinner show at the Tropicana, all expenses covered by my pretty winner. What a night, and guess who saw me there at a front row table? Yep, my friendly showgirls were waving to me from their stage. Unreality was about to set in, but your bubble always bursts if you stay any place too long, especially in Las Vegas. My Lady Luck had to return to L.A. and I had to go back to work.

I decided to supplement my income with a regular paycheck. So after weeks of trying to get hired, the Jersey mafia at the Fremont Hotel downtown finally hired me as a Shill. I looked like a tourist, so they paid me to gamble for the house and make the tables look busy. I was their honey to bring the bees to the tables. They were the bears that took the money from the bees.

What a job. My limit was one dollar per bet at the Black Jack or Craps tables. Some times I was asked to play Keno or the wheel. But the Poker tables are shilled by professional gamblers that weren't allowed to play at the regular gaming tables. They were allowed to play with House money while awaiting a sucker from Iowa to come looking to get into a game. You could spot the shills because they would have a $20 Bill under their silver dollars and chips. A tourist would never notice that they were the only player without a $20 bill showing. So it was 6 or 7 against one. Not very good odds.

But my job was not to fleece anyone. I would be told to go to a table, and there I would toss my shill to the dealer. It looked just like a chip the players had, but the dealer would recognize it. He would know to give me ten $1 chips. At blackjack I wasn't allowed to hit 12 or over. In other words I could not break, or go over 21 for that would be taking a card from the gambler after me. It was good for my health not to take a wrong card or let the guest know that I was playing for the house.

I learned a lot about gambling, casinos and people during this job. The craps table was one of my favorite spots to hang out. Especially when I got to shake and roll the dice as if I was a real gambling tourist. People would look at my young 21 year old face and bet against me. If it had been my money I was betting they would have been right. But I somehow could not lose when playing with house money. Some times I would pass coming out six or seven times before even making my point. And then make the point and start over again coming out. As you know, rolling a seven or eleven coming out is a winner. And I would see the faces of betters who couldn't believe how lucky I was as they dropped their money into the mafia's till. I tried to signal them somehow not to bet against me, but I guess I just looked like a loser to them. The House loved it.

On one occasion, I had gotten a cold from going into the air-conditioned casino from the 115-degree heat outside. I had my turn to roll coming up, but was about to sneeze. I forgot to clap my hands together before I reached into my pocket for my handkerchief. This is a must rule for us low life. It lets the men in the sky looking down at my every move through one way mirrors see that I am not trying to pocket any money. Well the pit bosses were notified and before I could blow my nose I was off the floor being searched. I was given my one and only warning allowed before termination.

By this time, the job was getting pretty old and for over six weeks I held down three jobs. From 10am till 5pm I had my sales job selling the Filter Queen vacuum cleaners. Then from 6pm to 2am I'd be gambling, or rather shilling at the Fremont. Then a quick 4 hours sleep before being at the TV studio where I did the morning movie.

The TV show had started by doing live ads for the vacuum cleaner during the morning movie. I called it the biggest sucker in town. Some other advertisers asked me to do their ads and soon I was doing the news and weather and ads during the Morning Movie. This was before the big studio days. The whole studio was in a 20 X20 cinderblock building. But the power of TV was still pretty heady. I'd ring a doorbell and people would recognize me and say "C'mon in Sucker." I'm sure they meant the vac, but I went in and did my pitch anyway. Well after 6 weeks, everything started melding together. They didn't have enough makeup at the studio to cover up my droopy eyes and hunched back. And I started making mistakes on the air, and at the casino. I was mispronouncing words doing the live vac demo, and this was before videotape, so nothing was ever edited out. They told me and my sucker to hit the road.

At the casino that night I was kind of dressed up and looking sharp. I had gone to the Sands for a popper to celebrate my loss of a job and also a sale that afternoon. As fate would have it, the "Clan" from *Oceans Eleven* were all there. In case you missed this movie, go rent it and catch the flavor of the times. Of course Frank Sinatra would have the Clan there, because he was a part owner of the Sands. So here I was down and out, and surrounded by Frank, Dean Martin,

Joey Bishop, Sammy Davis, and Shirley McLain. I let them cheer me up, buy me drinks and suddenly it was time to be at the Casino. Damn!

So off I run for an important appointment (sure) and show up at work 15 minutes late. I am reminded I have no more warnings left. But if they let me stay I owe them one. (Sure.) The "Jersey" Pit Boss says they have some high rollers in and are opening the Chemin De Fer Table and he wants me to go shill at it because I've got a suit on. I am told that I will be given $1,000 for my shill by the Croupier and that my bet limit is $100. I couldn't believe that I'd be so entrusted. I sat at the table with what appeared to be some of the richest people in town and therefore the world. I'd never played or even heard of this game before, but found out it is played with three decks in a shoe. One of the players is the 'Banker' and places their bet. The rest of us bid a part or cover the entire bet. The object is for the "Banker" and highest bidder against his bet to receive two or three cards and have the total of their numbers last digit be closest to nine. It is a very nerve racking deliberately played game. The house take is 10% of the pot, as it is with the poker tables. So they don't care who wins.

But the players care. Especially when they have a piece of the action. I was just there until the table became filled, which held about twelve players. I tossed in my shill and was passed my measly $1,000. Everyone else was betting $1000s, and I would bet $50 or $100. It didn't do much for my self-image again, but what would. One of the players, a Baron from Germany with a single monocle in his right eye, had won five or six hands and there was over $7,000 on the table, which he left as his bet. I had just lost $100 so I didn't think I'd be in on this next hand. But the Oriental lady with the pearl cigarette holder had passed, as did all the players. They weren't about to challenge the Baron when he was in the middle of a hot streak. In my sleepless state, I was shaken by the man from Holland next to me who said "Say Banco!" So in my best midnight daze I said, "Banco!"

My mouth turned into a sand trap, the croupier glared at me like I was dead meat, the chairs in the ceiling by the one way mirrors fell over and I expected them to come crashing right through them. I felt a stiff finger, or was it a gun, in my back. The Croup took his paddle and lifted my measly $800 and put it out next to the $7,000 that I had just covered. I was in a difficult position here. If I win and the Baron and his body guards find out I am working for the house, I will be Bratwurst tomorrow. However, if I lose the Jersey Mafia will make me a buzzard appetizer out in the desert tonight. I thought of my parents and how I would like to say good-bye to them, and thank them for all they had tried to do for me.

My first card was dealt. Slowly I reached out to turn up a corner for my eyes only. The longer to live my dear. It was a four. The next card came sliding in. It was a two. Not too good. Probably real bad. But my expression was meaningless. I looked into the Baron's eye. Nothing, not a clue. I had the option of taking another card, but would have had to stick on a 7, 8, or 9. He leaned back. He wasn't going to take a hit I thought. So I calmly said," I'll take another card." But nothing came out. My mouth was too dry, so I scratched my card on the table to get a hit. The dealer slid it out of the box; the finger in my back urged me to turn it over. I didn't hesitate and just picked it up and turned them all over at once. They totaled eight, I smiled the Baron didn't. The dealer turned over his cards, showed a ten and a seven. I remember the Croupier paddle picking up the whole pot to claim it. But I had two fingers under each armpit raising me up. I reached out to claim my winnings and grabbed some of the cash as I was persuaded into a back room. Suddenly I was flying toward a wall behind me and all I remember is cussing, and money flying about me as I sank down the wall into unconsciousness.

I came to quickly, and was told what would have happened to me if I had lost the $7 Grand and not been able to pay it back. Then the Jersey Mafia Boss man suggested I never be seen in that casino again and gave me thirty seconds to disappear. I'm gone, back to the Sands to see my new friends. Nowhere in sight. So home I go to the Raunch (Ranch) Motel where my divorcee friend nurses my wounded ego and tells me a better day's a coming.

Her name is Jackie, a blonde hair blue eyed beauty who looks like she should be adorning one of the pools on the hotel strip, not here at the Raunch Motel. There were some real derelicts staying here and they all had become my best friends. But she was different. She tried to keep aloof from me, but confided in Tiny and his wife that I was growing on her. She was falling in love with me, but she was afraid of the complications it would cause with the used car salesman who was paying for her divorce.

In Nevada it takes 6 months to become a resident in order to get the divorce legally. So during this period her benefactor visited her twice. That left us with lots of time to be together. But he saw me and I saw him. He was big, rich, mean and ugly. I wasn't. He may have guessed about us, but we kept our relationship as secret as possible. But did he see us kissing that night when she slipped out of her room and knocked on my door? My room consisted of a bed and two curtains. One covers the closet and the other the bathroom. My door opened out to the desert as far as the eye sees toward the sunset. I learned to check my shoes, sheets and clothes for scorpions, but this guy was different. It was tearing me up that he was with her on my turf, or sand as it was. And so, as we stole a kiss by my door, it must have lasted too long, because we heard him calling her. She ran around the other end of the building and appeared casually out by the pool. But he was suspicious.

He finally left to go back to his Used Car Lot in Bakersfield after a very long weekend. But he had yelled at her and threatened her and so she was scared but defiant. She tried to keep her distance from me but we were the only game in town as it were. The attraction continued for both of us. We didn't go all the way mainly because she had recently had some kind of surgery and it would have caused hemorrhaging. So that was not in the cards, but we came as close to it as passion could take us. And to me who was a closet virgin, it was distressing. I know in this day and age that seems impossible to be 21 years old and virtually still pure. I didn't even know the term let alone the blessing it could be. I just figured I had been 'passed over.' Till now. Now it was there but I couldn't have it. The story of my life. Lead me into temptation and then keep me from it. But such are some of the cycles life takes us through to see if we handle them any better the next time around. As you will see I continued to be tested not until I overcame, but until I was overcome.

But finally he was gone. The same day I get a letter from my parents that they are going to San Francisco on business and will be coming to Las Vegas in three days and want me to meet them at the airport. I told Jackie the news. This was exciting for me because I hadn't seen my parents in half a year or more, and I knew they weren't too happy with my adventures. So in order to impress them, I left Kid at the motel and Jackie and I took her car to pick up my parents. I dropped her off at the Sands so as to not shock my parents all at once, and drove the white 1960 Cadillac convertible to the airport. There they were, just like the letter said. Mom was carrying her mink stole as usual, and looked a little out of place here in the deserts 110-degree heat. She needed a drink fast, so after our initial hellos, off to the Sands to get her a Grants on the Rocks.

"Where'd you get the car?" the question finally popped. "I borrowed it from a friend. As a matter of fact she'll be at the Sands where I have a room for you. We can all have a drink together." My parents didn't say another word. Must have been the desert heat. Well their mouths dropped open when they see this gorgeous blond that is totally in love with me." They not only weren't polite, they were panicked. When the third round was ordered, Mom asked Jackie to join her in the ladies room. Dad had a chance to have a few words with me and they weren't pleasant. Something about getting on with my life, my future and Uncle Sam's army. That's when Jackie and mom returned. Mom looked fine, but Jackie looked like she had been dealt the flu. She looked sick because she had promised my mom that I would be out of town tomorrow and she would never see me again. She said she did it for me, but it was the hardest thing she ever did. I still wonder if Mom slipped her money, but no amount would have covered her pain.

We took the folks to the airport to continue on to Newark and home to Plainfield. And that's when I got the word. I couldn't believe it. I went into total shock as she tried to convince me that it was best for all, and that as soon as I got settled, she would leave used car salesman and drive her red Austin Healey convertible east to New Jersey, where we'd live happily ever after. After I got out of the Army.

To Be Or Not To Be

The desert looked wet, no saturated, as Kid and I drove off the Strip and out of town the next day. I think I never cried this hard in my life, but I had to remind myself that it wasn't over. Jackie and I each had to fulfill our predestined paths and then we could be together. Used car Salesman was to come in a few days and be with her for her divorce settlement, but I didn't know he would marry her the same day until I got her second letter. The first note she wrote as I was driving to San Francisco. This second one she wrote the 1st night of their honeymoon. He got drunk and she slipped out of the cabin and wrote me an incredible love letter while he snored. Every day of their 7-day honeymoon she wrote me, and every day I went to the General Delivery Post office and got my letter of the day. Had she been caught he would have killed her, I had no doubt.

On day ten they were to return to Bakersfield. I had been staying with a childhood friend, Fritz Bruce, who my parents told me was living in San Francisco. I hadn't seen him in fifteen years, but I looked him up anyway. We had a great time, and I am sure I knew a hundred people by name that I met there, and somehow they all knew me. I had never experienced such a caring, interested social scene anywhere. We had a great time. One Saturday Fritz had arranged a back yard clambake in my honor. He had had lobsters flown out from Maine with all the trimmings. A gang of his friends dug up his back yard and we had an old fashioned clam bake with steamed clams cooking in the seaweed, corn on the cob dunked in butter, and lobster on the *Chronicle*. It was unforgettable.

Two days later I was heading for Bakersfield for a final rendezvous with my love. I got a room at the first motel I came to, and started to call her on the phone. He answered and I hung up. I was sick. I looked at the letters from her again and at the pictures Tiny had taken of us that made us look naked, though we weren't. It got me so determined to see her that I found my way out to Country Club Lane and found her house as described in her letters. It was just getting dusk, so I parked and started the army four point crawl up the sun-baked yard to the house. I was about to look in a window when I heard him shouting at her. I couldn't make out exactly what was going on, but it wasn't good. I had to get out of there before I did something I'd regret. Back to the motel I tried to sleep. I couldn't. I got up to look at her picture again, and to read her letters again.

They were missing! Where the h___ are they? I tore the room apart, nothing. I took a chance and called her house again the next morning. She answered! "I've got to see you," we agreed. She said she would come out for a half hour, and then she would have to split. She used to work at this motel's office and people knew her there. I told her about the missing pictures. The next morning we have our final hugs and goodbyes. Too soon she has to go and wishes me a safe trip back across the country to home. She promises to write and when I get out of the army she will come to be with me. She left my arms like a dove and I was alone. I got it together enough to pack up Kid for the long journey and decided to have a sandwich at the motel restaurant on the way out. I ordered a BLT and as I waited I looked into the mirror in front of me at the counter and, bigger than life, there was Mr. Used Car Salesman glowering at me. The shiver of death went through me. The BLT arrived and I tried to be cool and started to eat it, but it turned to sand and I couldn't swallow anything. It took me a half hour to get it down with two glasses of water, hoping to outwait him. Finally he left. I didn't know whether to call the cops or make a run for it. What's going on? How did he know I was here?

Finally I decide to make a run for it. I don't see him anywhere. I pay my bill and had the funny feeling not only he was watching me, but all the waitresses as well. I see my way clear to Kid and make a straight beat for the door, key ready. Whew, I'm in. Lock the doors, and let's get outa here. Pulling out of the lot I see a white Austin Healey convertible pulling out behind me. A girl driving and, oh oh, used car salesman next to her. (I find out later it's his ex-wife driving who lives at the motel and had been given the incriminating pictures and letters by a maid who had recognized Jackie while making up my room.) Is that a gun I see flash in his hand? I put Kid's pedal to the metal and am going about 75-80 on this Boulevard, but I see in the rear view mirror that they're gaining on me. I let them get close and see a ramp going somewhere two lanes over to the left. At the last possible second I swerve over to the ramp and she starts to do the same, but because of her extra speed couldn't make it and tried to pull back. I see in the mirror the tail end of that nice used car hit the railing divider and spin out down below as my ramp seems to take me up up and away onto a non stop route to Reno some 300 miles North. With mixed emotions I am headed home.

In Reno I write her a letter, not knowing she is doing the same from a hospital bed. Reno seemed like such small time after living in Vegas for over a year. The dealers were almost all women, while there were none in Las Mafiosi town. After a couple of days here recuperating and wondering what I had left behind, I decided to head home and face reality. I certainly would appreciate the good food, clean sheets, and the love my parents tried to give me, but I had a hard time receiving. I didn't recognize that's what it was.

This area of the country sure was a lot prettier than Plainfield, New Jersey. I mean Lake Tahoe is a sight to behold with the mountains, green pastures, sheep being herded down the middle of the roads. And the female dealers at least smiled when they beat you.

I had a hard time leaving, with so much more to explore, but I was expecting a letter to be waiting for me at the General Delivery Post Office in Salt Lake City. I needed to hear from Jackie. I began crossing Nevada toward Utah when I got a stupid idea. I'd get some paint and brushes at a hardware store and on the way I would paint signs to Jackie for her to follow when she came to see me next year. I put PC LOVES JH on boulders that no one could miss. Then near dark I came upon a railroad trestle. I parked nearby and climbed up there into the middle of the bridge and hung over, upside down, and printed in my best letters "PETER LOVES JAC..." when a flashing red light and a loud speaker suggested I stop and come down.

The cop was real nice and said that if I could get it all off within a half hour I wouldn't need to spend the night in jail and pay fines for defacing Railroad property. I had also bought turpentine to clean the brushes, and in 29 minutes I was showing him a nice clean bridge. He laughed at my love sickness, took the rest of my paint and told me to get home.

That night I spent in Salt Lake City. And at dawn I was out looking for the main Post Office. They had two letters for me. The writing even on the envelope was smeared with tears. I tore them open, and nearly got psychotic with rage. It was here I found out about the missing pictures and that his ex-wife called him and showed them to him the morning of the very dry BLT. After their unfortunate car accident, the used car salesman got home and beat Jackie up after terrorizing her. I wanted to go back and kill him, but her letter forbade that. She also insisted that I get home as soon as possible, because she thought that he was on his way after me to rub me out. And I had left the perfect trail of roadside signs for him to follow. He could actually be here in town waiting for me to head east into the sunrise.

So I hit the town limits at full speed and drove non-stop toward home. What a dilemma my life had become. Here I was running home to keep from being shot by a jealous husband behind me, and the Army waiting to have people start shooting at me there in my future. Not a good spot to be in. Kid and I sped across the Great Salt Lake which seemed eternal.

But then I approached the beautifully majestic Rocky Mountains. To tell another truth, I wasn't prepared for what lay ahead again. I was just plowing ahead as usual, my invincible life not concerned. As I began climbing the foothills, I saw a lady getting fuel and decided I better fill up too. Good thing, as there's no gas until Denver on this route. I got to talk with her and found she was a schoolteacher heading back to her home to find a job. I think she was going through a major life change. It was none of my business, but I did feel somewhat responsible for her, so I let her go on ahead of me. Rumor had it we may run into the season's first snowstorm up on the mountain.

Well sure enough, it was an all afternoon and evening trip up the mountainous curves. Like most roads in the country at the time, the roads were two lanes. One in each direction. And the snow came, in big wet flakes you could hear slap on the windshield. And the road became illegal to drive onto unless you had chains. But we had already started the trip, and couldn't just fly up up and away. Kid and I talked to each other, me encouraging every inch not to spin or skid or stall, as my teacher friend did a few times, And while it was tempting to pass her I would nudge Kid up to her rear fender and keep on trucking until she'd get a grip and continue on, up up and away.

But as I subsided into a driving daze, running strictly on a prayer, large trucks were losing control coming down the mountain as night time turned wet snow into ice. I swear I saw at least three 18-wheelers just go over the side where there weren't even guardrails, and therefore no trace of their disappearance. And there were others that seemed to go past me out of control and heading for the quick way down. Nightmare on Loveland Pass was a reality, but again my Guardian Angel was as much of a reality. And today I can look back and thank God for His loving me, watching over me, and protecting me, as I'm sure he has done for you too.

I had a feeling that I had put a permanent barrier between Used Car Salesman and me. He was not about to cross the Rockies any time soon. Winter had come and sealed us apart.

Homeward Bound

Across the country I would keep trying to tune in the World Series. The Pittsburgh Pirates were up ahead of my trail and made the crossing go quickly. After 2 days of steady driving I was in Indianapolis. I was getting to the weary point where a cold beer would have kept me fueled up. But this was a dry town. The nearest beer would be just over the state border. I was given directions and off I went to quench my thirst.

Over the border I got off the highway to find the cold one. After a few turns there it was, the State Line Cafe. I locked up Kid and walked in fearless because of my thirst. Inside was a different world. Here were the locals answer to the Hells' Angels, which it appeared had been in a rumble recently and probably lost. So when ole preppy Pete walks in, the place shakes with interest in me. Guys with leather, chains, casts, crutches and bloody bandanas on their grungy bodies let me in past them. I head for the back of this hut for the bar. The bartender looks at me like I'm dead meat, and I was getting used to that. So I asked for a cold beer. He reached up and pulled a string which turned off the bare light bulb over the bar and said "We're Closed!"

I knew there was futility in arguing and shrugged and started stepping over crutches to get back to the door. The chicks seemed to be taunting me so as to get me in trouble with their restless gorillas. Somehow I made it to the door, which was blocked by the head Gorilla. I reached for the knob and he moved and let me out. That's when I knew I was in trouble.

Outside the bikers were sitting on their Harleys, just staring at me. I looked to see if Kid was all right. My orange madras jacket looked out of place in the rear side window what with six killers leaning on my car and sitting on the hood and trunk. I could tell Kid was feeling indignant. I turned to see the Head Gorilla coming out behind me, giving me the smile of death. So I went over to him and asked if he were the head mucky muck. He said he was. I said I didn't believe him. "Let me see you tell those guys to get off of my car" (and let me drive away) I said, to 'prove his rank' He just nodded his head, and all of them jumped down and moved away as I smartly went for the door, unlocked it, got in and started out of the parking lot in one smooth split second. I gave a thumbs up and a smile to the Head Gorilla as I went past him on the porch. I swore never to drink again.

I drove all night until I ran out of gas somewhere west of Pittsburgh, and finally let my head fall back on Kids soft cushion and fell asleep. I was in the middle of no where, but I could work on that problem in the…zzzzzzzzzzzzz.

The sunrise was so bright, and seemed so soon! I got out of Kid and walked up to the top of the rise ahead of us. And right there the heaven's angels must have built a gas station just for me last night. So I was able to get a can of gas and walk back to feed Kid. Then we drove up so as to fill each of us up with some delicious gas station victuals. I put it all on that credit card Dad gave me before I had left for Florida. That way if anything happened to me they would have a record of where I had last been. At least that was my reasoning at the time. It also made the trip a lot less complicated for me. So off we went full, and happy to be alive. I remember that Pittsburgh had won the World Series yesterday, so it was no surprise that the whole city was covered with litter and bottles the day after. Those Pennsylvania people know how to celebrate. I know, I majored in it at college. And that made me think, maybe I could spend this night there at Lehigh University with my old classmates.

I arrived at Lehigh in Bethlehem just in time for dinner, and I was surprised at what a big fuss these guys made upon my unannounced arrival. I had never joined a Fraternity, but was a social member at two: Chi Psi and Sigma Phi. They bought me a Keg of beer and we partied all night. There were a hundred questions about "What's out there?" It sure was nice to be recognized as a human being again. Yes, it was going to be good to be home. Except for that three-hour nap when I ran out of gas, I had been driving non stop for 2 1/2 days. When I put my head down to sleep all I could see was -----z-z - - - - white lines.

Am I me, or am I my fathers image of me? Am I me or am I my mothers image of me? Am I me, or am I what I've been the past two years? What am I to be, if not me?? One of my parent's best friends has a son here at Lehigh. I grew up most of my life with him and many other friends that have kept in touch through college. His name is also Pete, and I'm spending the night at his Fraternity these few nights. He wanted to hear all the juice about my travels, so I laid it on. It always sounds better than when you're going through it, because you leave out the part about working three jobs in 115-degree heat to avoid starving. But Pete was one I could tell all to, and he could fill in the blanks.

His Dad, now a partner on Wall Street is very well off. But that doesn't shield one from the hazards of life. His first two wives had died. Pete and I had lost some good mutual friends, from drowning in a skate pond and from an accidental shooting, and of course earlier to polio. And Pete was with me through a lot including when I broke my leg skiing.

That was our freshmen year and we had gone up to Stowe, Vermont for our midwinter break. The last run of the last day my left ski went under my right ski as I fell forward. A split second later I was looking at the bottom of my foot. That and the pain creeping in told me I had broken something. The ski patrol finally got me off the mountain, an adventure in itself. When finally delivered by ambulance to the little hospital there in Stowe, the Head Nurse said, "What happened to you? I never saw a break like that before!" And they treat a couple hundred breaks a month there. Well, the next morning Pete comes to visit as the Doctor says I'm going to have to stay there awhile. I said just as long as I'm out in time for the homecoming weekend and a very sharp date. The Doc said it would be more like 26 weeks before I could leave. "Twenty six weeks?!" "Aye-up.'

I was put in a ward with 8 retired bankers who moaned and made sounds only corpses made. After 4 1/2 months I wrote home and said if they want anything left of me at all, they better get me out of there. So my parents arranged for 7 ambulances to shuttle me home to Plainfield. Another adventure with blue lights and sirens all the way down through Connecticut and New York for a nine-hour trip to my house. Our poor maid's hair was wired when she saw all the lights and the extra long final burst of the sirens. They wheeled me in and upstairs to my own bed, where I laid for another two months. But Pete was there to visit and go all through this with me. He was the one who saw the date on my cast showing that the accident occurred on the 26th. Yep, that was accident number 5 on the 26th. I was starting to get superstitious.

I went through six more months of therapy and finally commuting to New York City by train, ferry boat and subway to do some college catch up courses at NYU while still on crutches. One school day a fellow student acquaintance and I decided to play hooky. We went everywhere, Rockefeller Center, top of the Empire State Building, NBC's *Good Morning America*, museums and back home. All the way traveling on crutches. That night my parents took an unusual interest as to how my day went. "Oh, same as usual," I commented on my way out some door. Later I found out my grandmother had seen me on my crutches outside the NBC show windows with her favorite Dave Garroway pointing at me. She called my folks to tell them the happy news.

Finally about a year after the accident, I was free from the crutches and could start building up the muscles in my emaciated leg. It was in February 1959, back in college that Ole Pete comes into my apartment off campus and says pack up my bags, we're going skiing. I wimped around about it, but he convinced me it was a done deal. So three days later we were on a plane for Innsbruck, Austria. From there we took a train to Kitzbuel, the most charming place on earth, as long as I didn't have to ski. But sure enough, the next morning I'm convinced all I need are good new ski boots and no more problem. I am made a bath by the maid at our pension to soak in with my leather boots on so as to form fit them to my feet. Then I walk in them until they are dry.

The next morning we are on a 45-minute Gondola ride to the top of the Valuga, some out of sight mountaintop. Then through the clouds on two more Gondolas to the highest peak in the sky. We are the only ones. Ole Pete says "Come on!" and shushes down, straight down to avoid causing an avalanche on this 'Pete's Peak'. He was tiny as an ant's rear end where he finally leveled off and disappeared.

Only a few people showed up at this remote pinnacle of the world, where I was trying for over an hour to get the courage to push off. I didn't know if my ankle would work or not. It was already giving me pains. Pete had brought me back on the biggest horse he could find so as to get me skiing again. I tried not to picture him in the ambulance with me on the way to that Stowe hospital. He put his ski glove in my mouth to chomp on to help me do a silent scream of pain. Oh well, that was then. This was now. I couldn't stay here forever. I took my skis off one more time to loosen up. After some jogging in place, stretching and having a word with my closest neighbor, God, I put on the slats and pushed off. Straight down. I'm thinking at 90 mph I could die if I fall, but quickly put that out of my mind. The slats were rattling and my knees were knocking. I was trying to overcome total fear with something. I was digging deep into my soul to picture getting off this mountain alive, so I could kill ole Pete.

Finally, it leveled out into a bowl in which I screamed "I'm Alive!" But oh oh, it's a catwalk about four feet wide curving around to the right with about a 2000-foot drop off to the left. After slowing to about 70mph I just hoped my edges would hold and keep me from going off the left edge. I just had to put the cliff out of my mind and picture the open valley just ahead. I hit something and started slipping and going down. But an angel seemed to push me ahead just enough to slide into an open area while tumbling every which way, yet my new boots and me were still one together. I started putting my trust in them to carry on. It was a six-hour run down the mountain ranges. The most gorgeous place I had ever been. This was one of Gods three places for me, next to heaven. The other would be scuba diving and the 3rd of course is anywhere in between. I was approaching over seven hours to get off these mountains. I was still scared, alone and wondering where I was. I had seen no one or nothing but sky and snow. It was getting dark, foggy and hard to see anything. "Yahoo!" I screamed as I saw some lights way down below. An hour later I was finding out I had skied down into the wrong town and had to take a 20-minute train ride to Kitzbuel. It was 9pm when I found ole Pete dancing at a favorite après ski place, the Post Hotel. Boy was he glad to see me! I let him live. Why I don't know. I guess we had a lot more living to experience together. We continued to have a ball skiing some of the other mountains, eating and dancing all night and just hacking out. But this adventure had to be one of the peaks of my stupidity.

Nevertheless, here I was staying with Pete at Lehigh for a few nights on my way home. He was going to finish college and I had to go home and face the future, including Uncle Sam. I had not finished college and I had flunked ROTC because of my demerits. The military life was not one I would choose, and ROTC had been forced upon me because Lehigh was a Land Grant University.

The Administration had made the mistake of letting Government onto the campus, not me. Therefore I rebelled by marching off the wrong foot, smoking in rank and putting my smoking cigarette butts down the guy's rifle in front of me. It looked cool, smoking barrel and all. This was the Army Mr. Jones. But all this was the most helpful part of my academic experience, as you will see later, when I arrive at Uncle Sam's Active Duty Camp.

After a few days of this reunion stuff I headed back to the future, to my home in Plainfield, NJ. This is not an easy transition for my parents or me. But they took it better than I would have if I were in their shoes. It was only a two-hour drive, but it seemed forever as I started recalling the road behind me and the road ahead of me. Is Jackie for real? Did I out run the bullets or am I running in towards them? Are my parents for real? Is anything for real? Where do I go from here???

If you sense the total out-of-touchness I was experiencing, then stay with me. We aren't alone. If you don't relate so far, please stay with me as we see the fun life has in store for us overgrown teenagers. We have a lot to learn. Give us time and space. But more importantly give us, yes, love.

Oh yes, the old slogan love. No, I mean the open dialog that comes with the ability of both sides to discuss and agree or disagree about all sorts of things, and not ever let the last word be the last word. Just talk, and then listen. That's all we want at this age. To Be rather than Not To Be.

Prodigal Son

I was not sure what kind of reception I was going to get from my folks, if any at all. They thought I had gone off the deep end a long time ago, but I really went awry when my Florida trip ended up out west. And I was gone not a few weeks but a year and a half. I was feeling real appreciative of how they had taken to my adventures, but also feeling very sorry for them also. I was not fulfilling their expectations of me at all. Even though I was Cum Laude my senior year at Northwood School up in Lake Placid, the ski accident had put me so far behind at college I just never caught up. And so I didn't finish. I know that disappointed them a lot. So as I pulled into the drive of the ole manse, 1210 Evergreen Avenue, I was surprised to find my father there with 'open arms'. He was not big on hugging. But he was there. And we had a big roast leg-of-lamb dinner that their maid, and my friend, Dorothy served especially for me. And that night they gave me a surprise party with all the gang that was in town. I was left alone late that night with an old friend Patti, from Texas. A crush was resurrected which lasted all through the coming Holiday season. She was always very aloof from me, but this night was different. Maybe I was different. I don't know, but it was nice.

I felt like the Prodigal Son whom I had heard about in Sunday School way back when. I had never been treated so undeservedly well by anyone, especially my parents. It has always remained a special memory in my heart.

The next morning, after a looong winter's nap, Dorothy fixed my favorite breakfast, poached eggs with creamed chip beef on toast, with all the trimmings. Then she brought me all the mail that accumulated for me since I left. [2]In it were three letters from Jackie that jumped out at me. I took them to read somewhere alone. The first letter was written the day I was leaving Las Vegas behind. It was full of love and hurt and brought back all the memories of that shattering day. She mentioned the Little Chapel on the Strip, that I remember

---

[2] I now get more junk mail in one day than over those 18 months

39

seeing on the way out of town, which was where she got married. If I had known, I would have done a Dustin Hoffman act and been there pounding on the windows yelling her name.

The second letter was from a Bakersfield Hospital where she was being treated for a nervous breakdown and some bruises she had suffered in a fall. Today it is called spouse abuse or wife beating. I wanted to go back and…The third letter was about how she would try to go through with the charade until I was out of the Army and she could ride east in her Austin Healey with her two kids. Oh, I forgot to mention she has children. That's because they were staying with friends during her residency term in Vegas.

The three year old visited a couple times. We took him up to the top of Mt. Charleston, a significant mountain visible from town. We had a special picnic and I built a circular rock campfire. There was a tree with shallow roots I just pulled out of the ground and we kept pushing it into the center of the hot coals. Jackie put Robbie in the trunk of her Cadillac where he was used to taking a nap. We laid down under the stars keeping each other warm near the fire until we fell asleep. We awoke in terror to the sound of a guttural growl. It was pitch dark, and while I couldn't see anything, I could tell it was very close. I leaned over and blew on the hot coals and whoof, the fire exploded like lightning. It reflected the fear in its eyes as we made out the form of a black panther. Its fear of the fire was at least equal to ours, and so we all split company at the same speed in opposite directions.

When we got to the car Robbie was not in the trunk and Jackie freaked. Was he the dinner of our unexpected visitor? We called his name. Again. Nothing. An eternity later we heard some fussing down the road, and there he was, sleep walking and had bumped into some bushes. Whew! This was my first experience with a youngster, and I trusted Jackie with that department. But I hoped I would take more precautions if I ever had a child.

Her letters brought back so many memories like this. We continued to write back and forth, but they became further apart, until we decided to just live our lives until it was time to get together again. Absence and time make the heart uncertain. My parents surely knew this. I wish her love.

Get A Job

The next morning I was awakened way too early and reminded that I had several things to do, such as tell Uncle Sam I was in town and find some use for my self. Well I joined the US Army Reserve, which met on weekends until January when I'd report for active duty at Fort Dix. I was the lowest ranking thing walking on an army base. I wasn't even an acting Private. I was a nebbish. My neighbor Hank joined with me. I was glad to have him with me through all this. I had lived next door to Hank since we were 6 years old. He spent most of his youth in a wheel chair because of some hip disorder. I would always get him on my basketball team and push his chair around the court and he could swish from anywhere with ease. Later he was hard to stop, because he grew like a weed when he got out of that chair. He was big, and his nickname became Moose.[3] He and I spent many good times together, fishing up at the Forest Lake Club in the Pocono's, and going to the skeet range.[4] I could hardly lift the shotguns at the age of twelve.[5] His family was always special, and set a very Christian example for anyone.

With the Army obligation settled I went job hunting. I didn't really want to go back to Wall Street. My Dad was 'famous' there, and so I felt whatever success I might have there would always be directly attributable to him. He didn't feel that way, but I sure did. Now many of my friends had no problem stepping into their daddies' shoes, or using their influence. I just felt that was my dad's thing and doubted it was mine. I didn't know what my thing was, but it had to be mine, not somebody else's.

---

[3] Moose now lives in White Horse, Yukon Territory, where every creature has thousands of square miles. He has built dozens of fishing cabins in the winters and takes tourists fishing on Virgin waters year round. He married a native Indian girl and he's big, "ugly" and happy.

[4] Pennsylvania

[5] The seed planted that let me be a skeet instructor. See High Hampton, NC in 2nd Arc of the Great Circle.

41

So the interviews started. The first was in New York with Bleachette Bluing Company. I was hired. An old man had bought a small division of American Cyanamid that he had worked in for most his life. AC was going to just dump it, but he saw his life going down the drain. so he managed to take it over. He was looking for someone young to succeed him, someone who would have learned the business and could buy it from him. I was his man.

The job demanded work in all phases of the business: research, development, patents, manufacturing, advertising, marketing, sales and customer satisfaction. I was also to learn all the office billing and shipping and accounts receivable and payable. I had learned just enough in college to understand what all these stages meant, and now I was going to get to use my judgment to implement my ideas, with guidance from the old man. For it was only he and I and one secretary. We had an even older man calling on wholesale buyers for the supermarket chains, and I was to go and learn with him also.

I loved it. My office was either on Lexington Avenue across from Grand Central Station or in my car Kid, going into every grocery store in Brooklyn, Bronx, Queens, Manhattan and Long Island. If Forest Hills was hosting the Tennis Championships, I was there to cheer them on. If Yankee Stadium had a baseball game going, I'd have a hot dog there for lunch while on my rounds. If new equipment came in, I was at our contract packagers helping to set up the new line. All this was because I asked one question during the interview. "What's Bluing?"

"Well, my son, that is a good question! Why is the sky blue? Why do sheets turn yellow? What is Bluing. Why did your grandmother's mother even use bluing?"

Yes, yes tell me! I found out that blue is the most fleeting visible color of the spectrum. The light from the sun is white, but as it comes through the early layers of the atmosphere the blue portion splits, and the remaining yellowish light proceeds to earth. Yep, that's why the sky is blue. The same goes for sheets and white shirts. With time and exposure to air, the blue splits leaving yellow linens. So even the primitives would block up streams and swish our ultramarine blue in the water. Then by soaking the whites in the blue water they would come out sparkling white. And we supplied the blue. We built our

42

distribution to 100% in the NYC area, but also in the Dominican Republic, Haiti and other 4th world countries. This kept me busy and gave me a regular paycheck. I was able to finally put some money away, in a real savings account! I GOT A JOB!

Uncle Sam finally let me know the date I was to go to his wonderful Camp. He called it a Fort. Fort Dix was to be my home away from home in February. This gave me a few months to enjoy my newly reached maturity. Many of my friends were also at home, doing jobs, going to night school and partying. There were a few groups I hung out with, much like college where I was associated with a few fraternities. I had different groups of friends, which had different interests of which I had common interests. I guess I had multiple interests whereas some had few.

Anyway, one group included Carlton Montague Barlow III, known as Cotty. I call him Repeat, as you will see his life's events closely mirror my own. You may remember my visiting him my first night traveling at the University of Virginia. Peter Van Ness, another old friend, at this time got a job stocking Nabisco Cookies in supermarkets. We occasionally bumped into each other making our business calls in different grocery stores. Jim Clevenger, a skinny guy who lived in a big house, liked music and NYC. He had just joined CBS Sports, as did Frank Gifford. It was difficult to tell which one had really taken the hit on the head. Jim was the type who would give a beggar in New York $5 and then change his mind and give him all his money in his pocket, usually about $200. He also usually regretted it the next morning when he woke up broke and wondered what happened. Hunter Lewis was a chemical engineer, though one would never know it. He loved to have fun, and we did as we'd drive into New York in his Army Jeep, dressed in our Army Parkas. The lack of a muffler made us sound like a one jeep war as we'd tear through the Lincoln Tunnel, rifles at attention, whip aerial banging on the ceiling and two way radio crackling out obscenities from his girl friend's car. That would be Joan, from Sands Point, Long Island. She had a new job as Fashion Editor for a magazine called *Mademoiselle*. These few friends will be coming back as we spiral through another arc of life.

MOTHA

Another crowd of friends included ole Pete, my best friend you remember from skiing. He wasn't finished with me yet. Then there's Howard Crosby Foster III, rich, and crazy like me. One summer we had had one of the most competitive gotcha contests. It was so close that one of us would have to drop trou at the Bay Head Yacht Club formal dance Saturday night to win. He tried to get our friends to stop me, but I won. He and I were a treat on Wall Street when we worked together there as well. He too decided not to take advantage of his fathers seat on the NYSE, bought a Winnebago and followed in my Fords tire treads. And Tony Haley perhaps was the craziest of us all. Tony was the instigator of a million laughs. One incident comes to mind when we were at one of our girl friends homes. He went around to the crystal glasses in the kitchen cupboards, would cut one in a glass, and put it back in the cupboard upside down. He'd also leave the cabinet door open, so when the Mrs came into her kitchen she'd notice and turn the glasses right side up. Well if that didn't raise a stink.

Diversions from the real world were main objectives. We all formed a golf group consisting of about 24 guys and 24 girls. We would go off for weekends twice a year to different Country Clubs and have just a hilarious time. We would practically take over country clubs, such as Baultesrol, Plainfield, and Fred Waring's Shawnee. We had hats with our name embroidered on them, "MOTHA". This stood for the "**M**etropolitan, **O**ut of bounds, **T**rap, and **H**azard **A**ssociation." There are dozens of stories here, just waiting to make Caddy Shack just that. Most of these guys were in their niche in the world as lawyers, doctors, stockbrokers and me: *the wanderer*, selling laundry products. Hey, I was my own person, and I knew there was more to life than what I learned in school. There were truths to be discovered and I was going to discover them, whatever they may be.

I remember one of the MOTHA couples would always make it to church Sunday morning, no matter where we were playing golf. One Sunday morning I saw them going down to the bank of the Delaware and crossing the river in a canoe, through the fog to go to church. I thought they were crazy, because I could hardly get my eyes open at that hour. They were devoted to something, but it wasn't for me. God was actually made a mockery by some of these guys, something I just could never do. I may have ignored Him, but I never made fun of Him. Just in case, you understand. I wasn't religious, mind you. But there was just too much perfection out there to take any chances like that. But some of these lawyers seemed to have found Him guilty of not existing. And He didn't exist in our minds or hearts. We were Lost and didn't know it.

No wonder we had no boundaries in our behavior. We behaved as our parents had taught us, which included going to church on Easter and somewhere around Christmas. But it also included drinking, partying and having fun in life, anyway we could, without getting locked up for it. If it were today, I believe we all would have qualified as authentic alcoholics. And all of us would have been arrested for DWI's. But thank God we somehow lived through the times when gas and alcohol were mixed more often than not. And emotions were mixed with hormones with equal disorientation.

Death was always a step away. Driving while intoxicated would be called an accident. Being done in with relationships would be called suicide. Just an afterthought. I used to wonder, "How did we ever make it?"

There's only one thing tougher than being a teen, it's being an overgrown teen. So I was going through all the usual rebellious "I want to be my own person" type of thing here. God, what an awful transition. If you are going through this now, just hang in with the best you can be, and you'll make it. Let go to your basest instincts and it will be hell. I was walking the tightrope and it seemed like I was the only one going through this at the time. You too? I didn't know what I was looking for, but *it* was looking for me and that's 'the rest of the story.'

The Odd Trio

Tom Pearce and I had shared a lot of experiences recently. He was from Poughkeepsie and had played hockey up there as I also had up in Lake Placid, New York. He was starting to date Dr. O'Neal's daughter, Carol. This was very daring as her surgeon father was more than very protective of her. His old buddy, Bill Clark, and I decided we should find a nice house and share the fun and expenses of having our own `home'. They had been living in a cruddy apartment in Elizabeth, NJ and I would see them on the commuter train to New York. I used to drive from Plainfield to Elizabeth just to go hit some local hangouts, like the *Dunellen Hotel*, where singles would go every Thursday night for a complete overhaul at the bar.

So one thing led to another and we found this nice house to rent, with a pool! The owner, Mary and her husband lived downstairs in the basement. That was ok as she would come up and clean her house constantly, and he was a truck driver for Pabst Beer and so we never ran out of beer. He had a fridge in the garage just for such product sampling. Try as we might, we could never get it completely empty. With all of this going for us, how could I remain pure? But sure enough, I continued to succeed at not getting what everyone else was getting. I couldn't figure out why then but hindsight is 20-20. [6]

This was the life, being on our own and doing what we wanted when we wanted. We'd have girls over and some would peel the grapes before they fed us, others would just hold the bunch dangling over our mouth and tease us.

And then we had a summer place called *The Shanty*. This was the all time perfect hideaway. We'd go out and meet girls at the Beacon Hotel in Point Pleasant on the Jersey Shore. Then when we'd rendezvous back at the Shanty where we'd party `60's style. I guess the worst thing we did was drink beer and decorate the windows with empty cans. Just about every window was blacked out, full of cans of every brand of beer under the sun. Just driving into the Shanty was

---

[6] See *"The Second Arc of the Great Circle"*

enough to spell danger for our guests. As we'd pull up to the stone pillars outside on the street entrance, we'd say "Here we are!" And the car would disappear as we'd pull into the front yard where the grass had grown higher than the cars roof. There could be six or eight cars in our yard and all would be invisible from the house or the street. I was surprised the girls didn't completely freak out. But they trusted us and they were ok to do so. (Not so today.)

We had fun just being shut off from the world. This Shanty turned out to be owned by an English couple who were acquaintances of Tom's mother. And Tom heard from her that the couple had this place on the Manasquan River in Point Pleasant, but were not going to be in the USA for at least five years. Well, we were there to keep their house safe We'll come back here and check on it over the next couple of summers.

It seemed a shame not to be able to see our cars parked outside the Shanty. Each of us had bought our own new cars. Bill Clark had his silver Porsche; I had a new fast back black Volvo and Tom's bright red Morgan with the wide leather strap over the engine bonnet. We looked fast wherever we pulled in. Especially parked in front of Mary's house up in Rahway with the pool and all. No wonder the girls fed us our grapes peeled.

One morning Tom and Bill had gone on to work and I could hardly get out of bed. My stomach was screaming and a high fever had me in a pool of sweat. I tried getting to my car to get to a doctor. I was all bent over as I drove twenty miles to Plainfield. The telephone poles seemed as if they were doing the hula. Somehow I made it and the doctor tested my blood count and said I had appendicitis, but he wanted another opinion. He sent me to the top surgeon Dr O'Neal, who said for me to just go directly to Muhlenburg Hospital and he'd check me out there. Upon arriving there, I was stripped and totally shaved by a bloodthirsty faggot. He got chewed out by Dr. O'Neal as the anesthesiologist gave me the needle and said count to one starting with ten, nine.

Doc O'Neal has known me forever but didn't realize my roommate was the guy dating his daughter Carol. Tom was getting her home late and Doc couldn't handle it. If he had known, I may not have woken up. As it was, he had me walking the next day down the hospital halls so as to show what a great surgeon's patients can do the day after he cuts on them. He said my appendix was about to explode but he got it out clean and with less than a one inch incision. Gag! I'll never be a doctor! But I appreciated that I was alive and mistakenly gave him the credit. He accepted it, however. Some doctors play God so often they start believing they are.

Doc said I would have to take it easy for a while and not to lift anything heavy. That became the stock line of many jokes. But not being able to go to work, what should I do?

First I called Uncle Sam and told him I was wounded and wouldn't be able to come to Fort Dix and crawl under live fire at night. He said he was sorry to hear that and seeing as how I was looking forward so much to doing that, he would postpone my induction for six months. Yahoo!

Second, I called Eastern Airlines and booked passage to St. Thomas in the Virgin Islands. I had seen pictures of this paradise in some magazine and felt I could recuperate there much better than in my bed at home. They said when I arrived at the airport they would have a wheel chair and my luggage taken care of all the way to my hotel. Where was I staying? Uh, duh. So they made a reservation for me at Casa Santana which overlooked the harbor of Charlotte Amalie, and I could have breakfast on my patio off my room. It all sounded too good to be true, but it was even better than it sounded. Tom and Bill took me to the airport and wheeled me to the Eastern Desk. From there they waved goodbye with tears of sadness for me. The Stewardess insisted that I be in first class so they could tend to my needs, even though I had a coach ticket with a student discount. They were able to keep me on my strict diet of steak and champagne all the way to Puerto Rico. There I was wheeled around to an ice cream store and treated to a tangerine cone covered with shaved coconut. Oh this was going to be tough. The pain, you know.

Then on to St. Thomas. I had never seen water the color of this below me. I could see the bottom of the ocean from thousands of feet in the air. I swear I saw whales, but no, I'm sure I was just seeing things. Baboom rrrrrt. "Ladies and gentlemen, please remain seated until the plane has…" I was first off in a wheel chair brought on board. True to their word I was whisked away in a cab, luggage and all, to my room above it all. I said to myself, you know how to recover. The first day I was still quite sore, but after awakening to fresh pineapple, eggs and bacon, coffee and juice on my patio, and then soaking up the vitamin C rays right there as I watched cruise ships come and go, I was glad to be sore. Other wise I would have thought I had died and gone to heaven. This was Paradise!

The second day I was able to move around surprisingly well and decided it was time to hit the beach. My hostess called a cabbie and I was taken to Morningstar Beach just outside the harbor entrance, a long strip of pure sand with that magical water lapping at my feet. I was getting better as I swam and enjoyed the day and meeting all sorts of neat people. But it was almost noon when someone suggested that I have a Sundowner to cool off with and to get in touch with the steel band playing calypso on the patio. That drink healed me! I felt no pain as I walked and talked and danced and swam the rest of the day. It was time to head back to my Casa and a young black native named Little John offered me a ride back on his Motorbike. So off we went into the wind high on a ridge overlooking Morning Star Beach. He said he would come by the next day and we'd ride out to Red Hook and do some snorkeling. And that we did too.

The rising sun saw us ride several miles over treacherous roads that twisted and turned over mountainous jungle. Flowers whizzed by in a blur of color. I freaked out as Little John screamed over a hill, on the left side of the road, and a jeep came at us to our right. I hadn't adjusted to our British habits on this American Island where driving on the left is the law. I later found out that a new mayor had once tried to change this at midnight so not many would be on the road. The whole next day was the biggest blood bath in the islands history and the mayors last day in office. The next mayor changed it back immediately. I'm glad it wasn't while I was on the island.

Red Hook was another picture book beach on the far end of St Thomas. The view was spectacular as across the blue turquoise water was St. John, the third of the American Virgin Islands.[7] I felt a strange drawing towards the Island, but it was not to be satisfied, not now.

---

[7] Little did I know that place, St John, would play in my future.

This life style was my recovery from the first surgery of my life. I improved each day to the point where I was better than I had ever been. But everyone had been so nice to help me get better, I almost didn't want to. But they were really happy to be a part of my recovery and I had grown very fond of my friends here. But just as that time arrives, it is time to return to my other life. It was time to return home. Ten days of paradise is almost too much to imagine, but I think I could handle it. How about you?

Back home at reality, the Odd Trio were just getting into high gear. Spring was turning into summer and the atmosphere was invigorating! We all made it to work somehow each morning and each night was a different location to party and then back to our house and into the pool. Somehow on Fridays we all managed to be down at the Shanty by 5pm and ready for a weekend!

Uncle Sam Wants You

This was the summer to beat all. And I figured it may be the last of my life because Uncle Sam was still waiting on my body to enter his most sacred killing fields. I had better learn to live before I die.

Some of the most favorite albums were still being played on our radios. Elvis was beginning to overtake Harry Bellefonte, and the Ella Fitzgerald sounds were being replaced by Barbara Streisand, while Benny Goodman's drummer was in a major drum battle at Carnegie Hall with Buddy Rich. Only time won, but the new talents never replaced the greatness of their predecessors. So it was that I would catch the great in New York City for one or two nights a week, do our New Jersey bar once a week, and be at the Shanty by 5pm every Friday. Then the odd trio would put their new and separate sports cars into action to see who could outdo whom.

In the heat of one July Saturday night, we all again ended up at a new dance bar together. We started playing on the same group of girls. I, for some reason, said to my girl friend of the moment, that if she would like to come home with me she just needed to go out the bar door and get into the Limousine that awaited her outside. I was kidding, but when she looked outside, as it would happen, a limo was just stopping outside the door. I stepped outside and opened the door and said to the driver, "Would you please take Miss Heather to the Shanty. I'll follow (in front) in just a moment." The driver saw my wink and decided he would play along. Beautiful Heather, with eyes and mouth wide open started to get into the limo. I gave her a kiss and assured her I'd be following her. She was puddy, and just wanted me with her, but I assured her 'James' was my bodyguard and would keep her safe while I led her to the Shanty. I couldn't believe how this limo had arrived at the moment of my 'lie' and exactly upon opening the door. And then how the complete stranger 'James' played along with me to this point. My Heather was impressed, but not nearly as much as I was. We behaved that night, and laughed at how 'fate' had played into our hands. She really thought it was my Limo, not just magic and luck. Well, it wasn't my limo, but the lesson was mine to believe and behold. This was the first memory of the magic I could call on for so many unexplainable things.[8] I knew I needed some answers to all this, and time held them all. And so the search began. I never realized that what I can share with you in moments would take me twenty years to discover.

The rest of the summer was filled with the unbelievable experiences such as this. At our annual MOTHA outing in Rumson, with my golfing buddies, I found myself cutting the deck of cards to whatever card they mentioned. One time it was seven times in a row. No big deal to the casual observer. But it was totally awesome to me, and therefore to my friends when they realized it wasn't just a trick.

On the eighteenth hole on the last day of this year's annual MOTHA outing at the Rumson Country Club, if I could sink a 40-foot putt all the way across the green, my partner, Tony Haley, said we would win, and that I could do it. I said I can do it, pictured the putt dropping into the hole and knocked it across the bumpy grass surface into the nest for a birdie. We won, and our team owners of which we were half owners, won around $1,500. This was big bucks for me in that day and age. If I had thought about the money that ball would have never rolled in. I would have choked for sure. And that is what usually had happened in my life. I had my sights aimed at the wrong target.

And Uncle Sam wanted my sights aimed at his targets. After this wild and fun summer, we had a party for Moose and I with the good ole guys who knew how to party all night. Hank (Moose) and I were enrolled to be at Fort Dix at 4:00 pm the following day. I was so 'sick' on Induction day that I just had to call Fort Dix HQ and let them know I wouldn't be there today as I was very ill. I was informed that I was to arrive this day in a body bag if necessary! They would take care of any illness after that. And so I arrived, by ambulance, ready for war, with my golf clubs, tennis racquets and some other very important gear. Some guy in kaki took all my gear and put it back into my friend's ambulance and I was left there with instructions from my 'Doctor' to have three days bed rest.

---

[8] *Hung By The Tongue*

A one striper helped me through all the sign-in procedures. He gathered all my uniforms and other stuff I didn't recognize, and was driven to my barracks. It was hours before the rest of the recruits showed up all dirty and sweaty. I turned over and went back to sleep. I had a doctor's appointment the next day and they agreed I finish my doctor's orders and rest for two more days. The rest of Charlie Company went through hell week in two days. I was helped to my appointments. I couldn't believe how nice all these army guys were treating me. I was impressed.

Hank (Moose) wasn't so lucky. He showed up in the expected way and they just made him eat his lunch from day one. He had to march, do KP, get all his shots at once and suffer other unknown inhumanities. I just wish they would have let me have a TV, but fortunately, someone brought me some books and the time passed pretty quickly between naps. By the second day I was feeling great, but they made me lie low another day. When we moved into our permanent barracks for basic training, some two striper moved all my gear for me. After I got an all is well from the dispensary, I finally made the morning muster. It was there we were asked if anyone had any previous military experience. I knew better than to volunteer for anything, but I had flunked ROTC in college. So I raised my hand, and that was the only hand in the air. I was told to fall out and taken back into the barracks. It was there I was told to move my gear into a private room and made Platoon Leader. This meant several changes, including doing the inspections, never doing KP, ordering the troops to do pull ups or push ups in order to get food; and so it was.

Hank was in **Dogbreath** Company, right near us in **Charlie** Company, but his company commander spit nails when he smiled. And Hank was the biggest 2 X 4 to spit at in uniform. He was nailed every day to the wall by this famous DI. But to overview my whole military career, there was Basic Training, and after Basic Training there was life, and after life, death. There was a kid, and then a very mature man. Briefly it went like this. After I sailed my way through basic, there was a two-week leave. I had found out that military personnel with leave papers could fly on military aircraft free to any destination. I had a cab take me to the adjoining air force base and within 30 minutes I was airborne from McGuire Air Force Base for

Texas. That's where the next plane was going and that's where Patti was now living, and I figured that was where I was meant to spend my leave. As fate would have it, the orders for the air force plane was changed in mid-flight to go to Cape Canaveral, Florida. That's where my buddy Cliff was living and we spent two glorious weeks fishing and scuba diving and sailing and cavorting with the richie rich there in Palm Beach.

This was my first time to do some scuba diving in the ocean. Clifford had just finished his stint as a UDT [9] specialist with the Navy Seals. And if he could live through that, I had faith in him now. So down we go after a few pointers on the how to's. It was definitely magnificent as the sunbeams shown down through the depths of blue, when suddenly a shadow came over us. It caught my attention immediately as it was a completely clear day. We both looked up together to see three huge sharks above us getting kind of jerky and anxious. Not as anxious as I got. I started to swim up to get out of the ocean forever, but Cliff caught my ankle and pointed down. No, I nodded, but he insisted, and on down we went. I was so anxious I thought I would inhale my whole tank with each breath. He got me to settle down with sign language and then pointed to a cave down a little further. He held his hand so I would wait outside. He disappeared into the cave when I heard him tap on his tank three times. That was our warning signal. Dang! Sharks above us and there's trouble in this cave. What could be in there, a bear? Suddenly another huge shadow appears with Cliff hanging on to it. He was trying to ride a sea turtle and it was coming right at me. I had no idea what it was and prepared to shoot whatever with my spear gun. The thing was scared of me for some reason and tore my mask off with its front paw as it went to swim around me. Cliff saw me in trouble and let go. I was comforted to feel his grip on my arm as I tried to breath without a mask. It worked and I thought I might live. Then he tried to teach me how to get my mask back on and clear the water out of it. Finally I got it half empty and I could see him clearly if I turned my head sideways. We're still at 60 feet when he signals for us to go into the cave so as to protect our back and flank. The sharks are closing in

---

[9] Underwater Demolition Team: now called SEALS

and my anxiety is their target. In the cave Cliff, with his mouthpiece hanging out, starts laughing in a high pitch. I figure it must be the bends and we're both going to die. He pointed and there went three sharks in a straight line never to be seen again by us. Back up in our boat I only suffered a bloody nose. Later he explained the laughing was a trick he had learned in UDT but had never tried. The laughing was supposed to sound like dolphins which terrorize sharks. It worked and off they went. Whew! Basic was a cinch compared to this Navy stuff.

We had some more good laughs over this and other water sports as we entertained some pretty listeners in the evenings. Clifford was always the ladies man and never really took advantage of it. I probably wished I had half his good looks and money, and he probably wished the same. Maybe the truth was that neither of us had either?

Time passed so fast that I had no sooner forgotten about Uncle Sam than it was time to be back at Fort Dix for my next assignment, Advanced Infantry Training. Somehow that didn't fit into my vision of the future. But I went out of Clifford's driveway and stuck out my thumb and got a ride all the way to somewhere so I could get a bus to Cape Canaveral. Once there I started asking about flights going north. There were no military flights scheduled for two days going my way. So I did my mental thing and within minutes 007 comes up to me in a black suit and dark glasses and asks if I'm "Looking for a ride North?" "Sure!" "Well," he apologizes, "I'm just going as far as Virginia, would that help?' "Sure would! I could buy a commercial ticket from there!"

So he carries my duffle bags and off I follow out on the tarmac to this small 20-passenger jet. Whew, definitely nice! He heaves my bags up into the underbelly of the plane and they disappear somehow. Then he and I climb up these neat stairs and into the cabin. There15 men, all dressed like my friend, are staring straight ahead, not talking or moving. Was I walking into a movie set? I was introduced to a gorgeous young lady who looked positively excited to see me. She was our hostess for the flight. Ginger brought me anything I wanted starting with champagne, then a sizzling steak with all the trimmings, and she was desert. Seriously, she came over to me and asked if I would like a blanket and sat down next to me for most of the rest of the flight. Ginger is sweet.

This was the nicest flight of my life, and it was free, and when I get home I'm going to write a letter to East Coast Airlines and thank them. (When I got around to doing this days later I found there is no such thing listed as East Coast Airlines.) We landed in Virginia at Langley Air Force Base (which I found out later is the home of the CIA) where my friend the pilot had called ahead and had a C-120 patiently waiting on the tarmac for me. I didn't know what a C-120 was either, but I was really impressed with how nicely these people were helping me get to the Fort Dix area. Upon landing and a sweet farewell from Ginger, my friend carried my bags to this giant plane that looked like a flying elephant.

The air force boys had been waiting a half hour for me and were ready to take off for Delaware. They stowed me in the back like cargo and off we went. I thought this beast would never get off the ground and the roar was deafening. I was scared and wondered where Ginger was. I was surrounded by some heavy equipment and 10 air force gunho's who looked at my Private's Army uniform like it was less than lower class. They pulled out a net bunk from the cargo wall and said I could lie down if I wanted. I did and was asleep in seconds. Later, all I remember was a screaming wind sound and these guys shouting, "We're going down, jump! You've got to jump!" as they rolled me off of the bunk. The floor of the cargo bay must have been an elevator that they had lowered enough to let the air whistle and when the floor wasn't where I expected it I panicked! They started laughing at ole Army boy, and I started laughing too, just cause I was still alive and not floating down through the sky without a parachute.

These guys turned out to be just as scared as we avoided a crash landing at Dover Air Force Base in Delaware. We came in too low and almost hung it up in some electric and phone lines. The pilot gave the beast full engine power to try to pull us out of our landing plight. Every rivet in the plane was vibrating along with me. Somehow we started turning and finally climbing and cleared the disaster below. Turns out my jokers had loaded the heavy equipment all the way forward with out telling the pilot, so we came in front heavy. We felt the surge of gravity pulling at us as we went from going down to trying to go up. We banked around the Air Base and came in for a safer landing. I saw the pilot after finally disembarking, spilling his guts in the airport toilet. He said he always does that after nearly dying. But these flyboys had arranged for another flight to be waiting for me there too.

This turned out to be a four-engine turbojet with some real live sky cowboys on board: the pilot, a wandering sergeant, and a sky girl. I think they call her a WAF. What ever they call her, I called her beautiful and she loved it. She might be the last girl I see for a long time, as they don't have any of those pretty things in Advanced Infantry where I was heading. She went and offered me a beer and seeing as how the sergeant already had one open, I said "Yaess!"

We were out over the ocean and the pilot wanted to see if he could barrel roll this monster turbojet without us spilling any beer. It didn't work at first so he tried again. Never did work, but it got me as sick as an ole hound on brandy. They laughed all the way into McGuire Air Force Base where I was sworn to secrecy. They got me a cab and off I went to Fort Dix, three miles away. Whew, what a leave! I had never had such a good time as these last two weeks, and now I was going to pay for it. I was dropped off at the AIT barracks and went into a bustle of men getting their lockers ready and their bunks tight and their boots shined. They started yelling at me that I better get up and start getting ready for inspection. I couldn't do anything but lie on that bunk I was so tired and disinvolved with their burden.

Then it happened. A Master Sergeant came in and yelled, "CANNON!" It was all I could do to get my arm to raise up off the bunk. When he saw my heroic effort he looked at me with bayonet eyes and said, "You don't belong here!" I said, "You've got that right Serge," and mustered up enough strength to drag my duffle bag down between the row of bunks while I gave the recruits the usual, "Polish that buckle soldier, tuck in that shirt, blouse those pants, tighten those bunk sheets," until I had made my escape. The sergeant drove me in a jeep across the base to this real nice area which I found later to be the service area of Post Headquarters. I was put into these real nice air-conditioned barracks with the golf team and the band.

Then Serge took me over to Post HQ where I was interviewed and given a typing test. I had to type out a page of military orders. After reading mine over and over the past two days hoping they would change to "Honorable Discharge" I knew how to type orders. I was hired on the spot to work there as an assistant to the General. My first job was to retype my orders from Advanced Infantry to Post HQ. That was easy, as this is just what I had pictured in my fantasies instead of crawling under bobbed wire at night with tracers skimming the air above me in my gas mask and cradling my trusty M1 Rifle. Actually the M14 was probably just out, but I remembered when I joined my reserve unit that I had been asked what I could do best in the Army. I said that I'd love to jump out of planes behind enemy lines, but since I broke my ankle skiing the doctors wouldn't let me do that anymore, but I can type!

And this duty was the life. I was now a PFC, one step above nothing, and yet I had the Uncle in my back pocket. Or so it seemed. Every night, at 4pm I would be heading for the shore to party, catch a few winks at the Shanty, wake up and drive the two hours back to Fort Dix in the morning mist. I never made my bunk the whole time I was there, so I never had inspection and was never missed in roll call. I'd show up around 8 am and drive by the ranks and hear "All present and accounted for Sir!" and go on into work like any other soldier. I have to admit I was burning the candle at both ends, but I could handle it.

After a few weeks of this grind I saw my next-door, growing up, hometown buddy Moose, who had survived Uncle Sam's distasteful cooking very well. We decided to go to the shore together the next day and get a real meal. It was payday, so we went to go get our checks, but the military aficionados had misplaced ours. We had begun a wild goose chase and so I said, "Let's roll. We'll come back tomorrow and get them. We'll just tell them at work that we were trying to get paid all day." So off we go on the two-hour drive to the beach. We get to Point Pleasant and a couple blocks down from the Shanty was *Jersey Mike's* Giant Subs. We grabbed a couple #5s and went to look at the ocean while we ate them.

Then we moseyed down the boardwalk to a bar I sometimes enjoyed. The bartender remembered me and then we met two very pretty stewardesses. After a drink I asked if they'd like to go to Hanniwald's Diner for some coffee. They said, "Yes!"

The blonde got in next to me and Hank put the brunette behind her in the back seat. As we traveled down Atlantic Avenue there suddenly appeared a very large black wall in front of my car. I hit the brakes and slid off the new pavement onto loose stones and crashed straight into a tar covered lane-paving machine. Geahhhh! I felt numb all over. I saw blood all over my blonde friend; the pain was mixed with numbness and unconsciousness. When somebody finally arrived it was the bartender asking me if I was really 21, not "how are you?" It took them almost two hours to get me to the Point Pleasant Hospital, a ten-minute ride away. I realized the engine of Kid, my trusty Ford, had pushed the steering wheel into my chest crushing my sternum. Hank, or Moose, had been thrown forward into the back of my seat pushing me into the onslaught of heavy metal. I broke the steering wheel with my face. And I hadn't signed out at Dix. I was AWOL if caught.

At the Hospital they found out I was a soldier at Dix and would not, therefore, treat me, unless it was an emergency. So they called Dix and told them they had a transfer patient. The Army sent a truck with a couple lackeys who went to the beach and had breakfast before coming to get me. There was a tag on my toe that said Fort Dix, like I was dead dirt. I told Moose to say goodbye to my parents, I love them and I'm sorry, just before I passed out again. The soldiers were irate at finding me in such a condition without being told. I found later that if I had wanted to sue for this negligence I'd have to have died there in order to prove it was an emergency. [10] I came to as I was bounced back to Dix in a truck, with Hank there trying to comfort me. He came through it all with just a chipped tooth. Do you think God was trying to get my attention?

There was a team of eight doctors staring down at me for hours after arriving at Dix. They were wonderful as they encouraged me. The twenty some stitches in my face were carefully done, they said, so I'd be able to shave over them. That meant I might be alive to shave! They didn't tell me I was bleeding internally so bad that I must have used up most of their type O blood. For a week I was half in and

---

[10] It was at this same Point Pleasant Hospital that 30 years later my mom died, and my dad a year after her.
Whoa!

out of consciousness, on I V feeding and transfusions. I remember this WAC that stayed with me even after her shift was over. She'd be there holding my hand, telling me I was going to be ok. It was she that saw my vital signs going zippo. She called Colonel Stone who came at 2am and gave me an illegal shot that coagulated the blood internally, hopefully where I was bleeding, and gave me heart massage to get me going again. I learned all this from this very special WAC months later after being discharged from the hospital. She even came to see me at home where I told her I owed her my life and what did she want. She wanted to be with me for a night. She stayed.

I was on medical leave for several months before returning to Active duty, where they gave me a soft interrogation about whether I was AWOL. They decided I wasn't and gave me that pay check they had misplaced and several others that I had earned since then.

Three days later I was heading for the shore again with a friend driving. I was quite uneasy about getting into a car, but had to do it. And as we traveled through the dark pineys, as the area is called, suddenly at 60 mph the headlights short out and we are thrown into pitch darkness. I opened my door to see the edge of the road meet the grass and guessed at telling her go left or right as she slowed to a stop. After I thought we were ok, I swung open the door to run back and warn any cars that may come upon us. I no sooner got one foot on the ground when I realized we were off the road and still moving. A pine tree was pushing the door shut on my head. I shouted loud enough for her to instantly hit the brake all the way and the squeeze stopped. I was shaking but ok. We found the battery cable that had jumped loose and were on our way, still heading for the shore. The draw that Mother Ocean had on me was smashing!

My friend's car got us to the Shanty. She was looking strikingly good to me too, as I had only seen her as a superior officer. She was a Lieutenant and I was next to nothing, but we had met in the hospital, she as my nurse, and I as her patient. We quietly had arranged this time together long ago if I made it out of there alive. We really had a nice evening together, which was a living oxymoron there at the Shanty. We really liked and respected each other and she did have an investment in my hide.

It had been interesting to see her stand up for me when my AWOL interview occurred. The Captain who had to interview me about why I was at the shore the night of the accident, called in this Lieutenant at my request. She gave me a character reference that even knocked my socks off. The Captain said that I wasn't AWOL and that ended the matter. I owed her my life twice.

I never saw her again after I got the word that I was being given an early honorable discharge from the Army. I wouldn't even have to go to Reserve meetings after my active duty time was up. So after four months of military excitement they decided to get rid of me, honorably. Good decision Uncle Sam.[11]

After all, this death defying accident on March 26th was the 7th year in a row that I had a progressively worsening event culminating in this final one in which I technically died. I had made a promise to God, as I lay dying in that Point Pleasant Hospital, that if He let me live I would give the rest of my life to Him. To me it wasn't worth much, so I really wasn't giving up that much.

God continued testing by fire, and molding me until I was ready to keep my promise. Thank God for His perseverance, patience and love of me before I ever loved Him. This whole story is His story, of how He took this ole bag of bones and assigned a thousand angels to protect me until I kept my end of the promise, to love, and yield to Him. But I had so much to learn, and it is very exciting to see how it all unfolds. There are many more stupid adventures I'm afraid, but thank God for His Grace and Mercy on my body and with my soul!

---

[11] Let me state here that I have every respect for the men and women of our armed forces, and I never took them or our missions lightly.

Back To Bleachette

I had been given a second chance on life, or was it many more chances than that. After having seven accidents on the same date seven years in a row, I wondered, and I wondered. God really had my attention, but I didn't know where to find him. Someone said all the answers were in the Bible, but that never made much sense to me.[12] So I continued to look in this world for answers, and a way to make a living.

I was offered my old job back at Bleachette Bluing in New York, right at Lexington and 45th Street. I went in every Friday and when needed. Otherwise I was on the road from Montauk Point to Philadelphia seeing retailers and wholesalers. A pretty rough bunch in the grocery trade, mostly Jewish, with a little Mafia here and there. I learned to get along with all of them.

This also was my creative era, as I was to eventually take over this business and let the ole Boss retire. It was my idea to modernize and come out with new exciting products. He said go for it, and was a great help.

First I worked with a chemist to change the bluing product from just a cloth wrapped block to be swished in the laundry water to a liquid product to be poured in. This created many challenges such as stability on the shelf. The product had to look just as good a year from now as it did when just shaken up. The shape of the bottle, the label, the fragrance, the advertising, the selling to wholesalers all were laid in my lap. The packing was done in Pompton Lakes, in northern New Jersey where I worked for weeks on the packaging lines. I was working for coolie wages, but I had all these responsibilities. I had to believe it would finally pay off big time. Finally we went to market and it was a great success.

Can you remember doing laundry before fabric softeners? I had seen enough laundry to know stiff pants syndrome. I went to work

---

[12] Many years later I realized it was because I didn't have the 'Great Translator' within me.

with my chemist acquaintance and voila, a wonderful new product named Fawn. It was thoroughly thought out between my mentor Boss and I. I might be able to make enough on this one to buy him out and let him finally retire. We had researched even the name and found the most pleasing word in the English language was **dawn**. We went for the copyrights and found it had already been reserved by Proctor and Gamble.[13] We then came up with the name Fawn, and within 6 months we had100% distribution on the shelves of stores all over the metropolitan area. Three months later P&G put a free sample bottle of Downy on every doorknob in the country. This was a first of this kind of marketing and it knocked my shelf space from 8 rows down to two, one or none. And then their TV ads knocked us off the shelf almost completely even though our surveys revealed that people preferred Fawn.

During this great depression I went out to lunch on the streets of NYC. It was like Orson Wells had done his thing again. People were running down the street screaming, sobbing, just miserable. In a bar where I could get my favorite hot corned beef sandwich nobody wanted to wait on me. What? Then I heard the TV talking about how our President Kennedy had been assassinated in Texas. I couldn't believe it could happen here in America. Personally I didn't vote for the man, but I had had pleasant run ins with Jackie, and this murder completely removed my appetite. I went back to the office and we closed for the rest of the day. We didn't know if a missile was coming next.

This was the beginning of an unstoppable crime wave that has made ripples from political high places ever since. "Hell's base here, Satan has landed." Everyone alive that day remembers just where they were and what they were doing. Bleachette Corporation decided with the rest of the country to close its doors for the day and go home. The whole country was in mourning for a week.

(Now, decades later, we are so desensitized we would hardly miss a stroke of work or play. It would be especially ignored if it were a Republican Conservative murdered by a liberal left wing murderer. Our 'impartial' media would insure profound noncoverage these days.

---

[13] It was over ten years later when their product *Dawn* hit the market.

But we'll look into that later in the future, and now back to the present.)

Reality had sunk in as we watched John John salute the casket and John's Son took the oath of office. At least that's how the Chinese saw it. It was logical to them that the new President would be John's son. (But to Americans it stank as bad as a lawyers 'suicide' in Fort Marcy Park. There I go again into the future.)

Bleachette Bluing started looking bleaker as I realized how the giants of the industry could squash a small company's tremendous achievements. The Boss started looking for a buy out from a big company as he saw my interest waning. I had given this company five of my good years and they were heading down the proverbial drain. Where was I going to go from here? A new career? Unimaginable! My father had worked for the same company since the depression. Here I was into my 5th or 6th different job already. And I wasn't even married yet. Who would want a flake, a floater, a loser?

The Boss urged me to stay on and I would have a great opportunity with this new 'parent' company. I did, and worked extra hard to prove myself. As it was to be, the day of the take over, all three of us in the office were on the street with two weeks severance pay. Someone asked me 'what now?' I just said, "Don't know, something better."

Ya Mon

I had to get over these negative feelings that I was putting on my insecure self. I tried to forget my problems by drowning them at every party I could find. And if there were no party, the Odd Trio would head out to the Dunellen Hotel, the Park Hotel, and the Somerville Inn. We were still living in the house in Rahway, NJ, which also saw its share of parties. But one day, soon after a company that made ant traps bought Bleachette Bluing Corp from under my sweaty brow, I came down with a nasty fever. I tried driving to my parents while the phone poles were weaving and doing a hula dance again.

Some how I made it home where Mom drove me to a doctor to find that I had Mononucleosis and had to rest, rest and then rest some more. My dad heard it was called the kissing disease and said "What the hell Ya been doin?" He had said the same thing when I came home after one week at college with a throat infection I had gotten at a cruddy restaurant. But he thought I had gotten it from some VD pusher. Fortunately both times, the doctors told him that it wasn't from some woman.

I was then allowed to recover there at home, and after a few days with no fever I started making plans for recuperating elsewhere. I started looking at travel magazines and some pictures of aqua green oceans hugging white beaches.

That did it. As soon as the doctor said I could get out of bed I was on a plane to Jamaica! No reservations, just bags in hand. I jumped into someone's limo at the airport and got out at the first resort there in Montego Bay. They were full but had a cancellation as I stood there, and they gave me a room with a view of the aqua-green ocean that was in the magazine. I had to pinch myself as I enjoyed pineapple on my patio balcony. "Oh ya mon. Dis de good life!"

After a day of laying low and only thinking bad thoughts, I made it over to the beach. There I was introduced to a fire eater, a coconut oil vendor and a beautiful girl with a rum and coke in hand. I managed to put them all together in a funtage only found in Jamaica, mon.

I was greeted onto the beach of aquamarine water by a six-foot spray of fire going across the path of sand leading to coconut palms and paradise. "Whoa, wha's happin, mon?" I was ready for any thing, but not this. His toothless smile made me smile and I let down my guard again. After some small talk he wanted me to sip his magic potion so as to also become a fire-eater. Actually he was looking for money, but the natives still had manners in the 60's. His lady friend convinced me that my pale body needed the protection of coconut oil on my body. She sold me a coke bottle full of the pure clear lotion, and it gave me the best tan ever over the next two weeks. Next I met a girl more beautiful than anything I had ever envisioned in paradise. She was a blend of Eurasian stock and was a native Jamaican as well. Her light brown skin and easy smile made her fun to be with. She knew everyone and everything, but she was modest about her apparent notoriety. We made a date for that night, which was unforgettable. I was to pick her up at the Harmony House, a small hotel complex. Later I found that her family owned it as well as the very popular Brown's Rum factory. But what I wasn't ready for was the really good time I had with this island girl. We danced and cavorted all night until she took me to the stables where she kept her horses. When she heard that I had done some riding she got us two beautiful Palominos that were just as happy to cavort with us as we were. On this unforgettable night we rode bareback on the empty beaches as the sun rose over the ocean. The spray from her horse galloping through the surf sprayed over me as I tried to keep up with her. We laughed and kissed and never saw each other again.

After sleeping well into the next afternoon, I was greeted back to the beach by an arch of fire. "Hey Mon, you have hot time last night?" "Flambe le bush" I urged, trying to say 'close your mouth' in French. It went over his flaming head. I was upset because I wanted to see her again. But she had said she was afraid of seeing each other any more, because someday she would have to stay and I would be leaving the island. What did that have to do with anything?

The next morning I checked out with my memories and hitched a ride on the airport limo from Montego Bay to Ocho Rios. On the way

I remember passing a big house up on the right. Our driver said that had been the home of the White Witch of Rose Hall. She would run slaves underground below the sugar cane fields from the sailing ships in the harbor into her dungeon. She would use them for slave labor, fun or torture. Whoa! And she would put their heads on the stone posts marking the entrance to her home. Later I went there and saw the hairs sticking out of the mortar in the dungeon where chain shackles still hung. Is this is a way of life here?

The limo driver took me to the Sheraton Montego where I lucked into another room. It was not the normal room on the 2nd floor or above, but on the beach next to where the tennis pro stayed. We became good friends, as I was the best tennis match he had had in weeks. He also had a lovely young thing trying to put the make on him. She was not the type of hotel groupie that would put the make on the native employees, only the staff. That gave her class right there. She, was Beverly: Blonde, blue eyed, sensuous, Canadian, and very deserving of my company. Her last name was Hills: aspiring actress which made my New York knowledge very valuable, not. However Beverly Hills would go out with me if I had wheels. Good ole Walter, the tennis pro, had a personal car, which he gladly loaned me so he could pursue other interests.

We tooted around the tropical paradise and went up to the rain forests in the mountains, able to pick orchids from the window as we passed through what seemed like Eden. We climbed and slid down Dunns River Falls laughing and falling finally into the ocean at the bottom. We went rafting, water skiing, visiting the Rose Hall where we saw the torture chambers and had the Rum Special at the beach bar and learned to dance the Ska. I think I was getting better. We had three beautiful days together before this Hollywood bound beauty had to return to her Canada. But we did it all, eh?

I was so distraught at my loss that I went out on my own that night to a native bar. I was the only white there and everyone was really nice. Then I was told that a woman that had come in wanted to talk with me. Turns out she was the islands great bwana, the Queen of Jamaica, very famous and very respected by the natives. She invited me to join her for the night. We went to several different native bars where there was music, dancing, dining and drinking. At one such club, a fight broke out with broken bottles and blood aflying. A ring of natives headed for us and put a ring three people deep around us. I thought we were about to become hairs in the dungeon, but a large man said in my ear, "No problem, Mon. We be here. No problem. Just stay where you be mon." I was impressed. This was not to protect me, but Queenie. And I was with her. Whew!

Our driver wanted me to stay with his sisters. It would be an honor. Especially since I had no way of getting back to my hotel at that hour, I agreed. She was fat and ugly; her 'house' had no running water with a squatty potty under the bed. I was finally nervous as I had to face her gigantic brother the next morning and he would want to know if I had fun, and want money before I get my ride back to the hotel. I went to sleep regardless, right under her wall portraits of John F. Kennedy and Jesus Christ. I guess she wasn't half bad.

I was sure grateful to get back to my hotel with all its amenities and with my life. There was a man named Oleg Cassini on the dock who told me about a new hotel opening up just down the beach. It was going to be a Playboy Club. I grabbed my PBC membership card and jumped in my borrowed car and sure enough they were carrying in the room carpets and redoing the whole place. Also there was an intense Bunny training school just ending for the day. It was then that I saw the other interests that ole Walter wanted to pursue. He saw me and invited me to join he and some friends. Well we had a Bunny good time. Tennis anyone?

The natives here in Jamaica on the whole were friendly, helpful and charming. They loved their ocean island, although most of them couldn't swim. They knew their bread and butter, or rather rum and coke, depended on tourists coming and spending big bucks, and coming back again. But every morning my young native buddy Nigel would come see what I wanted for breakfast, what I wanted to do that day and make suggestions. Then he would arrange everything, never wanting anything. He just enjoyed serving someone. The day before my departure I insisted he tell me what I could give him. Instead of money, he said he would like a pair of my white socks. I realized he wasn't kidding, so the next morning I wrapped up a $5 bill in some white socks and gave them to the old man in the beach chair out on the dock, Oleg Cassini, to give to Nigel. I hope that he got his socks. I arranged for Walter to give him another gift just in case Mr. Cassini never saw him again.

Jamaica was my new Paradise. I had felt so at home here surrounded by the beauty, friendliness and warmth. Now it was time to return to Newark, NJ where the January temperatures were below zero. Do I have to? "Ya Mon. You come back, Mon."

Back To Reality

The transition from virtual paradise to actual nausem is hard on the body in the middle of winter. Still it is even harder on the mind and spirit. But it had to be done, and as usual I tried to make the best of it.

Bleachette Bluing, as my life project, was gone. What next I didn't know, but I felt confident I could get a job anywhere in those days. It was just a matter of what I wanted to do. A friend who I had known growing up, Don Luce, had been very successful in Life Insurance dealing with businesses. I went and interviewed with his company and was hired. It took me a while to say yes, as I remembered how hard making sales out in Las Vegas had been. I wasn't sure I was cut out for full time commission sales. Then they offered me a draw program where I would get so much money each month for two years, and my commissions would go towards paying that back, and then I would get a draw plus commissions.

I had a real hard time calling the number of people needed to get one appointment. Then I was scared to death of going out and trying to sell my friends insurance. It was never a priority for them, and they just saw me so I could 'practice'. I made some sales and some very good clients and my confidence started to gain hold of my whole manner of business. It was very hard and slow going building this business while building myself. I immersed myself in positive thinking books and seminars. I represented one if not the oldest of Life Insurance Company in America, Mutual Benefit Life. My office was right in downtown Newark, New Jersey. It wasn't the end of the world, but you knew it was near. Eventually, to be competitive I represented about 10 Life Companies and then I got my Health Insurance License, which added another 20 companies' products I could sell.

Then I started being a real maverick for that time. I was very surprised I had been hired because of my work history on Wall Street. The Insurance Industry frowned on the mix. But I saw an opportunity. After a few years, I studied and passed the NASD exam, which allowed me to sell stocks and mutual funds. Then I designed some plans for my clients who had whole life policies to take the cash value, buy term insurance and invest the balance of their premium into mutual funds so their money could grow at a much faster rate over time than in an insurance policy. This was radical and I would be fired if the insurance industry found me out. I placed all the stock fund orders through my Uncle Bill McLeod's office in Plainfield. Little did I know that this combination would later become the highway to super millions for A.L Williams. Buy term and invest the rest.

I also became licensed to sell a new product called Variable Annuities, and teachers were allowed to purchase this for their school retirement plans. I had to go from public school to school educating the teachers as to the benefits of this great new product. None of them bought.

Pension and Profit Sharing Plans and Group Health Insurance Policies were where my friend Don was making big bucks, along with Key man Insurance and funding Buy-Sell Agreements with Life Insurance. Man, I was up to my ears in this stuff when it all came tumbling down. But that's another story. Let me back up and get into my social life during all these insurance years.

I had not been dating anyone in particular in these early sixties, although one young lady, Jackie, was catching my heart, my eye, my ear and my tummy. Different friends had given us each a ticket to a Princeton football game, and our tickets were right next to each other. I shared my two thermos jugs of whiskey sours with her and we had a really smashing time. We all jammed into a local motel room and we ended up sleeping on a small bed together with our clothes on. It was better than sleeping on the floor alone like the rest of the room mates we had. My buddy Cotty was there and my date's cousin was there and I'm sure a few others. We dated like this for years without breaking the rules of fidelity. It was a great time, although we did have a few arguments just to see if we could survive them. Then she didn't want to date anymore. After five years she wanted to get a ring.

So Christmas night I took her out and we parked in the middle of some woods and I gave her the ring box with a note. She said, "Aww, you shouldn't have." And I said, "I didn't." She opened the box to find a tiny diamond 'engagement' ring to put on her charm bracelet. She did not know whether to laugh or cry so she did both. It was very confusing for her, but I knew that I had the real ring in my pocket. Just then, as we were hugging and consoling each other, we heard a stick snap in the woods. I started the car and lights hit us from all angles. I was ready to run over what ever was holding the light in front of me blocking my escape route. But just before I ran it over I saw a badge and a gun about to be drawn. I stopped and we got interrogated for ten minutes. I'm sure they would have bigger criminals to go after these days.

I just knew they were going to call her parents and spill the beans about us in the woods. I told Jackie when I dropped her off after a twenty minute goodnight kiss, that if the cops call her house, that she should tell her parents I was proposing. The cops didn't call but she told her parents anyway. I was soon invited over for a very fancy dinner. Her father, a surly Irishman, called me into the smoking room after a wonderful meal of roast leg of lamb, roasted potatoes, wines, and deserts. He poured me a brandy and said, "Peter, you have been dating my daughter for five years, you've been coming here eating my food for four years, letting me beat you at golf at my Country Club for three years, drinking my booze for two years, and making me lose sleep for one year. Just what are your intentions toward my daughter?" Gulp! This man was about to make me serious about something I wasn't ready to be serious about. I loved his daughter, but I was still not making it as an insurance salesman, and I wasn't the independent person I needed to be. Would that accomplishment ever arrive?

We were in a party mode at least every weekend and there was no reason to change. But this future father-in-law was trying to jolt me out of my advanced adolescent juvenilisms. Some of the goings on during this era may explain my reluctance to conform. One of the outrageous groups of guys and gals I would hang out with would go into New York for theater and dinner at the Playboy Club, or we would weekend at Cotty Barlow's grandmothers mansion on the Long Island Sound in Madison, Connecticut.

This is where we have celebrated the rites of spring every year so far since the late fifties and through the sixties. We would all arrive Friday evening and stake out one of the 15 bedrooms, depending on our needs. We'd have the fireplaces all ablaze with the huge kitchen abuzz with us cooks and bartenders. We would have a formal dinner Saturday night in the dining room where we could easily sit us twenty to thirty friends at one long table. Cotty would always sit at one end and often I would be at the other. Many of the first time dates would just freak out at the wonderfulness of the weekend. Others would take it in stride. Jackie handled it well as did Linda Eastman. She had her daughter Heather with her on weekends and she was the youngest at less than two years old. I'd love to see her now, as she was adorable then, just like her mom. Linda was someone I would have liked to get to know better, but in her casual way she let me know otherwise. She married one of her subjects that she captured with her camera, Paul McCartney. It is still fun seeing her bang tambourines and enjoying life with him in their Wings albums. Of course the Beatles were still together at this time, and so she was suddenly unavailable after Paul swept her away.

She has always intrigued me and maybe that is why a Linda was to be in my future, just as another Jackie was now taking my interest, as did that lovely Jackie in Las Vegas. Cycles in circles.

73

The Invincibles

Another outing that still remains unforgettable is our two-week cruise from Maine to Essex, Connecticut on *Windfall*, a 70-foot schooner we chartered. This was so much fun as we planned and shopped and filled a trailer to pull from New Jersey up to Maine. It was somewhere in Massachusetts that our paper plates got loose and took off out of the trailer as if we were launching flying saucers from the expressway. We got them under control and relashed down the tarp over our duffle bags, food and 24 cases of beer. Hunter and Joan Lewis were the oldest by a year, so they were our chaperones, while Sam Moody, Peter Van Ness, Peter McGonigle, Cotty Barlow and myself with our dates were the chaperoned. This was our first major overnight type of sailing together on the ocean. It had to be the hairiest, scariest, prettiest, most wonderful two weeks of my life to date. There was just our Captain, Chever Rogers, and we were the crew. It takes special people to come together like this and function as a team, but we ended up having all the bases covered, 'weather' or not.

Our first landfall on *Windfall* was on an island 30 miles off the rocky, fog enshrouded coast of Maine. We found there an island with artists living with nature and across from where we anchored was a hermit on another island with a lighthouse and sheep that kept the hills of grass trim and green.

The early morning chill slowly worked to warmth as *el sol* burned its way through the Maine mist. A cup of coffee was the first order of the day, and as we all arose at the same time, we all were on deck to see what would appear next to our wondering eyes as the fog retreated. We couldn't wait to go exploring, and so we started shuttling the crew ashore in our tiny four man dingy.

Peter Van Ness handled the shuttle and so was the last on the island where the hermit lived. But he was the first to make contact with this old recluse, who hated tourists but for some reason he saw us as creatures from the sea. He told us stories of wrecks and screams he would hear out on the ocean. We learned that all the natives that work the waters of these coasts carry a boat dog. That way the dogs would bark at each other. The skipper could see where the other boat was in the fog by which direction his dog was barking. If the dog kept barking at the same direction the boats were on a collision course and the skipper would take evasive measures. We kidded him about his sheep, but he didn't know of what we spoke. He told us of other legends of the sea lions, and sea gulls and flying fish. We explored the two islands and decided we could shove off for the open sea early the next morning. We set up our watches and chore lists and got good nights sleep to be ready for our next adventures. Some of us stayed awake to chat awhile with a mug of hot buttered rum as the evening chill returned with its shroud.

A day and night later we put anchor between several deserted islands. We spent the day here exploring the rocky crags and hunting seafood for dinner that night. We found mussels, and snails for hors d' oeuvres and lobster for the 'maine' course. Upon approaching one of the larger rocks, we saw it was occupied by a bull sea lion and dozens of his lady friends and family. They were quite possessive of their home and an army of them slipped into the sea as we approached. With the timing of an Olympic water ballet team, they emerged around our dingy in a perfect circle at the exact same time. Their eyes pierced ours as they warned us not to go further. One order from the bull seal and we would have become capsized toys for them to play with. The water was a little cool for me. So we just stayed cool and watched them watch us.

Back on board *Windfall*, we had the shotguns out and were practicing some skeet, when a couple real birds came within our range. Thinking no one could ever hit them, Hunter and Peter both shot at the same time, and darned if one of those shots didn't down one of the birds. It reminded us of one of the hermit's legends that whoever kills an albatross will not live long. We were freaked and brushed it off as superstition and to be forgotten. That was easy with our Lobster and seafood dinner all cooked up on deck over coals. What a night. But would the beer last?

After two more days at sea, we started encountering severe weather. This was something new and called for a different mode of operation. We had to sail sober with every move a matter of life and or death. We got everything lashed down below and up on deck. We had our foul weather gear and harnesses on for those running around the deck to clip on to the ship somewhere. These waves were coming over the sides swamping the deck, and grabbing at your body trying to take you back into the sea with it.

We had the sails reefed so as to reduce the amount of sail to the gale force winds. But we were still pitching and making awesome headway. It was a sudden lurch and snap that had us all look astern to see that our only dingy had busted loose from its tow line. We decided to try to save it, and went about to try to find it. It suddenly popped up next to us and Cotty jumped into it as it disappeared under our pitching bow. He tried pushing with all his might against our hull as the sea raised the dingy back up, but he was no match for the power of the sea. It was a miracle that the sea sent a wave and bashed our bow away from him and separated us to avoid a disaster. But we were fast sailing away from Cotty in the dingy. A crew member quickly started climbing the mast to get above the waves but even he lost sight of Cotts as we went about to try and find him. Finally, we saw him pop up on a wave and started to head for him, and we got a line to him but he had to let go as the strain was too much. Again we lost him and kept circling until we again spotted him, threw another line to him which he quickly tied onto the seats. We all pulled up and he just barely made it onto our stern as if a whale had spit him up on us. We couldn't believe he was alive. It was less than an hour later that the sea ripped the seats out of the dingy and the waves splintered it into flotsam and jetsam. Cotty was somber for a while.

Finally the storm broke and we were able to sail into Booth Bay Harbor where Captain 'Chevas' was able to buy another dingy from an old salt on the dock, pick up the new dingy and be on our way without even stopping. This dinghy was larger, stronger and even had a working motor. We were in heaven. The next week was equally as exciting but not as dangerous. We were able to enjoy every bit of our time at sea, and this was a life-changing event for many of us.

We went to other islands, some deserted and some like Nantucket and Martha's Vineyard full of charm, history and salt worthy people. We would land on an island and run all over it as if we were an espionage team and reconnoiter to report what, when, where and who is everywhere. At one island we found a yacht club type building that was closed but open to our perusal. We made this our headquarters and did search and report type of missions. No harm was done and it was great fun. It also gave our sea legs some much needed exercise of running up and down hills. Now that we had conquered the sea, it was a challenge to reconquer the land.

And just as we had gotten used to a way of life at sea, we now had to face the reality of going home and going to work. After sadly disembarking in Essex, Connecticut, we went to Cotty and Pam's grandmothers Mansion in nearby Madison for the rest of the weekend before heading back to New York and New Jersey. This helped. There was no way I could have just disembarked from the yacht and gone right to work. Too much of a culture shock. While we reminisced about the cruise, Peter Van Ness, Cotty and myself each said we could do that forever. Peter said when he got home he was going to give Nabisco notice that he was quitting and get back on board the schooner *Windfall* with Captain Chever Rogers and help him deliver her to St Thomas in the Virgin Islands. Cotty and I said we would fly down there after we quit and we'd all be together to take charters out around the Caribbean all winter. This was getting real exciting. Cotty worked for International Paper and I was turning people off selling insurance.

After we all got home to our ruts, Peter immediately gave notice and quit a week later. Cotty and I waited, but the excitement was building. After Peter packed and we had a big going away bash in Plainfield, he headed for Essex and left toward Bermuda in late October. We planned to meet down there right after Christmas. It was almost like a blood oath that we took.

Then came the big Kahoona. The big lesson in life. We, as overgrown teenagers in our twenties, were invincible, and that was that. Then we got a phone call. The schooner had run into a late hurricane and had not been heard from. A freighter had seen the yacht in trouble as had a sister sailboat that had made it into Bermuda's treacherous inlet sheltered by an arriving tanker. The Navy and Coast Guard were to start searching the next day after the visibility improved and the Hurricane passed. We were just positive all would be just fine then.

Two days later the Coast Guard said they had salvaged some wreckage, but had no sign of the boat or any survivors. Word from the freighter was that they had come about after spotting the schooner with her main mast broken and towing a dingy with what appeared to be a body in it. By the time the high seas let the freighter turn around again they were never able to see anything again. Cotty, Hunter, Bob Henry and myself drove to Norfolk, Virginia to view the wreckage they had found drifting. When we arrived, we were still sure all would be ok. As we all entered the empty room with the Coast Guard commander, our eyes simultaneously saw half of the helm, bunk drawers and other very familiar debris. They asked if we could identify anything, and we all shook our heads no. They had explained earlier that if these ship parts were from our schooner that the search planes would be called off as there was no chance for survivors. We had to just pretend in the chance that they were still out there somewhere...

We called Peter's parents and we were so choked up that none of us could talk. They thanked us for doing what we did and assured us that they had resigned themselves to Peter's fate and were being consoled that Peter had died doing something he really loved. I cried for two weeks.

We continued going to Peter's family farm in Hopewell. Being around his folks, just as if he were there, which he was in spirit, became a healer for us all. We'd all whitewash the riding rings and just be around his folks and brother and sisters. It was good for us all.

Hunter and Peter had both shot at that albatross or sea gull at the same time. We'll never know for sure who hit that bird during our cruise, but the old hermit could make a case here. We just let it be.

My parents were very patient thru all this, and after I got a grip on things, they had three of the pictures Hunter had taken of us during our cruise enlarged and framed exquisitely. They still have a prominent place in my life. Peter is still invincible.

Wedding Bells

If you will but look back at the ground you and I have covered together, you will see the pieces of your life coming together. Like a puzzle, you are still waiting for some of the key pieces to be in place so that the design can be revealed. Don't fret- I know where the pieces go, and they fit together perfectly.

One of the steps toward maturity seems to be the consideration of marriage. Yuck! How can anyone get that mature? But the thought first grabbed my brother Bill. He started the mess by marrying Nancy, a girl we've known all our lives it seems. She used to be a tomboy growing up and she and I would go at it, wrestling and pulling hair until one of our parents broke us up. We really liked each other but just didn't know how else to show it. So when I heard my brother was dating her some ten years later it was not understandable. So Nancy invited me over to her house to have a brotherly talk with me. She gave me all kinds of grownup advice and told me she loved me and I told her I was happy for her and hoped she would be very happy. They asked me to be their Best Man, which I found carried a lot of responsibilities.

One of them was to protect the groom from his chosen ushers. And to the last man, they were all out to get him. My brother had pulled pranks on these guys for years, and now it was get even time. I foiled all of them until at the bachelor's dinner, the usher next to him had put his false teeth in Bill's red wine, and then proposed a very nice toast, which demanded a bottoms up chug. As my brother chugged down his wine you could see his smile go to panic as he saw this guys false teeth coming after him down the side of his glass. Other than that I had things under control.

I got him to the church in Summit on time thru snow and sleet. I got him to the Plainfield Country Club in one piece for the Reception. I proposed the toast in front of hundreds and I got them out the door hours later to the awaiting Limousine. Bill locked the doors and gave me a thumbs up as they pulled away. It was just pulling away when I got a chill. I saw the limo driver, without his hat and jacket, being held captive by three of the ushers. Bill later told me that Sam, his best friend, turned around in the Chauffer hat and looked into the back seat at he and Nancy, and said "Where to Boss?" My brother freaked. He was had, and it was all my fault.

Apparently word got out of my expertise in this occupation, and I was invited to be in at least twelve more weddings. We all thought we knew what we were doing, but who could know what they were really getting into. It seemed getting married was just the thing to do after an uncertain check out period. If you were still dating after a year or so, get married. I only remember the fun we had at everyone's wedding. I mean real fun. Some highlights might give an overview so as to plan the perfect wedding and reception.

Sands Point, Long Island is where Joan grew up and where she married Hunter from Plainfield, New Jersey. It was the meeting of two high societies. I met the daughter of the President of PepsiCo who is Joan's neighbor and who had horses. And Perry Como, and the list went on. We, Hunter, Cotty, and the rest of the sailing crew were all there and quite socially inebriated. We had made sure Hunter got plenty to drink during his bachelor party, and I had arranged a customer from the bar to come into our private party room when she heard applause. I proposed a toast so that Hunter, after finishing his rum soaked dessert, would have to chug his scotch-laden water. We all applauded and in came our ploy, slinking her way toward Hunter. He has been told she is a hooker and she to pretend that is what she is. Each step closer to Hunter made his mouth drop open even further until she made a move for him and Hunter passed out, falling backwards. His last memory of the night.

He made it down the aisle in spite of us, and after the reception at the Sands Point Country Club, we all ended up at Joan's parents house. The champagne was still being poured. Mrs. Allen told us we needed to take off our tuxedos and get comfortable. I just had to show off and took bets as to whether I could do a flip off the diving board without spilling any champagne. I made the perfect flip and held the glass high with champagne. And as proof to the cheering crowd, I chugged the pool water laced champagne. Now the whole point here is not to teach you how I did this, but rather to see I should have heeded Mrs. Allen orders. For now I had a soaking wet rental tuxedo. No problem, I just threw it into the dryer and went back in the pool. A half hour later I heard a scream, "Whose tux is in the dryer!!?" I thought it must have been that little ring bearers, as the vest was tiny. O oh. I had to return that tux. When I got back to New York I wadded that little vest inside the tux and laid it on the counter with a bunch of others, thanked them and was gone. They never did call to thank me for the new size they now had to rent out.

Hunter and Joan were married and could now be our legal chaperones. That became real handy as we traveled as a crowd to places like the Hamptons, the island of St Croix, or skiing up in Bennington, Vermont.

Now that the ice had been broken, my friends started falling like dogs in heat. Tony, Crosby and Peter, three of us 'Fabulous Four', went down one after the other. Tony was the leader in this nutty group. His dad was a top gun with Pittsburgh Plate Glass and while we had partied together for years he decided to marry this girl he had met at Bucknell. Barbara lived outside of Philly in Media, a main line town where you had to have substance, fortunes and then some. Barb was from a recognized family. So it was surely news when Tony ended up after the wedding in a brawl with the manager of the hotel where we were all staying during the reception. It had something to do with not having drinks brought to their room. Good reason, or so it must have seemed at the time. The reception was somewhat shortened, but they were married, and that was the end of that.

Crosby was much smoother in his approach to life, and managed to get the lovely Sally from the upper crust of Cincinnati to say yes. The fabulous four were once again united in the middle of another posh society where no one could quite appreciate our sense of humor. I was a guest in a mansion with an indoor swimming pool right off my quarters. I had breakfast served poolside just so I could be sure I was there. Crosby was married in style and made his great escape to Bermuda, pipe in mouth, and antique car as their getaway fling. Why not!

Then Peter, my buddy. He went down too. So off the fab four went with about a hundred others from Plainfield to the Gentile assemblage in Virginia Beach to marry the sweet Penny. The home in which I was the guest of honor had gold coin collections in every lamp table, and antiques unknown to even dealers throughout the house. I could have pocketed some very valuable loot if I was so inclined. Too bad I didn't as my host was ripped off about two weeks after the wedding by some pros and lost just about everything. Had I lifted a few grand of stuff, I could have given it back, and then they would have still had some of their valuable collections. It must be hell to be this rich, I thought.

I did fall in love with most of the southern belle bridesmaids as well as the beautiful plantations with horses roaming the rolling pastures. This was a way of life I could adapt to with just a little coaxing. I made myself available, but the belles ended up the evening giggling and gossiping. I found a pillow and settled into dreamland again. The parties lasted a week, ending two days after the wedding. My buddy Peter knew how to pick them. My parents and all our parents were here in Virginia Beach for the big wedding day. The only time they saw us was when we ushered them down the aisle. The night of the wedding, Peter and Penny decided they wanted to hang around and continue to party with us. We all ended up in the ocean under a full moon at mid tide, riding waves and stripping from our tuxedos and belle outfits til the patch of dawn appeared to our wondering eyes. Next!!?

Ahh yes, my housemate at the Shanty and in Rahway was to marry my surgeon's daughter, Carol O'Neil. We had another exceptional Bachelor Party with the ole gang of Cotty, Hunter, Sam, 'Dog' and several other friends at the time. The Party was a replay of several others, but because it was the night just before the wedding, we all wanted to get decent nights sleep. At least that was my game plan.

The next day at the beautiful Crescent Avenue Church, the Bride finally arrived, on time. But none of us had seen Tom. One of the guests at the bachelor party said that he heard Tom had gone into New York City with some of the boys and hasn't been heard from since. Another rumor that was passed on to the panicking bride was that the boys had left him in NYC without money to see if he could make it to the church on time. It was getting very late, and Carol came to me in total distrust and asked where Tom was. I said with fear and trembling, "He'll be here." She didn't buy it either, but later I told her to walk the aisle, he'll be here. That was just to buy some time and create a moment of truth for Tom. She walked, and walked, all of us looking for Tom and hoping. But the Minister stood alone with the bride, and he stood. When Carol was ready to bolt, the huge doors at the back of the church creaked open and there was Tom, dressed to kill. The wedding came off without a hitch, and we never heard how Tom made it to the church almost on time. We just know Carol was ready to kill. Not a very weddingly emotion, but it got her through the day.

Cotty was one of the ushers for Tom and Carol. He also had moved from Plainfield and had a rent control apartment in New York City. We had grown up also since high school. We partied together, played street football in front of his home with a future quarterback of the Denver Broncos, attended the same prep school in Lake Placid, NY, and were co-conspirators of many a good time.

He was dating everyone and we were all surprised when Marin Gustafson, cover girl on *Madamselle* Magazine and model with Wilhelmina Agency, captured the heart of my buddy. As it was, my girl next-door type of girl, Jackie, was also modeling with the Wilhelmina Agency. Cotty and I just live parallel lives to an uncanny extent. I called him Junior at Northwood School through high school. Now I call him Repete for just that reason. When ever we'd get together and catch up on happenings, we had both gone through the same experiences. And when we went to plan an evening or party we just complemented one another and time and motion flowed. So did the alcohol. We seldom had an occasion go by where we were without adult beverages. It was just as much a part of life then as was smoking cigarettes. Illegal drugs never entered the picture. That is what made these the good ole days.

Marin and Cotty were engaged, and it was shortly after that Jackie and I decided to do what I was still reluctant to succumb to. I loved her, but my main concern was economic. There was the very good possibility that she, as a model, could be making more than me. This was a new phenomenon I was not comfortable with yet. But I was all for liberation of all, so I finally proposed, with a real ring. That set the wheels in motion for my parents to meet hers. Plans for every aspect of my life were made for me. Many by the families involved. Jackie and I did enjoy the buzz and had fun looking for an apartment. We finally decided to live outside New York, in West New York, NJ. We rented a seven-room apartment on the top floor, overlooking the Hudson River and the Big Apple skyline. Jackie and I would be able to drive or ride a bus into New York in ten minutes. This was important.

With the nest located, the wedding was next. We were to get married in her church. Jackie was Catholic, and I was sent to Presbyterian Church by parents that went there every Easter and Christmas. But my father had been brought up Catholic, and was excommunicated when he married my Protestant mother. Now I was, I thought, fulfilling fate by taking my family back to the 'Church'. I was indoctrinated during several meetings with the good Father. And then Jackie's dad got special dispensation from the Pope so we could not only be married, but in a High Mass. My God, I never thought I would live through an hour and a half of calisthenics. It was enough to wear the knees out of every pair of pants in the church. I think I was embarrassed for my friends. They had no idea what was happening. I pretended to.

The reception was very gala at Mr. Carlin's Essex Fells Country Club. We had a sit down lobster dinner for about 300 with open bar forever. Everyone probably had a good time, but my best man brother had provided the limo which came early to the reception and was awaiting outside. Brother Bill asked five times if we were ready to leave. Finally I said yes and we did the garter thing and got in the limo under a shower of rice and rose petals.

The Honeymoons Over When...

We were exhausted as we settled back into the limo. I checked to make sure it was the real driver this time, and cracked open one of the champagne bottles. Giving a glass to Jackie for a toast, she refused the drink. She was quiet. Later I find out that she is really irate about leaving early. She wanted to stay and revel with her friends, while I wanted to get the honeymoon started. Leaving before the reception was over was the unforgivable sin, and I lived under that cloud forever. What a way to start a marriage. It was like our wonderful dating days were suddenly left outside the veil of grief. (We had fun and did many wonderful things together for five years, but this sin was always boiling under her surface.)

Our honeymoon was great. The first night we spent in New York at the Plaza Hotel in a suite with fireplace and a view looking over the skating pond in Central Park. We had room service cater our needs in first class fashion. But something was bugging her, and at the time I didn't know what it was. The next day, Sunday, we wandered the streets of New York in the snow. Talk about true romance, this was it! Then we headed for the airport to fly to Grand Bahama, a new resort area. It was raining there for two days and very boring, so I suggested we go to Nassau. We agreed and we scooted all over this paradise on a moped buying china and crystal and spending most of my life savings. Anything to cheer her up.

Jackie was quite different than the Jackie in Las Vegas. No comparison. I had to handle her entirely different. My new Jackie had grown up to be a very attractive model. But to just go to breakfast, it would take an hour to get ready. It was like she was always auditioning. And she would tolerate the beach, but she had to either be in the casino or touring Market Street buying. Our relationship seemed to have changed, but I was willing to be patient and accommodating. Loving had to be mutual. We'd see. We had had our share of arguments over the five years we dated, but we had worked them out. So, I thought, we could work anything out in marriage too. We really did have fun on our two-week honeymoon, even with its ups and downs. But the honeymoon doesn't last forever, and so after completely doing Nassau we flew home with memories of a lifetime.

We put the memories on our wall, in the china cabinet, and in our picture album. But she never put away the limo that took her away from her party.

We went to church, Catholic Church, every Sunday. We were able to walk there from our apartment on Boulevard East in West New York, New Jersey. It felt good doing this for some reason, although I would never become a Catholic. I had promised during my indoctrination that if we had children they would be brought up Catholic. It really didn't make any difference to me. One religion was the same as any other. Little did I know.

We had some great evenings with friends at our apartment, eating and drinking to capacity. And we'd dance to stereo sounds and 'screw' the neighbors, especially those underneath us. Two of our friends were Dennis and Mimi. Jackie had known her at school, and Dennis was an Assistant Prosecutor in Jersey City. What an existence they had, with his being so involved fighting criminals that he always packed his pistol.

Mimi was also as pretty a blonde as they come. When the four of us went into New York eyes would follow us as people tried to figure who we were. We hit the bars, restaurants, theaters and clubs. We never had to wait in lines, as we would just pretend we actually were somebody and we'd get in the secret doors.

Jackie and I would attend the different modeling parties as well, and I have to admit, my eyes were always searching for the ultimate female specimen. Some would say they were just admiring the Creators handiwork, or thought a particular lovely was someone known in some previous life. I just was full of admiration for the variety and quality. I made few new friends with this attitude. But I wasn't supposed to be making friends with these single girls, only with married couples.

On one occasion we were invited to go on a ski weekend sponsored by *Madamselle Magazine* for all the models in their recent issues. I got to go along on the bus because the Fashion Editor was Hunter's wife from Sands Point, Joan. So there Hunter and I are, the only men to help these three dozen snow bunnies get their skis on and then pick them up when they fell off. We both almost ended up divorced right there on the slopes. We tried not to be jerks, just helpful. But our wives were out to make sure we remained faithful and forgotten.

Our Hostess for the weekend in Vermont was Maria Von Trap. You may remember her story called *The Sound Of Music.* She had shed her Nun's habit for cross-country skiing duds. She was charming, but one of her guests was a monk from one of those Monasteries in Colorado which calls for silence. These guys never talk when in captivity. But this joker was constantly trying to feed lines to my wife and actually chasing her to the point of really annoying her. I had a little chat with Sister Maria and warned her of his near future demise if he continued. She immediately bussed him back to Colorado.

We had the opportunity to do some beautiful cross-country skiing, but because of this creep we decided to get away from the lodge and get up on the mountain. Jackie and I were not expert skiers, but we could get down a mountain. Not the case for most of the bunnies from our group. And so it was my chivalry in action when I would help them up off the new fallen snow. When Jackie saw my politeness in action, she flipped out protesting that I was "married!" I knew that, but I didn't know I couldn't be polite. I found out otherwise. I was not there to tick her off, but it sure was easy. The rest of the weekend I felt quite constrained. What ever happened to the fun?

Jealousy had reared its ugly head, and I took the responsibility to make sure it reared no more. She had played the card and called my bluff. She had me in spades. Ok, I was a wimp. But to me, my marriage meant more to me than any macho, ego trip.

We really loved each other and this was one marriage that was going to work. Our folks were still married after decades of better and worse. We could do it too. So with that mind set and a deep down love in our hearts, we set out to make it work in an imperfect world.

Money pressures were evident, but they are there for any newly wed couple to some extent. The biggest pressure was that I was on commissions-only now, and she was on a per job pay. We didn't have regular paychecks as it were. Our hopes were that between the two of us enough would come in.

She would make an average of $60 an hour (which would be about $500 to a $1,000 in today's market.) That was just for the actual photo session. Now TV commercials were the real gravy. She would make a couple hundred $$s per hour and residuals each time it was on TV. Her Coke ads would bring in several thousand dollars before it went off the air.

My Insurance commissions would be several hundred and very seldom a few thousand. I paid the bills and she saved her money. She needed it for makeup, clothes, and miscellaneous expenses. We tried to keep a grip on things, but we had nothing to hold onto. The Catholic services we went to every Sunday left me empty, but I figured they were better than nothing. So we did plenty of working and drinking.

Then to improve her market share Jacqueline quit smoking, and started yogi. I would pass her in our hallway standing on her head, with a facemask on. It was scary as hell. But after putting on her make up for an hour and a half, she looked really good. That is for the second I got to see her before she dashed out the door to catch a bus out front to go into midtown Manhattan. There she smiled at guys all day for her supper.

The Fame was coming for her. She was now hobnobbing with some of the top models in New York, though she wasn't quite in that league. Jacqui Carr was her 'Stage Name'. Her agency, Wilhelmina, was growing very fast to becoming the Number two agency in town. I was discussing with Wilhelmina and her husband Bruce, the possibility of a division for sports stars, and I would handle all the fringe benefits for them, such as tax sheltered pension plans. Then Jackie wanted to go with the Ford Agency, the number one in town. I stalled her on this for several reasons, as she would be new at Ford and not be guaranteed as much work. Besides, she was being treated well where she was. But Jackie thought she should be a super star model and Ford was making her overtures. We had to get away from all this for a while.

Globetrotting

We had Hunter and Joan over for dinner and they were ready for a break also. Joan was semi- famous as the Fashion Editor for *Madamselle Magazine*, and Hunter was selling chemicals for Rhykold Chemical Company. We decided we all needed a vacation and put our fingers on the globe. It came up, Majorca, Spain, Lisbon, Portugal and Northern Africa. Why not?

Two weeks later we are on a transatlantic flight, first stop: Lisboa. We ate and drank very well thank you. Hunter and Joan, Jackie and I had plenty of practice at that wherever we were. After shaking off some of our jet lag with a nap in Lisbon at our hotel, we walked the city streets. It seemed like a time warp of some kind. A Middle Ages sensation, as we wandered on cobbled streets and went into centuries old restaurants. We finally had enough brandy to kill anything we might eat, so in we go to the type of dining establishment with long tables, and big crowds at each. The language dumbfounds us, but they graciously helped us. They had live sea animals in a huge aquarium. When I ordered crab I pictured a little cocktail dish with a few bites in red sauce. When our waiter brought it to the table the crab hung from his upraised hand and the other crabs feet touched the floor. This was supposed to be an appetizer for one person. It was big enough to eat me, and if the waiter let it go, it may have. Well he killed it and had it cooked and we all had a good bit of the crab. It was the first of five courses. The rest of the dinner was normal fare, for Portuguese. A course of Chicken, another of Fish, then the Beef and finally, would you like dessert with your cafe and brandy. And thus the eating went for two weeks.

Our flight schedule allowed us to buy a ticket to the furthest destination and then fly to any places in between at no extra charge. We took advantage of that big time. Our next stops were Madrid where we did museums and churches, Barcelona where we wandered down the flower lined Ramblas and went to discos, and finally Mallorca, the island paradise off the coast of Spain. I took Spanish in school, and I never really had much luck using it until I got to

Barcelona. All of a sudden it was like a familiar language, especially after Portuguese. But the Spanish I had studied was Castillian, which is the most proper dialect, and the one spoken in Barcelona. I felt very at home here in that way. I was able to converse and understand basic conversations immediately. I had never experienced that in Puerto Rico or Mexico or New York.

Now Mallorca was a real treat. Jackie and I had found a cute motel our second day there and moved our stuff into it. It was an ivy covered stone house and matching motel type units that were situated around gardens and a swimming pool. This Iberian island was the paradise that Scandinavians came to for vacation. And this quaint resort must have been one of their favorites. The poolside was lined with beautiful people. They were all watching me stalling to dive into the pool, but I was actually taking deep breaths. They were all watching as I finally dove into the cold water and went the length of the sub-Olympic sized pool underwater, seven times. There was a big round of applause as I surfaced as if they had just seen a miracle. Jackie even seemed impressed, but she just took the credit with humility as she got me a towel. I couldn't believe I did seven laps myself, but it was a piece of cake as they say. Well, everyone there said hello to us for the rest of our stay as if we were some cat's meow. When Joan and Hunter arrived from their side trip they figured we had been up to something that everyone knew us already, and in so many languages.

One of the beaches we discovered looked much like I imagine Monte Carlo. There were wealthy looking nude bodies everywhere, and some with bikinis that were even sexier. Out past the swimming ropes were some yachts anchored. It was out there that I headed with Jackie on a mattress. There we met an Italian on a speedboat who spoke the same hand language that we spoke. Within minutes we had him towing us on water skis across the harbor for about five miles. There we had a picnic with wine and bread and fruit and cheese and more. Then we skied home. What a day. We saw our new friend a few days later at the Africa Lounge in the center of Palma. Little did I know the coincidence in the making by this chance encounter at the Africa Lounge.

Mallorca seemed an endless source of fun. But Jackie and I were restless to get in some more travels and caught a plane to Tangier in northern Africa. Talk about going through the veil of mist to another world, this was too weird. We managed to get a room with a balcony over looking the Med Sea. It was quite picturesque as we could see the alleyway to the Kasbah with fez-topped men in robes swarming down the alleyways to nowhere. From behind, they all looked the same to us. Where have I heard not to say that? But they did. We stood on our balcony and had a smoke and a drink and were over taken by the romance of it all. 'Let me take you to the Kasbah Dahling.'

And so off we went to become part of the swarm. The market place is incredible with the hundreds of booths selling everything except the camels hump. Or is that what they made those ottomans out of. It was tempting to go to each booth as each vendor would say, sssst, do you want…whatever. But when we heard…mint tea it seemed appropriate. What I didn't know was that this is an afternoon ritual, which included sitting on the ground and sucking on a hookah stem. That is a water pipe with some kind of toe bacca in dere. When we tried to stand up I figured they had some really fine tea here. We wandered deeper into the alleys of the Kasbah and came upon a snake charmer. His buddy suggested Jackie take the camera and take a picture. She did and then the snake charmers buddy took up a snake and put it around my neck for Jackie to take a picture. Then another. My first instinct was not to smile or I was dead. To these snakes I did not look like an Arab, or its basket, nor could I whistle Arabian Nights like a flute. I just stood there, cool, as you would be. Jackie took some pictures and I said enough. The buddy peeled the snakes off me with a stick (more than one because once they got one on ya, they add more) and put them back in the basket carefully and quickly put the lid on top. Jackie thought I was so brave, (I thought I was so stupid) and I let her think so. The next day we saw the snake charmer's buddy was playing the flute. We asked where the snake charmer was, and he said in sign etc that he had too many bites on the face and finally died last night. My condolences.

This was a strange land for sure. It seemed every few minutes the Rams horn would blow, like an air raid signal, and all these robes would hit the dirt and bow toward some unseen thing in the north. I don't mean to be insensitive toward their religion, but at the time, I had none to count on. And this just seemed to be even less of an attraction toward the spiritual life. This was weird. I expected a magic carpet to soar over their heads at least.

Jacqui and I decided to do some sight seeing. We had our guide get a cab and off we went. The car climbed up the hillside above alleys and masses of humanity to the Governors Palace. The cab stopped to let us see, so I got out of the cab and with camera in hand walked into the Gov's courtyard. The welcoming committee all greeted me with shouts and automatic machine guns lowered at my head. The cabbie and our guide were frantically yelling at them and me some kind of gibberish, while I ran off a couple of shots of the fancy mansion. Then I got the word, no pictures no pictures! I was apologized for by the cabbie and grabbed by our fez-topped guide and forced into the cab. The cabbie got in trouble for letting me out. Can you imagine doing that to Saddam Hussein's Palace today? Same same. Our escorts told me, "I very lucky they not shoot. Bang. No problem for them." Dang, touchy touchy.

That night we decided to try Coos Coos and some other local taste treats at the spectacular Arabian Nights Cafe. This was to be the big night. Our guide said this is the best of the best, with music and belly dancing and mmmmmmwah, good food. Well, the cushions were flat that kept you off the floor, the belly dancer was a guy, the music wasn't, and coos coos means pigeon something. None of this really got me excited.

Meanwhile, everywhere we go some Arab is trying to put the make on Jacqui. Apparently they don't see many girls with their face showing, let alone what Jacqui was showing. These guys are starved for whatever. And they act mostly like juveniles or Humphrey Bogart, not.

We were getting pretty tired of the whole act around here, so we made one last pass through the Kasbah to shop for goodies. We got a few (touristy I'm sure) items and had them shipped home. You know, the leather ottoman you see at the foot of every tourists favorite chair, and the rugs and china and the Jalobas and embroidered shirts and the who knows what else. We were wrecked when we got finished and went back to our suite and slept while the masses passed several floors below our window balcony on their way to nowhere. We did not engage in any illegal inhalations, but that second hand smoke is, whew! Enough to wreck a camel.

We decided to go to Madrid and check out the museums and cathedrals, and took our magic carpet called Iberian Airline, and flew up there the next day. We arranged a room and went out to eat. We found the whole diet here is based around ole Olive Oil. The *huevos*, the *pollo*, the popcorn, everything is cooked in Olive Oil. I smelled cooked Olive Oil for weeks. Also. I thought New York was noisy and smelled bad. It is a quiet paradise compared to the streets outside the pensione. At least the NYC sewage is piped into the Hudson River instead of the back alleys. Actually, Madrid is not that bad and does have some very interesting historical landmarks and parks. It is very Catholic, which was a cultural shock as well after being with the masses at Mecca.

Hunter and Joan joined us here and we went to a bullfight. Now I had studied some about España at school, but what I had learned about Bull Fighting no way prepared me for the real thing. One can watch in horror, or in suspense, or in admiration for either the Matador or the Bull. But in any case it is very intense. I don't think we are capable of seeing a bullfight the same way a Spaniard does. I think the male Spaniard focuses his own testosterone into the Matadors pants. Then when the moment of truth comes it is not just the Matador out there, it is every male Spaniard whose eyes have witnessed the trial and now the final challenge. The Moment of Truth. To me it was just another hood with a four-foot blade about to put down a foe that has been wounded by a dozen other gang members already. But as each battle took place, and they dragged another bull out the door without its *cajones*, I just thought how peaceful New York really can be on a Sunday afternoon.

Thinking of New York gave me the idea of looking in the Madrid phone book for a model agency. Dang if they didn't have 'Yellow Pages" there, and Model Agency was right there under the M's. I called the biggest ad and told them that I had a famous Model from

New York with the Wilhelmina Agency. Would they be interested in an opportunity while we were here for the next few days to put her to work? I did this all in Español. They said "Si". I understood and we made arrangements on the phone for work without even a go-see. For the next three days I was surrounded again by models from different countries including Spain, but my Jackie was the center of attraction. They work a lot different in Europe. In NYC the rush is on, and either the models are already on something or they have a joint to get a session going. (We were not part of the new drug scene.) In Europe there is an all day wine, chat, aperitif, chat, shoot, liquor, shoot, chat, cafe con leche con cognac, etc. (This we could barely handle) If the shooting is not complete we have wine in the morning and start over, even though we are paid by the day. The challenge for me was to do all the wheeling and dealing in Spanish. The challenge for Jackie was to be humble, what with all the groveling over a 'famous New York Model'.

Small talk could be done with a combo language using hands and grunts and toasts and nodding. But some of the Spanish Models did not know how to be subtle, and would flash me some skin and Jackie would get all bent out of shape. Then everyone would whisk the offender away and we would have a drink and shoot again. We did three billboards, two display posters, one TV ad and a couple magazine ads. We more than paid for our vacation, we also wrote off all our expenses. I said to 'J', "This I can handle!"

And with that event, time was running out on our little tour de España. We boarded Iberian Air for our flight home. They seemed to get lost a few times at sea as we seemed to keep swerving and changing directions over mid Atlantic. But finally we touched down at Newark Airport, always a cultural shock no matter where one flies in from. But the abrupt contrast seemed to bring forth the vivid recollections of an incredible journey. Would it ever be possible to return to such a magnificent experience, or was I doomed to hell here in Newark, NJ?

Life's Ups and Downs

The cultural shock of returning to the States from Europe is impressive enough, but when the event becomes almost depressing instead of uplifting, lifestyle needs to be rethought. If you have ever been to Newark, New Jersey, you may not have thought you were at the end of the world or the rim of the toilet seat, but you could feel it was there. And in the daytime you can see it on a cloudy day. It was a cloudy day as Iberian Air flight #111 dropped below the smog and immediately screeched as air met land. I had the same reaction as my feet hit the tarmac. We were unable to disembark into the airport due to construction. So we had to duck down and make our way below the smog across unknown runways to the safety of the terminal. Newark had recently grown from a single building to a confused mess. I'm sure it will all be completed some day in the game of progress.

Jackie and I had grabbed hands so we wouldn't become separated in this endeavor to get to our hopefully transported luggage within the Jet Set HQ. Once we were announced as one of the lucky people who had all their luggage arrive, we were out of there and on our way to our home Sweet home. *Nos Casa.*

I couldn't wait once home and overlooking the New York Skyline on an unusually clear night, to call Cotty and let him know we were home. It was then and there that my Buddy told me he was married. This was really great news, as he was the only bachelor left after I had gone off the deep end. Carlton Montague Barlow was married. Eloped at that. What a guy.

Cotts had been dating and married his model friend, Maren, and we were invited over for the first dinner in their new apartment. It was one of those large 300 square foot apartments on the upper east side of 62nd street. As we all four squeezed into his living room, we could smell the roast beef roasting. When Maren disappeared around the corner to check on her first dinner for guests, I heard her open the oven door, with a shriek! With that getting our attention, we all had eyes riveted on a rolling roast beef heading our way, with Maren chasing it with a fork and washcloth. The roast won as it made it to the center of the living room rug and finally spun in a tight circle before laying dead before us. Poor Maren was mortified, until we all cheered the good show, picked up the winner and rinsed it off under the faucet before slamming it back in the oven.

I had a good laugh about this on the way home, but Jackie did not share my sense of humor. We had had a few drinks and the discussion became an argument. She was shouting at me to let her out of the car. I said no way, it is the middle of New York City at 2 am and I was not…At the next light she jumps out of the car and disappears. I circle the blocks looking for anything moving and finally decide to head home, as she must have taken a cab there. Sure enough she is home and I have to beg my way in. Geah! What is going on?

Our marriage lasted five years, as had our dating. We went through good times as well as these rough times. But we never thought we would end. Until the late sixties when the whole country was going through a divorce epidemic. It seemed 8 of ten friends were getting a divorce.

Jackie, or should I say Jacqui, had been asked to go to Paris for the second year to do the Paris Collections. She was to have a girl friend from Wilhelmina Agency to room with her. But the roomie flaked out after a couple weeks under the shadow of the L'Arche de Triumph, and Jacqui was left alone and running wild. I knew this because I was close to a French photographer known just as Frank, in Manhattan, who had connections all over the Paris underground. He told me of Jacqui's moves everyday, and that she was running with a guy who preyed on American girls. A gigolo.

I couldn't believe it, but she stayed on even after the collections were over. She called one night and said she wanted to stay there. I said for her to at least come home and we could figure this all out. She said no, and I kept getting reports of her activities. One day my French friend said he was going to Paris and was there anything I wanted. I told him to bring back Jackie and to also get me a pair of suede pants.

While he was gone, I spotted his girl, Ingrid, who had been Miss Sweden, running across midtown Manhattan. I stopped my car in the middle of 5th Avenue and took after her. She was on her way to a modeling job and looked great. She asked me to come to her place for dinner, as she knew we were both alone. Why "Sure!" I got back to my car as traffic was getting angry at this roadblock sitting there with the door open. I just casually got in and drove away, looking forward to an extraordinary night.

I was next to worthless all day wheeling and dealing insurance deals, as my total focus was upon meeting Ingrid and enjoying dinner in her company. When it was finally time to be at Frank's apartment, she was awaiting me in the most receptive mood. She made me feel very comfortable, as we sat near the window and had some adult beverages. We talked about her home where she was a national heroine, what with being Miss Sweden and all. She was most casual and humble about it which made it all so cute and interesting. She also told me how lonely she was and how Frank was just a convenience and tried to control her. We moved to the dinner table in the middle of the living room with a candle and two chairs. She served a delightful dinner, not overloading me with food, but making sure I was not thirsty. Later we opened a bottle of French Champagne, which we took to the pillows and fell asleep.

The sharp knock on the apartment door at dawn was more than I could comprehend. But I finally realized where I was and saw Ingrid going for the door. She signaled me to just be quiet. I heard a discussion in French, and figuring I was dead meat I went back to sleep. After I heard Ingrid come into the room and get clothes out of the closet and then more discussion in French, I finally heard the apartment door close and felt Ingrid move near me. She said it was all clear and I could come out. I was perfectly comfortable where I was and remained under the dark covers.

Frank's accomplice had come to get some things for him to take to Paris. Had Frank heard I was there, I may have been served up as an appetizer in one of New York's finest French Restaurants soon. But Ingrid said the intruder didn't see me. But upon finally arising what do I see on the apartment doorknob but my favorite necktie. Oh, I bet Frank is just about to hear about this tie seen in his apartment. I felt like scum. Not because of Jacqui, because she had already broken our trust, but because of me moving in on Frank while he was in Paris helping me. Yes, my priorities were screwed up, but what wasn't. I had nothing to stand for, so I was fair game for anything. This is how to make life a mess.

Had I believed in God and His Word, I may have had a chance. But I was putty in the hands of the Devil and didn't even know it. I did recognize his dirty footprints on my path of life, though, and so I didn't make it a habit of seeing Ingrid much after that. A shame to say the least. Especially as when Frank returned from Paris a couple of weeks later and somehow mentioned my relationship to Ingrid. He actually thanked me for looking after her while he was gone. He also said she was getting too possessive for him. Naturally, he liked the variety New York's Fashion world had for him to enjoy. He even wanted me to take Ingrid out for dinner in the new suede pants he had brought back for me from Paris. He told me she couldn't keep her hands off of leather. Oh well, what the heck. We all went on up to Madison that weekend and partied with Cotty and a couple dozen other friends.

I was fighting off the depressions as Frank had told me about Jackie's living with a French frog, a gigolo of the worst kind. Well I knew this, but he just filled in the details which I'll spare us. It seemed she was going to be over there for several more weeks.

Every weekend I spent partying somewhere just to try and forget the emptiness and pain I was suffering. Many weekends I would go to the Jersey shore and either spend the weekend at my parent's house in July, or at Jackie's parents house in August. It was pitiful, as I would make the rounds of bars trying to fill the void in my life, and then pulling in to the house around 3:00 am and sleeping til noon. I don't know why either set of parents put up with me, but I guess they just felt sorry for my circumstances and me. I wish one of them would have shaken me up and told me to shape up or get out. But they just put up with my stupidity and let me get drunk and stagger in whenever. Neither parents were very good examples for a potential alcoholic. This was not the end of the world, but again I could see it from here.

My insurance business was suffering something awful. Here I was, a family financial consultant and I couldn't even hold my own world together. I had one very loyal customer who had me doing all his Group Health Insurance for his factory personnel, the officers Buy-Sell agreement funding, their Pension and Profit Sharing and lots of referrals. If it weren't for Bob Ehrlich, the President of Pompton Lakes Packaging, I would have been on skid row. This was the factory where I had had *Bleachette Bluing* manufactured as well as *Fawn*. He did other products there such as *Parsons Ammonia* and *Woolite*. He became a good friend, and I don't think he ever knew my plight. I was proud to bring him a big check to cover his eye surgery. Bob was all bandaged up for days and appreciated the visit to his home to catch him up on the happenings in the news, and to read the check to him to put in the bank for disability income. This was no big deal for me, but he remembered this day for years to come. I can't wait to tell you how this small service came back to me.

But other than helping Bob and Tom Pearce and a few other friends, I was having a real hard time relating to anyone that wasn't perfect. I was feeling very out of it and insecure. What was happening to my world? My perfect world? I was meeting people who were more miserable than me, and we got along just fine. But I didn't want to go there, or did I?

One night of dining and dancing at the Plainfield Country Club and being loaded, as most every one was in those days, I made some passes at the Head waitress. She and I had always made smiles at each other during dinner there as she would bring me lamb chops or roast beef. But now was different for both of us. She was married to a bad guy and needed some attention, and there I needed the same. I waited outside the Club for a long time for her to come out and she reluctantly got into my car. I didn't know her husband was coming to pick her up. But she got into my car and we just talked. I wanted to kiss her so bad, and felt she did too, but we both fought it off until a thumping on the car interrupted our intimacy. It was her husband. I got out to let him know we were just waiting for him, and that was the last I saw her. I don't mean to say she is not ok, just that we both culminated in those few moments together a long time of mutual respect and friendly love. It happens and I was glad that nothing else happened. She had her problems and I had mine. It was time for each of us to go handle them.

Well, what was I to do? Fly to Paris and shake this woman whom I had married? And say to her, get your butt home and take care of our life together, and stop all this nonsense? Tell her I forgive her and let's start over? What?

I'm sure many of my friends had their suggestions, but even in hindsight, none of them would have worked. Jackie had been seduced into a world that even her Catholic upbringing would have said NO to. Finally I got her on the phone at a number Frank had brought back to me. She wanted to know how I had gotten her number. I just said "Through connections." This freaked her out as if I was threatening her immediate life or something. I told her she better come home before I come over there and do something her gigolo friend definitely would not like. Like change his voice level. She promised me she would fly home next week and would send me the exact time. All right!

I called Cotty (aka Cotts, Junior, Carlton Montague Barlow, or Repete) to tell him the good news. He didn't seem overly excited, and I guessed it was just that he had been worried about me lately. We got together at a pub near his rent-controlled apartment in the ritzy section of Manhattan. We got loaded together as the black and white couple that sang there twanged my heartstrings with their blues. I went and cheered them up after their session. They told me they were on the verge of busting up, and that's what they were singing about. I told them to hang in there with each other and it'll be all right, just like my situation was going to be all right. This wasn't going to be the end of the world.[14]

I mean, here I was awaiting the return of my loving wife, driving around on this spring day listening to Paul McCartney singing with the Beatles "I want to Hold Your Hand," and "Hey Jude" which I thought was a nice religious song. Duh! But life seemed to be taking an upturn. As soon as I got her home she would forget this French Frog and we could pick up where we left off. Maybe even better.

---

[14] Months later I received a post card from them saying they had hung together and to come see "Barbara and Ernest" at the St Regis Hotel.

I got the apartment all cleaned up, and prepared a major dinner with guests like Cotty and his model wife Maren, and Dennis and Mimi for the coming home celebration. Time passed slowly awaiting the big day, until I was suddenly finding myself on the way to the airport to finally pick her up. The flight was late and so I parked and went up to the arrival gate. My big smile and jubilation was greeted with a stoic quietness. Still I grabbed her suitcase and threw it over the railing and picked her up and carried her down the stairs to the parking lot. She laughed as I spun her around and I went for a kiss which seemed to die in mid air. She wasn't there. I told myself it would take time. Let her get adjusted. The dinner party was a fiasco as Jackie was distant and uncaring about seeing her friends. The next week was a living hell as we laid in the bed together and she would not let me touch her. She wouldn't even talk, until she finally said it, "I want a divorce." It took my breath away. I couldn't even talk. My whole life since ten years ago came crashing down around me like broken mirrors. Pieces of broken glass were everywhere as I saw flashing back at me a past that could have led to a wonderful future. And now all was just a worthless mess. I wish I could say I didn't cry and weep from a deep grief. We were one and now it felt like my flesh was being torn and disfigured. Only those who have been joined in a committed so called Holy Matrimony can know the pain of separation. But for those people who have been here, or will come to know this pain, I won't try to describe it. Just know it is not the end of the world.

It was a couple weeks of hell until she could move out. We had decided that she would move and take what was hers and leave what was mine. I trusted her on this. How stupid of me again. Then her father called and asked me, "What the hell is going on?" He was in his cups, and all I could say was "I wish I knew" and hung up sobbing from my depths. That was the last I heard from him.

Jackie and her mother came with a moving van when I wasn't home and cleaned out the apartment. When I came home all that was left was a couple sticks of furniture, an old air mattress with a small hole in it, and a dirty towel to try and curl up under. This may have been the most miserable night of my life.

Not The End of the World

One thing Jackie left me was my telescope which let me look out upon New York City. I remember one night, during the waiting period before her day in divorce court; I looked over at the 79th Street Marina and saw a break-in in progress. I couldn't believe my eyes. I was just debating whether I should call the cops and clue them in when a team of New York's finest showed up with their canine crew of German shepherds. I was able to see these incredible dogs working and they actually caused the capture of those turkeys. I laughed. I hadn't heard myself laugh in a very long time. It made me think I had better get out of my misery and get on with my life. I called on my buddy Cotty again, and he said to come on into the city and we'd go out and have a few drinks and talk. This was just what I wanted.

My insurance work was the pits. I just didn't want to talk to anyone. I found through my conversation with Cotty that I was blaming myself for this divorce and that was not the case. He said I needed to replace Jackie as soon as possible, get back on the horse, so to speak, and gittyup. And so I set out to meet anyone and everyone to try and replace her. This was fun, I have to admit. It was like being a very wise 18 year old. I met so many girls and many came back to my refurbished apartment for one or two nights and left notes and poems about the great time we had. But none of them replaced Jackie, although it was a lot more fun.

I had stockpiled some of Jackie's mail and had found from the French Underground in the NY City where Jackie was living. She had gotten a pretty posh apartment in midtown and her Gigolo friend from Paris had been flown in at her expense and was now mooching off my wife. I decided to play Godfather and pay them a visit. After parking my car out front, I rang her door phone. No one answered. I rang it again. Nothing. I leaned on it until I finally heard, "Who is it?" It was Jackie. This was the day before our Divorce was to become legal as she would go to court and lie about me. This was our lawyer's idea, our friend Dennis. He said it would be the easiest on both of us, and all she wanted was her maiden name back again. I was 'getting off easy' he said. True compared with the 34 charges his cute wife Mimi was bringing against him in her divorce charges. He was going to be paying her off forever. His case was coming up in a few months. So he coached me to be cool, don't do anything foolish.

So when I heard Jackie's voice, I thought 'Be cool'. So in my best Italian accent I said "I got a special delivery for Jackie Carlin." I think she knew something was up and sent her Gigolo friend to fetch. When he opened the door, the hair went up on the back of my neck as I stared deep into the depths of his black dead soul. I had my trench coat draped over my arm and the mail in my hand. It did look like a gun being concealed I suppose. He freaked and went screaming down the hall, "Shakie, it is your usband!!" This frog had no backbone at all. Now it was Jackie's turn. She gets on the intercom and asks nervously, "What do you want?" I said I just want to reason with you, and I have something for you.(Like a bullet) She tried to have me just leave it, but I was very persuasive. Finally she showed up hiding behind the door. I said come out here, with my back to her. She was freaking, but she inched her way out and I turned and pointed my outstretched trench coat toward her and pushed the mail into her stomach. She about died, but I guess it finally felt good to be in control. I said. "What are you so nervous about? All I want to do is give you your mail and talk for a minute. Who was that snake that answered the door for you?" As if I didn't know. I had shown her what he was made of, the yellow bellied sucker that hid behind her skirt. (I found out later she shipped him back to Paris the next day!) After that I was cool and cordial. I told her that after tomorrow there was no going back, this was last chance for us in this moment. She had nothing in that frog to keep her, and I might be able to get over it if she could. She said no, closed the door and ran to her apartment crying. That was it.

I drove around the city, tears blinding my vision and so numb it was unreal. It reminded me of when I left another Jackie in Las Vegas and how miserable I was then. I went uptown to try and find Dennis at his favorite lawyer hangout called *The Gavel*. He wasn't there but some of his friends were there including Jimmy Breslin, the reporter. There was only hopelessness in all their eyes, and so I left to go home. It was starting to rain this cold autumn night, but even the wipers on my car couldn't stop the tears. One more bar. I didn't have more than a couple bucks on me, but I knew if I could find Dennis he'd buy his poor client a scotch or two. I parked a few blocks from *The Gavel* and ran across the street to another one of his haunts. Not here either and no one had seen him tonight. He must have been preparing for his big case tomorrow. Getting back in my car, I turned the key and my heart sank. The key broke in half in the ignition. There was nothing to grab onto, no way to start the car. I used some precious dimes to call a locksmith, and was told it would cost $200 and tomorrow was the soonest.

I walked back to *The Gavel* in the rain. I looked like a cold wet hobo when I got there and found no one I knew. No one would loan me any money. The bartender bought me a drink just to warm me up and see if fate would deal me a better hand. No luck. I had to walk from 73rd street to the Port Authority on 33rd Street at 1 am to get a bus home. There was just enough money in my pocket for that. I was so miserable I was tempted to end it all some how. But I kept walking numbly as the rain kept falling on my head. I glanced into a large bank window and there was a big cardboard cut out of Jackie modeling an ad for something. I wanted to put a brick through the window and shred it, but I just screamed something at her and went on.

It seemed like an endless nightmare before I even got to 42nd street. There the junkies and pimps were waiting for a sucker to come down the street. I played every trick, looking at them and then at an imaginary person across the street and nodding 'NO' as if to signal not to shoot them, or pretending to be an undercover cop to them and whisper at them something and nod my head. Some how I made it through what seemed to be an endless field of landmines, and got to the bus terminal just in time to see the last bus to New Jersey pulling out in a cloud of black smoke. I sank on the floor just where I was, looking and feeling like a homeless bum, and cried myself to sleep.

I finally departed on the 5am bus home and had to wait till 9am to walk around to get money and try and get my car back. I had to move it by 4pm or it would be towed away. My local little deli cashed a small check for me, so I jumped on the bus and was back into the Lincoln Tunnel and the Port Authority in a few minutes. Then I subwayed to the area of my car. When I arrived the police were there, not for me, but a pet store had been locked up next to my car and all the pets were dead. As if I weren't depressed enough already. After they left, and I still ran into only money-grubbing locksmiths wanting hundreds of dollars. So I ended up pushing my car across the street to keep it from being towed away in the alternate side parking zone.

This scenario went on for two more days and nights before a Good Samaritan off duty policeman helped me out. Whew! I had hundreds of NYC parking tickets that I had studiously collected over the years in my glove compartment. I would have spent mucho time in jail had my car been towed and the tickets discovered. I did get another ticket in the deal to add to my collection. But I decided to have them stored elsewhere than in my car. Also New York was starting to use their new computers to find scofflaws in New Jersey and drag them out of bed in the middle of the night and drag them to jail. I never want to go to jail! Maybe it's time for me to get out of Dodge. We'll see!

But I had 'gotten out of my marriage' during this nightmare. I didn't even have to go to court while Jackie swore that I had committed unpardonable offenses against her and she wanted an annulment of our marriage. Dennis was there with her and so she got off with out a scratch and so did I. I only suffered the lacerations due to one body being torn apart from the heart out.

Dennis took me out to 'celebrate' and we went to *The Gavel* for some serious legal libations. All his lawyer friends were there just like the night I went and needed a few bucks and a friend. I was able to tell them they were flakes and it felt really good. They seemed to respect me for it. I didn't lose one friend. Dennis wasn't even embarrassed. But he told me again that I got off really easy. That Mimi, his ex-wife to be, Jackie's friend, was out to take him down to the bowery. She wanted everything he had and will ever have. Shame. She was so cute. A divorce epidemic seemed to be breaking out all over the country. About half of my friends went through this dreadnaught in the next year. Everyone in my apartment, except the nasty landlords, was getting a divorce. (Was it an article in *Madamselle* that triggered all this mess?) These women were getting weird.

Fortunately, my buddy Cotty still had a few contacts for me to meet in New York. And through them I met a girl named Erla. Now Erla was Norwegian, but she could speak enough English to carry on a very interesting conversation. She was an aspiring actress with a difficult future facing her. She either made it big or back to the land of No Sun. I dated her twice and asked her to marry me. She laughed and so did I. She also had a great sense of humor. And so we pretended to be married for several months. I was still on shaky ground, but she was helping me stabilize some, and she knew it. We had a great time. I was free to be free! I never asked for this, but here it was. Could I handle it? Watch me.

On The Rebound

Erla was the Norwegian's answer to Miss Sweden. She was to be my stabilizer and new love, of which I was so filled. She and I would go to little French bistros and restaurants in New York. And we would laugh and cry at off Broadway skits that taught her theater improvisation. She would tell me how she was shy and had to overcome it to be an actress. It was then that I realized I didn't need Jackie anymore. I had Erla. We would sometimes sleep at my place in NJ, and some nights under her Norwegian comforter in NYC. We would just submerge ourselves into the arts and croissant happenings around us in the big city till I wanted to scream.

So I went to a travel agent and screamed, HELP! It was just approaching the Christmas Holidays and we decided to give ourselves a present of three weeks in the Caribbean Islands. We would go down there on a snowy day and arrive in Puerto Rico in the warmth of Paradise, where I had met Maria! Only this time I was bringing my own West Side girl. There was one problem. All the flights down that way were booked solid for the next two weeks. So I called a Vice Pres of Eastern Airlines who said there was nothing he could do, but to hold on for a moment. It was a moment later that we had reservations to Puerto Rico. Ya HOO!

I packed a knapsack with bathing suit, towel, tee shirts and shorts. I wore sandals and Erla did the same. We drove to Newark Airport and were on our way! We were actually late getting to the gate, but they reopened the gangway and let us on. The stewardess said, "Oh, you are together? Let me see if I can find something back there together." So when she returned to the front of the plane she said there was nothing available, but that she had something nice worked out. She walked us back about four seats and put us together there in first class. We ate filet mignon and drank champagne all the way to San Juan. We were two happy travelers. The stews enjoyed the joy they had provided us.

Upon our arrival in balmy San Juan, Erla wondered what we were going to do for the night as we had no reservations and every hotel was jammed. "Not to worry, something good will happen" I encouraged her. It was just as these words were spoken that I saw a limo with the Hotel name of *Dorado Beach* on the drivers badge right under his name. I pulled Erla over to him and said is your name Carlos? He said "Si" and I said how soon are you going to Dorado and he said immediately. I said wait, I will get our bags. He said "Si". I had heard of *Dorado Beach Hotel* as my parents had stayed there for golf vacations for many years. They never took me, but here we go. When we arrived outside the luxurious entrance, the Bell Captain saw us as ruffians I'm sure. Then when he saw our knapsacks in the trunk he wouldn't even touch them, He actually asked us to put them over in the bushes out of sight. That was fine with us and then we proceeded to the beach bar out front of our hotel and started our vacation. Piña Colladas never tasted so good. We sipped till sundown when everyone seemed to disappear to their $300 a night rooms to get made up for their Showtime dinner.

So we decided to get one more toddy for the night and carried our drinks through the lobby and out the main entrance where we were able to quietly retrieve our knapsacks out of the bushes. We hiked down along the first and second holes and then along the coast to the most beautiful beach overlooking the impending sunset, just between the fourth green and the fifth tee. We were totally alone out here for the night, so we decided to just go swimming out here and let the sun watch us as we watched it disappear. We learned how to slow down to the tune of nature, to the ebb and flow we enjoyed the huge red sun as it exploded a blue flame while disappearing at the horizon.

Erla was impressed that I had packed so many incidentals that we needed that night. We put up a lean to in case of rain, showered ourselves with bug spray, started a fire and had cans of hors d'oeuvres for dinner. We were so tired that we collapsed under the lean-to I had tied between two coconut trees, on our sleeping bags and rocked each other to sleep.

It was a big thud, then another that woke us up in the same position we had fallen asleep. I looked up and saw this foreign looking guy with a machete up in a nearby coconut tree, chopping at the coconuts. We saw each other at the same time and both screamed, "Yo!" He started calling on some kind of radio he had up there with him. Next thing I know the head of security of this Rockefeller Resort arrives in his car and demands what we are doing there. I said in my stumbling Spanish that I was looking for my parents who are guests, but that they had left and we were leaving the island to fly to St Thomas on the first flight. He said we had better hurry and he personally drove us for an hour to the airport, free, and we got on the next flight out of there. Whew! Was he evermore glad to be rid of this big security problem at the gracious Dorado Beach Resort?

We laughed all the way to St Thomas until we saw this skinny runway out in the Sea like an aircraft carrier on which to land, with a mountain at the end of the short runway. Good thing the brakes worked on this airbus. But we made it just fine, and a cabbie was waiting for us to take us to where ever we wanted to go. I said, "Morningstar Beach Hotel please," and off we went.

When we arrived at this old haunt of mine, they were full, no occupancy, ocupado. So I asked if we could put our knapsacks behind the desk while we looked for a place to stay. Then Erla and I sauntered out to the beach and then all the way down by the inlet to Charlotte Amalie and put on our 'bathing suits'. We had our private beach again. Yet we could walk back down to the casual beach bar and look like we belonged there, which we did. I mean we really did belong right there, in paradise. The water was so blue and green and clear that it is only describable by pictures. We spent five glorious days here with out it costing $40 including food, drinks and our free 'room'. We actually found that we weren't hanging out with the tourists but the people who lived here known as the Continentals. Basically they were just white Americans that had left the rat race to live here. Not a bad idea, I thought to myself. The front desk personnel kept our knapsacks and toothbrushes for us so we wouldn't need to hike each time we needed them.

We met so many good people that we wanted to stay forever. But someone said we should check out St John, the other American Virgin Island. So Erla and I hitched a ride out to Sapphire Beach where we could see the island of St John. This was where I had been before. Sapphire Beach! I saw a new hotel with gorgeous girls working out in a group on the beach. Their Guru was a guy I remembered, only now with touched up grey hair, and giving the fatherly touch to these women. I gagged and headed for the dock before Erla got interested in her health.

The glorious boat ride over to St John, across the Sir Francis Drake Passage, over the waves with forest green mountains silhouetted on deep blue skies over aquamarine waters, was right off the cover of a favorite travel magazine. We arrived at the Red Hook Dock where friendly natives and continentals greeted us and made us feel at home in minutes. We went to a local bar and had a rum and coke with lime over which we learned from a park ranger that there were only four choices to stay on the whole island: two small hotels, another $200+ per night Rockefeller Resort, or Cinnamon Bay Campground. The reservation lists for each are over a year old. But I still felt the magic. We saw an open bus with the name *Caneel Bay* on the side. That was our ticket…I grabbed Erla and we jumped on like we were Mickey and Minnie at Disney World and off we went to the only resort on St John. We knew from our experience at Puerto Rico just how to handle this new opportunity.

Our magic was still working as we called the Campground manager from Caneel and he said he was full, but to come out anyway and he would see what he could do. The first car we hitched gave us a ride all the way, and upon arriving our 'luggage' was put in a golf cart and we rode through the paths to a brand new tent they had just put up. It was like a Hilton Hotel to us as there were clean sheets on twin bunks, towels, and all the cooking and eating utensils a camper needed. The commissary was well stocked with groceries, beer, ice cream, diving gear and you name it. The beauty of it was that you shopped for what you wanted, and wrote down what you took, and paid for it when you departed the campground. It didn't amaze me that when surrounded by nature that such an honor system worked. I realized that stealing or dishonesty had no place in nature. The vibrations here didn't want to be short circuited by any unnatural static. So for two weeks we were the children of Mother Nature. No one could argue that this was not one of the most beautiful places in the world. The greens and blues of various hues gave love and peace a chance.

To me love came back into my life in the image of my beautiful Norwegian soul mate, and I gave her a peace of mind she had never known. We were both in tune with nature. But I didn't realize the full extent of how in tune we were until the hour of midnight on New Years Eve. We had brought to the beach a candle, champagne and ourselves. We sat talking peacefully of life for the first time I can remember. The Caribbean sky was milky with stars and the small waves set a rhythm that slowed the hearts beat. Then for an hour or more we silently held hands.

My mind was still cluttered as I thought of my New Years resolutions: Quit smoking, get up earlier, make more sales, work harder, make more money. My conditioning kept coming through. None of them fit. None of these old resolutions put my busy head to rest. So I silently discarded all of them, blanked out my racing mind with anything to do with the New York Carousel and tuned myself into the frequencies around me.

After about a half hour of listening, four feelings came to me and became my resolutions. 1) To be aware; 2) to be creative; 3) to be motivated and 4) to do. I thought only of these four feelings, and I have never felt such peace of mind, even though I didn't yet know what they meant. I only knew they fit, they were natural, they ended the static and my total being was at peace. I knew I had touched upon a stream of life which was as almighty as nature, but of which I was a small part. I was one with the universe.

This is not a revelation one takes lightly. I explained to my soul mate what had happened and she quietly held my hand, smiled and the silent communication let me know she understood.

The next day my long time friend Cotty and his ex-wife-to-be showed up. His very appearance let me know that compared to the natural peaceful frequency surrounding us at this campground, he represented the same sort of static that I had been before I had found peace in my resolutions. His background is incredibly similar to mine up to this point. I had felt we were brothers in some way. His birthday is a year and two days after mine, (Aquarius) we were born in the same hospital, went to the same prep school, left college at the same time. We both married models, whose birthdays were a year and two days apart, (Scorpios) who are in the same modeling agency, and who

111

divorced us two months apart. As he shows up many times in my life cycles I'll give him the name RePete.

So here was RePete, a living example of myself before I had discovered peace. He, with his typical high strung cover girl, were the last people I wanted around me now, as they were a living looking glass of my all too current past. They were not full of love, but hate; had no serenity, only static; and their only communications were complaints. They were blind to anything natural around them because they themselves were so short-circuited. They knew it, but because of their old conditioning, and habits of existing in a marriage of expectations and disappointments, they were incapable of achieving a common relationship with even this paradise of peace.

Even being a neophyte at my type of peace, I was aware that they were a drain to me, and if I stayed I would slip into their kind of rush around, up tight, bittersweet lifestyle. I loved them, but I knew I could not help them, and they could only hurt me. Nothing went right for them and everything was going 'perfect' for us. My soul mate and I left.

I have since learned and seen many people try and stay to correct, help or cure a toxic situation. Most of the time, they become as screwed up as the situation was to begin with. And because the nourishing person has invested so much time and energy to the toxic situation they feel they must continue to stay and help, to finish the job. But the nourished person becomes drained, undernourished and finally toxic; so that they can't even help themselves. This is a trap I remain aware of and walk away from. So we left.

Immediately we refelt the harmony with nature return to our breathing, our senses, out timing and our joy. We returned to St Thomas and checked our knapsack at the Morningstar Beach front desk and strolled to the end of the beach where we rediscovered peace. I really didn't understand completely why I felt so serene, but I knew that I did, and that if I pursued my resolutions, it would be everlasting.

On our last·day we went down past the end of our beach where a rocky cliff marked the entrance to the Charlotte Amalie Harbor. We hiked out around the rocky crags and came upon a cave. There was a guy living in the cave and knew who we were, his neighbors. So we chatted with our neighbor and looked out upon the sea and across the inlet where an island he said was called Hassle Island. I would have called it No Hassle Island. It had about two dozen people living on it in a sort of commune, or community type atmosphere. The only way to the island was by boat. Wow. And straight up the rocky cliff, our neighbor said he had just heard that the Holiday Inn had bought the top of the hill all the way down to the beach at sea level, and they were going to put an elevator in the cliff and his cave would become the lower level doors. He was having a hard time handling this.

The day had come to return to New York. I was not as upset or apprehensive as I had thought I would be. I now knew what I wanted to work on: Number One-to Be Aware. I figured if I could accomplish #1, possibly number two: to Be Creative might just follow naturally. I've always believed everyone has a creative seed within them, but if I had one it was so buried that I had never found it. So I am figuring that my 'cosmic resolutions' would all fit into place if I worked on them in the order that they came to me. With that in mind we were ready for New York and work, and sub-zero temperatures and my up and coming divorced life for which I felt finally qualified.

In Charlotte Amalie I bought our quotas of duty free liquor and also a wristwatch for my soul mate, as she had never owned one. Two hours later, as we sipped our last Planters Punch before going to the airport, I noticed that her watch was forty minutes slow and not moving. We had missed our flight. Rather than get excited, we ordered another punch, as we figured there's a reason for everything. We finally headed for the Harry Truman airport leaving our waiter a new watch as a tip.

We were able to get a flight to Puerto Rico on a small Caribair plane where we discovered the chaos of New York was omnipotent. For three days thousands of people had been waiting in lines to get on a flight out of San Juan. Apparently blizzards of the north had cancelled all flights, and the hotels were already overbooked with reservations. So here in the airport were all the wealthy vacationers whose luxurious 2, 3 or 4-week vacations were being completed in long lines by day and hard benches at night. Some had been here for two nights already. I couldn't help but find a chuckle here somewhere.

With peace still in my soul, I went to the head of one of the 15 long lines at the Eastern Airline counter. Interrupting a complaining businessman who was demanding a stand-by ticket to New York, I asked, "Where's your manager?" The agent pointed to a lone Puerto Rican at the far end of the counter. I walked back around the 800 people and back up to this man and said, "Excuse me, what is your name" He said, "Mr. Morales," and I immediately walked back around everyone and back up to the head of the original line. I told the agent that Señor Morales said to give me a standby ticket to New York. The agent looked down towards the manager who I saw nodding his head in a succession of three quick sneezes. The agent gave me a stand-by ticket saying it wouldn't help because there was only one more flight out and there were already 100 standbys waiting to get on and that the flight was full. I said thank you and took our tickets to a pretty girl who looked like she needed a smile. I gave her one with my tickets and asked if it were possible to get a flight out tonight. She said that was doubtful as she put our tickets on the bottom of an eight-inch stack. But I kept my distance from her and the hundreds of screaming tourists, and smiled a bit of encouragement to her. At the time of the last planes departure, her phone rang. She said nothing, just nodded her head, hung up, opened her drawer and pulled out two tickets and called, "Mr. Cannon! Gate 57, and please hurry." I gave her a big smile, blew her a kiss and off we went, the only two in the airport running to go somewhere.

The stewardess asked my soul mate and I if we were together, and I said "More than we've ever been." So she said she'd try and rearrange some people so we could sit together. A few minutes later she returned and with a smile she graciously said," I have two seats together Mr. Cannon, please come aboard." We were ushered by a series of three stewardesses to our seats, in first class again, and then treated like VIPs with champagne, cocktails, filet mignon, wine, desert, after dinner liquor, and finally all the unused champagne that these lovely girls could find. I guess they found us as special as we felt, even though our shorts and tee shirts and in my case bare feet, were hardly a sign of first class. Our entire three weeks had gone so beautifully that this flight was like putting whipped cream on a banana split supreme. But like everything else that goes up, we had to come down, in Newark, New Jersey. It was dark and below zero when I realized my bare feet were stuck to the runway and the icy winds were piercing my golden tan. Home, sweet home.

Peter B. Cannon

On The Mend

In the airport we put on all the clothes we had and got into a taxi to go to her nice warm apartment and her Norwegian comforter. We needed it. People might say that I was back to reality and my previous three weeks were a dream world. But I knew better, and it was this knowledge that allowed me to cope with the pitiful realities to come.

My love had to rush off early that first morning to go to her theater class, as she aspires to be a Norwegian actress in America. But I knew she was in the process of breaking ties in Norway and was too vulnerable for me to suggest that she be what she is, a beautiful Norwegian.

So off she went to learn to be an actress. That night she asked me what I thought of her taking off her bra in front of her class to overcome embarrassment of herself. I felt this was stretching my reality too much and that her class was just after a cheap peak. I was not hep to the artsy scene it would appear. After a couple of weeks of our trying to get back into our own scenes, we were finding differences in our perspectives. She wanted a loose arrangement and I wanted a tighter relationship. I knew not to push it or I would lose her, and remained my charming self.

Erla had been such a blessing, because she had helped me 'let go' of my wife, but also instilled a confidence in me that I was not an incompetent in life. Nor was I a subhuman. Such an experience as divorce can leave a person so low that a dog won't even recognize him, and the scars could lay hidden in the stomach for the rest of a man's productive days leaving him an obscurity to even himself. I had thought that had Miss Norway left me, I would have been ready for the 'pipe' or a deep six of some kind. So it was, needless to say, a thin sheet of ice on which I was skating. But skate we did, over mirrors of time, space and motion, without losing a stride. She toward becoming the essence of an actress, and I toward becoming 1) Aware, and maybe somewhere, somehow 2) Creative. Both of us were essentially

116

working toward the same direction, except that she was learning how to become someone else, while I was learning to become me.

"What is awareness? Who am I? Where is reality? When do I find truth?" I asked myself. And my answer was "reality is truth, and truth is I, and I am awareness." But how do I become aware? It is learned. Developed and practiced. I realized I had five senses which I could start with for development and found a course at the New School For Social Research called 'Sensory Awareness.' I had never heard of a course like this before, especially at a college. All I heard of were Economics, Business Math, Accounting and such.

I had no way of knowing what to expect, and therefore was wide open to whatever lay ahead. The teacher was a disciple of Charlotte Selver, who was a disciple of Fritz Perls, whom I had heard of by chance. My new love had given me a beautiful wall poster picturing a couple in a field, lightly embracing, and it said:

> I do my thing and You do your thing.
> I am not in this world to live up to your
> Expectations
>
>
> And You are not in this world to live up
> To mine.
> You are you, and I am I
> And if by chance we find each other
> It's beautiful!
>   Fritz Perls

And on that basis the class proceeded. After the usual hassle of driving into the city, finding a parking place somewhere near Washington Square, and getting into the basement classroom vacant of desks and chairs, each person would sit, or better yet lay on the floor completely stretched out with eyes closed, just getting into themselves. After five, ten or 20 minutes of this pacifying self indulgence, the guide or teacher would ask us if anyone had any feelings during this period they would like to express. She would recognize everyone until no more hands went up, listen to each person and then call on another. There was no grade for this credit course so there was no obligation to raise your hand unless the individual wanted to express themself. We then usually went through two or three exercises per two-hour class. Simple exercises that each person would get out of them what ever they could or wanted. If one raises their hand slowly with the hand open each finger can feel the changes in temperature. Also muscles and bones and blood can be felt working. Balance in the body changes and sometimes unnecessarily, which leads one to find we waste energy compensating for various motions.

We find our muscles are tight, shoulders held too high, postures off center because of psychological hang-ups and unawareness. We got into exploring every non-sexual area of the body one at a time and then integrating each with the whole. I would literally float out of these classes with a smile for each person I passed, and it was a smile which would always get one in return. One night I thought I saw myself walking toward me, and just as we passed we spun around and both pointed at each other smiling as we backed into the night with a mutual recognition. It was none other than a local resident, Dustin Hoffman. This experience was a natural high which precluded any hassles that the big city had to offer.

As the class progressed we did exercises involving another person or the whole class. We would hold hands with a partner and with our eyes closed we'd walk sideways, front and backwards, and then in any direction. I found that if I tried to get into her thing, I would lose step, get uptight and the harmony of movement would disappear. If I didn't worry about which way she was moving and just got into myself and did my thing, and she did the same for herself, then we moved in harmony. And it was beautiful! I was able at the same time to be aware of my total experience, from the changes in temperature to the joy that almost overwhelmed me.

Many times I thought, "Why don't the public schools teach such a course?" I have seen so many kids screwed up on drugs to get high or rebel against people who love them, because they have never had this chance to discover their individuality. They are living in a plastic bubble created by the social environment which says, "You ought to be this," or "You shouldn't do that!" So a kid is always seeing himself through someone else's eyes and not his own.

I realized the public schools are run by the government and that the men in power are afraid of only one thing, individuals. That is why, for example, all heads are shaved and bodies are uniformed in the military: to eliminate individualism. The prevailing climate being "You are not you, you are what we want you to be, or else. And thus goes the theory of government of the people, and let the masses believe it's by the people. Besides, say the bureaucrats, the people are too stupid to know what they want or who they are. Big Brother can take care of all of that for them. All Big Brother needs to do is to create a crisis, get them in a state of dependency and Big Brother will make it all well. No more individuals. Just people divided from each other, rather than living in harmony.

After giving a speech one of these nights to an insurance group of mine, I talked with the co-speaker, Jackie Robinson. He was one of my heroes as a kid and now was an advisor to President Nixon on drug abuse. He spoke of his son, Jackie, who had been busted and was in a drug rehabilitation center. His father's love and closeness to the situation was admirable, but he had no idea why young Jackie had taken this self-obliterating course on drugs. The father had done everything a man of his race in his time could dream of doing, and did it beautifully. And young Jackie had excelled also in athletic abilities, even in baseball. Except in the clutch. Because young Jackie Robinson would hear the bell ring in his head every time an important double play ball was hit to him- "I got to catch this ball and get it to second base fast, cause these guys know I'm the son of the greatest star and they expect I ought to be the same." Nobody told young Jackie to be himself, play his own game, so he had made up his own, one his father never played. He only had one way to be a separate individual from his father, and to this day I'm sure Mr. Robinson doesn't know where he failed his son. He simply believed that if he could do it so could his son, and even better. If only he knew of the growth potential for a person just like his son in a class such as awareness. I'm sorry Jackie, I really am. I wish I had had more time to get through to you.

But fortunately I was not mixed up in Jackie's son's crowd, or I may be lying next to him. Because I felt the pressures he had in my world, as I'm sure everyone does in their own. Yet the hard drug pusher is a man I've never seen, and for both our sakes, I hope I never have the displeasure. That's not where it's at. If you're buying hard stuff, next time you see the man, see if he's on big-H. And if he is, look for help, because he isn't going to be around long. And if he ain't sticking, why ain't he? Cause he knows better sucker.

The message from my class is two fold: a trip on awareness is a free natural high, one we can always get and it won't let us down. And second, I don't have to live up to anyone's expectations, and rarely do I create them for myself, because big expectations mean big letdowns. Too many people set their sights from point A to point B, and see or feel nothing between those two points in time, space or motion. Their expectations of point B leave them unaware, and therefore missing a good portion of the enjoyment life has to offer. This ability of lacking expectations takes a bit of deconditioning, of unlearning. But once learned, this unlearning is extremely mind expanding.

While in the process of these classes, I felt I might find some reinforcing ideas about who I might be through astrology. I had no expectations, and I had no faith in the typical horoscopes found in the daily newspaper. Yet I wanted to explore this mysterious field further and get what astrologers called 'charted'. I gave my place of birth and guessed at the exact time. Three days later I was reading my analysis and was amazed at the closeness and accuracy of describing me. However there were some points which seemed irrelevant or incorrect. I checked my birth certificate and found that I was twelve hours off on my natal time. So I reentered the correct time and three days later I received a personality portrait, which to my astonishment was 90-95% correct. I was elated to find that an astrological computer program reaffirmed the semi buried feelings I had as to who I am.

I will mention here an important fact brought out in the charts summary which states, "Remember that in the long run the stars do not dictate your future, you do. Man has free will, and basically controls his own fate. We trust you will find a way to use this analysis constructively toward that end." And thus armed with yet another vehicle toward self-awareness, I set out to do just that, to use it constructively.

My soul mate was so impressed by this service she even sold subscriptions for the astrologers who also offered an up to the minute audio analysis by phone of the next 24 hours. Many times I would call this service and give them my code number, and a computer would say, "Good afternoon Mr. Cannon. This afternoon the sun and mars are benefic. Flattery will get you everywhere." By coincidence I had just finished flattering my secretary who was sitting on my lap and listening with me to the audio analysis. The computer then went on for another two minutes completing my personal analysis. The coincidences such as that were incredible, and even obvious to many skeptics who would listen in with me. I'm sure such evidence of the plausibility of astrology would not hold water in a court of law (the stars made me do it) or in an empirical scientific laboratory, but I was won over. (Actually I was fooled and didn't know it). I thought society has to prove everything within our three dimensions, or it is not fact and therefore not believable. But I believed there are more than three dimensions, a feeling which allowed me more freedom of thinking and depth of awareness.

With this new astrological awareness that who I thought was me, is me, I began getting even more out of my awareness class. The exercises began unifying previous simple exercises so that all the senses were being integrated as a whole. From head to toe we became aware of ourselves with all of our senses. I was still new at this type of experience which is much like developing any ability. Practice makes perfect. So I was not as together as I would like to have been when Miss Norway said, "Peter, I don't think we should see each other anymore."

This dreaded night arrived when she also said "There is someone else." She had raised my red flag and twisted and tore it to shreds. There was a shattering feeling to my brittle life as she had wounded me in my most vulnerable sore gut, making me reel off balance again just as I was getting my feet under me, almost feeling confident enough to walk through life. But I needed her at my side!

"Who!" I had to know! Reluctantly she started telling me it was just some one that didn't mean anything to her. But she had to do it. She wished she had my emotions, but said she had none. I wished mine would just finish me off. I wanted to die.

I guess Erla recognized I needed help and invited me into New York one night to explore something she had heard about that was called Scientology. I checked my astrological message on the phone that day and it said to be ready for anything. I met her at a bar restaurant and cried in my beer. I was a mess.

She held my hand and we walked a few blocks to a weird neighborhood full of creeps. She said all would be okay. We entered a very old spooky building. The elevator inside was announced by clinking chains. Was this Halloween? Then I realized this was the building where 'another suicide' was described on the TV news last night. The same building where Rosemary's Baby was filmed. A real witch got on our elevator on the 2nd floor. She was all in black with gold jewelry and long nails and I was freaking as I squeezed Erla's hand until we got off on the fifth floor. We went into an apartment with just a number on the door like we owned the place. Inside was a lobby full of books and a nice looking girl that made an appointment for me to see someone in five minutes. I was asked what I knew about Scientology, and I said I didn't know anything. That was probably their ticket to a live one. I asked Erla what all this was about. She said she didn't know either, but someone in her class recommended that it might help me. I knew I needed help, but Erla I thought, was all I needed to help me. She said she couldn't do that.

Two men finally gave an introductory class to about five of us. Then they focused on me and offered to let me test on an E meter at no charge. That was ok, as I had no money to waste on this stuff. They asked me questions that got pretty personal and the ole meter was jumping all the way over. They said I was on the brink, that I needed to get help from them immediately. I was an emotional danger to others and myself. I needed to get an E meter for a mere $500 and pay $700 to get started on the road back to what they called a clear. Then eventually I could grow to be with Ron Hubbard on his flying saucer. It would be several thousands of dollars later, but that was later. Now I needed their help. How much money did I have on me they asked? I could not progress with out an E meter, which to me were just two tin cans held in the hands with low voltage wires to some box with a meter. My illogical mind even knew this was a scam and this cheap toy they wanted $500 for could be made for ten bucks. I wanted out of here. But Erla made me just check it out.

They suggested I buy some of their books and do some self help research while I located the money I'd need for them to start helping me. They wanted me to hit up my parents, relatives. Anyone interested in me at all. Oh boy, what was I into here. I bought a book called *Dianetics* and we headed for the dreaded elevator that took two minutes to go from floor to floor. Weirdoes would get on and get off. Remind me to thank Erla for this wonderful experience. I headed home to get out a bottle of scotch and cry till I was dry. I was a mess and that I couldn't afford to do anything about it was the message I was being sold. So I was doomed.

I didn't have enough answers as to why my marriage failed so I was still vulnerable in one place, and Erla hit it right on the head with that comment. "Why?" I asked her. "I don't know" was her reply, "but it has nothing to do with you." God knows I found that hard to believe. The whole world turned upside down and everything I had learned in life seemed an unexplainable darkness. "Why? Why?!" my insides screamed as I drove home alone in a cold rainy blackness. My mind screamed for an answer:

I wonder how it all fits together.
    But the numbness in my heart
    In my whole body won't let me see,
    Won't let me feel, won't let me know!

    The streets are so dark, so empty
    The tears on the windshield won't
    Betray the secret of it all. The
    Pitiful reality of awakening in the dawn

Peter B. Cannon

Of despair, the anesthesia of shock
Protecting me from myself, the peace
Without love is death when apart.

Is there any hope that man can find
A dream that can last forever?
Or must he know before he sleeps
To know that love & peace has been,
And may never be together again?

Why can't they live life together?
It can be so beautiful when they do.
But man has always been at war
To torture and burn and to kill.
Even those he calls his brothers
Or sisters, yes even the closest lovers
Can trample a garden so beautiful
That colors are gone forever.

What then without the flowers
Even when the fighting is done?
No flowers, no bees and no birds
To sing loves tunes? But we have
Peace, and what way to enjoy it?
It's hard to say, it's so dark and dumb
We can't get it together,
To see or hear life's songs.

Go back we say, rerun the reel
But we can't, we're here and now.
We've dug our hole, so cold and damp
Now cover us, we've seen enough!
I thought love had a chance awhile,
But peace is no place for that.

Hey wait! Don't sling that mud
I see a seed within it. If there's
Still a chance a flower might bloom
I want to see it clearly
No! Don't bury me yet
I've still a dream!
To see love and peace together.

It can't always be a question
Of one or the other.
There must be a common bond.
Where is it hid so well today
And since the beginning of time?

Could it be, but no, sure someone
Would have found it.
But yet we're blind,
For there's one thing we don't ever see.
It's that which is closest to us...

Right now, it's there, a seed- a blooming seed!
Let's plant it! Let's water it everyday!
We'll scratch the ground with our nails
And help it on its way. Let's nourish
It with warmth and care, with tenderness
And affection. And maybe love can bloom
Again while peace is in the air.

And then the birds will come again
With the bees and other things
To remind us of our freedoms
And our pursuit of important flings.
Oh please, dear world, let nature
Have its way, let harmony win over
What we can ever say.

As words are places to duck and dive
And hide what we really feel.
So false and yet so handy,
It's hard to let them go.

Whoever heard a flower say,
"Love I must leave you now, I've
Got my growing up you know
And so little time for you.
The sun only shines a few hours
And the breeze is being blocked.
The bees will never find me
If you're here around the clock?"

Of course you've never heard that,
It isn't nature's way.
Cause love is all those things to him
And peace is needless to say.
It's the harmony of life
Which wants love and peace to stay.

It's the harmony of life that wants love and peace to stay. What is harmony, the harmony of life? It feels right, but what is it?

I felt so many answers from my thoughts that I knew I was going to keep on living, and learning, and growing. I was going to be aware and be creative and be desirous to do. I realized there was a seed in my soul crying to come to bloom before it was buried, a creative seed which I had never seen before...because it was me.

And I knew that the harmony was like a balance of nature. But I didn't know I would fit into nature unless possibly I might be a part of nature. And if so, where do I find the balance for I have been thrown off balance. In other words I was out of control of myself. I was actually thinking of death as a way out from my problems. Now that is what I call unnatural, off balance, out of control.

While scratching the ground to plant my new found seed, I continued my drive of developing awareness. I saw the book I had picked up at the Church of Scientology. In my searching I thought the

Church could help. I was right, but in my blindness I didn't know one 'Church' from another. And as you know, many dead ends have many truths along the way, but if there is 1% poison the death is just as final and eternal as any other. I had found this Church of Scientology organized and administered much like a regular church, only with much more arrogance. If you don't 'join' the 'ministers' try to make you feel inferior, incompetent and a complete psychological miscarriage. At this time I was quite vulnerable and quite shaken by their test on their e-meter that showed me to be at sub-apathy. This, they had pointed out to me, was as low as one could psychologically go.

Being treated so 'compassionately' I had no intentions of returning to their haunted house of horrors and paying out the nose for their sake. That turned me off completely but I did find some of their ideas useful to me hundreds of times, and especially at this particular time when I was out of control.

Control, I read from the Scientology propaganda, was defined as being made up of a balance of three stages: Starting, changing and stopping. If one of these stages is out of balance, we don't have control. A natural balance is birth, living and death. A preoccupation with death would make 'stop' top heavy and we lose control of ourselves, and our lives. A policeman represents 'stop' and we can temporarily lose control as noticed by our sucking wind between our teeth as we sight a cop on the highway. So it is important to know that in order for us to have control over something we must be able to start it, move it and stop it, each equally well.

It is just as important, moreover, to realize that some things just are not within our sphere of control. And if we try to control something or somebody outside of our sphere of control, we will lose control of even that which is within our sphere of control. Picture an experienced motorcycle or car racer who is leading the field by one lap, when out of nowhere another racer rams into him. After crashing into a wall, the would be champion spends three months in a hospital being put physically back together. Then several months later our champion is back on the racetrack, but he is not doing as well as in his last race. He is shaking and unable to control his own machine. He pulls into the pit unable to go on. Why? He used to have perfect control before the accident and in practice runs by himself. But now with other drivers around he has lost his superb control even though he is able to start, move and stop himself. Then he realizes it's those other drivers. He was trying to control them, and they are outside his sphere of control. As long as he tries to keep them from running into him he could not control what otherwise would be within his sphere of control. Realizing this, he pulls back onto the course and finds he has that good old feeling again, he has control.

I spent many months thinking of this lesson and each time would realize that something or somebody with whom I had been in contact was beyond my control. Miss Norway, my ex-wife, my parents, the weather, politics, clients and other cars and crazy drivers were all out of my sphere of control. And by realizing this I began to regain control of myself and those things which I could start, change and stop.

With the help of awareness, astrology and scientology I was unlearning much of my previous conditioning and becoming me: an integrated awareness of a redefined self over which I was learning control. I felt that although my life was a shambles I was able to handle all the miserable situations I was now in, and become a better me for it. I did not realize at the time, however, how rough a test it was going to be, and how miserable things can get.

I had a six-room apartment overlooking the Hudson River and the Manhattan skyline under a full moon, and no one to share it with me. I called Repete (Cotty) in New York and he was going through the same problem and we'd go out on the town looking for whatever diversion we could find. We might even end up around 42nd street like midnight cowboys. But this night we went to the classier bar circuit, one of our regular haunts called Timothy's. It was not that I was just miserable, or lonely, but I wanted some reflections.

It amazed me that now I should hear the words of a black girl and her white husband who were doing the gig there. They played and sang their own material, and in their songs I found that I was not alone in this world with the pain that love can cause. And no one could express it better than this couple through their music. I asked her between sets how she could sing those songs and she said, 'Cause we've been there too," as she looked at the tears in my eyes and smiled.

They sang songs that made my soul burn, songs that I identified with, one of which was entitled "Play With Fire (You'll Get Burned)." This night I decided to play with fire and went over to a beautiful girl who I could see had also felt her soul stir from the music. With a few words we communicated to each other many common realities. She had missed her flight to Seattle and was debating where to stay. I asked her to come stay with me for a night or two and she said she felt she would like that.

We talked of me and we talked of her and we talked of life until the wee hours. I left her asleep to go on an early fruitless business appointment. I rushed home early in the afternoon to see her again and to share more of what we had together. I knew she was going to fly home to Seattle soon and so I was, needless to say, crying as I read her note that I found on the breakfast table:

"My Dear Peter,

I feel so warm, so clean after having had such a peaceful sleep in your bed, and to wake up in this beautiful place with such a wonderful breakfast awaiting me. There is such graciousness here. Thank you for sharing so much with me.

I have made plans to be in New York tonight. I will see you again at Timothy's. I want to tell you that you are a giving, loving person and your desire to be, communicate, express and understand what is inside Peter Cannon warms me, excites me. Keep digging, questioning - keep those eyes and senses open - wide open - have confidence in your self. There is no need to fear being alone - the sunshine comes from deep down inside. Have faith in your overwhelming goodness. Would it not be such a wonderful world if all people were proud, aware of their soul and had your desire to share it - had your desire to realize the essence of us all - It is up to you Peter to help people understand, to help people feel and open up - to be that kick - to be that breath of fresh air to those people breathing that poison. Do not be afraid of yourself- play with fire…

My Love to you,…Chris…

I cried not only because I knew she had come and gone like a spring breeze, but because she had also told me what I could not tell myself. I do want a better world, and Chris had left me with a way that I would have to live to maybe accomplish that. My peace to you, Chris.

I knew by this time that if I were to live my life rather than exist through it, it was going to have its highs and lows, its peaks and valleys, and its ups and downs. I started believing that I could handle both again. Especially the highs. But the valleys are in our lives so there can be the peaks. We just have to focus and refocus on what we want, the highs or the lows. I wish I were so wise here in my miserable days.

As I kept seeking the peaks where I could find reflections of myself, I realized I wouldn't find a total reflection of myself in anyone. But I could find a part of me in most anyone. My secretary Linda was such a help. She gave me daily encouragement as we listened to our horoscopes. She even gave me her dog, a Hungarian Vizulla, and we took it up to our farm in Pennsylvania and gave it to the caretaker. He trained it up to be a great bird dog, which it was meant to be. And Linda and I bonded in a way that could never have happened at the office.

On weekends, I would get together with dear Sherry. She was so soft and beautiful, and rich. I remember weekends when I would pick her up at the Bay Head train station Friday nights and we would barely see daylight till Monday. Sherry was the first lady to do floor sales in the garment district for a top designer house. The guys were a bit apprehensive about their wonderfulness when she started outselling them. I taught her everything I could, and she did the same for me. But then she wanted me to be like her father and my red flag went up and I said ta ta.

Then Patty showed back up on the scene from Denton, Texas. She now was divorced and with two kids. She was going to a shrink who I am sure was using and abusing her while he diagnosed her as amoral. That meant whatever was ok. But she and I went up to the farm and visited my dog and spent the day climbing the mountain on the property. It was called Pinnacle Peak and I thought maybe this was the peak I had been dreaming about. I promised her a good time once she climbed it to the top. We were just about to go over the edge of the butte where Indians used to scout the area for hundreds of miles, when we heard little voices. Hundreds of them. Oh no, the cub scouts and boy scouts were using their free day on our mountain. We couldn't believe it, and so Patty and I climbed back down and went into the farmhouse. There we had a great time cooking and eating, wining and dining, and reminiscing about so much.

We continued seeing each other, just for the fun of it. Patti was a Lab Technician in the blood lab of the hospital where I was born a lifetime ago. She would get off work around midnight and I would pick her up and out we would go somewhere to pop a couple drinks and maybe listen to some music until the wee hours. Then after a few hours of sleep I'd be out trying to sell insurance. One night we went out to The Ole Straw Hat, a new Dixieland nightclub. We were sitting at the bar talking when this very brazen girl came up to us and said to me "You should smile more often - I saw stars when you smiled." Patti said, "Hey, we're both married, but not to each other. You can have him tonight, but tomorrow he's mine." The mysterious girl said, "I better be going," and started to leave. Patti said she was kidding and that we were both divorced and were just friends. And that was the last time I saw Patti, the cowgirl from Texas. I believe she moved to the mountains of Arizona, and I wished her well.

But it wasn't the last time I saw this mysterious girl. Her name is really Barbara Regina Modzewlewski. The first two names mean Strange Queen of the Heavens. I never could have made up the rest of the story to which you can be my witness. Even that night we were thrown out of the Straw Hat because "We do not have co-ed bathrooms here!" Some lady had complained to the manager that there were four feet in one of the stalls. So off we went to her house where we sat out under the moonlight under an apple tree in her parent's back yard. We were both in need of each other and had so much to share from our different worlds and common realities. She too was recently divorced from her artist husband who lived in Washington State.[15] So we immediately knew of one thing in common. I didn't know it but we were about to make a bunch of common realities.

---

[15] Little did I know that some day I would live there too, during the *Second Arc of the Great Circle.*

Make Money Having Fun?

One night that same week, I had a knock at my apartment door. I thought it was my neighbor down the hall who was also about to get divorced, as the intercom had not rung. So I was caught by surprise when who should be there but Barbara with a guitar case in hand. "Can I come in?" She cooked dinner, and played the guitar and sang until I cried. I really had never heard anyone play, and then sing so wonderfully in my life. She even introduced me to AMORC, which became a very interesting study. The *Ancient Mystical Order of Rosecrutions* taught from the ground up many of life's mystical mysteries. This is where I learned about zapping people. More on this later. Then I didn't see her for quite awhile.

On weekends I was still going to the Jersey shore and occasionally partying at the Bay Head Yacht Club. My annual membership that last year there made each drink cost about $400. I kept hoping business would turn for the better, but I was just keeping one step ahead of the bartender. But sweet Miss Sherry was still meeting me at the shore and we would party with the best of them at the Bluffs and the Beacon Hotels and what ever closed last. Then, oh well, it doesn't matter. Except to say we'd have breakfast together and chat merrily about life, work and her father. She still wanted to marry someone like her father. Why not, he was talented, good-looking and very successful. I just didn't see myself able to fulfill those shoes, and therefore, I didn't.

Back at my apartment overlooking the golden sun rising above the New York City skyline, I pulled up to my trusty telescope and zoomed in on some activity at the 79th Street Marina. I could see some people laying in all positions on a beautiful sailboat and a monkey was running up the rigging and jumping from mast to mast, and everyone was just laughing and having a good time. I wondered, "How come those people are having so much fun and I am so miserable." I decided to go over there to the marina next Saturday and just see why.

When the long week was over, instead of heading for the shore, I scouted out the marina area Friday night. Then Saturday morn I had a good breakfast while I gazed upon the yachts again through my scope. I was getting excited just watching the lifestyle that had been right under my nose for years. Finally I got up the courage to just go over there and walk out on the dock, trying to look like I belonged there. I sat down on the dock and just got into the peace of being there.

Finally someone came over to me and asked if I would like a drink? It was someone I recognized from the monkey's sailboat. I smiled and said that would be great. We all got talking and someone said, "Pete, if you liked sailing so much, why don't you get a job on a boat?"

I had never ever even thought of it. I said, "You mean you can make money doing something you love?!!" They said sure, all you have to do is want to. Well I had the want to, now the how to. Someone suggested I go to a place they knew of that rents uniforms for crews on the fancy yachts. I went down there first thing Monday morning, but first let me tell you I had never sensed such peace and camaraderie and inner excitement as I did that first day on the docks of the 79th Street Marina.

So my heart was pounding when I actually found this marine uniform place up in some God forsaken building somewhere in lower Manhattan. In his dark dingy quarters I wondered what am I doing here. Then an old man asked the same question. I told him the truth and he asked me some questions, mostly about any boating I had done before. Well I had been out many times on Mr. Scott's 1933 yacht (yes, he had invented paper towel), and Mr. Wanamaker's, and Mr. Mennen's as well as having done some sailing on Lightnings and Sneak Boxes. None of this, I thought, qualified me for anything, and he said if he heard of anything he'd give me a call.

It was three weeks later when I received a strange call and was asked if I could take a 63 foot Chris Craft down to Miami. I said let me call back, and got his number. He said I was recommended by the uniform place. I was going to do this or die trying. I called Barbara and she said to do it. I called Sherry and she said, "Do it, and I'll go with you" as far as she could before flying back to work. I called this guy, Rusty, back and got some more details like I was going to get paid real good, all expenses paid underway, and yes I could bring a friend. We'd be shoving off in two weeks. I said I'd be there; I just had to rearrange a few personal things. He said he understood. I sent all the old Oriental rugs in my apartment to a cleaners for storage and arranged a warehouse to store all my other stuff. It wasn't more than a couple small truckloads, but I had to boil down my lifestyle to a suitcase and a duffle bag. My cousin Mark came and helped me move. He was excited for me. I emptied the apartment except for the telescope, plants and some furniture which my now divorced neighbor John wanted to borrow until I returned.

The two weeks passed quickly, and I was ready. I went to pick up Sherry as I passed through NYC on the way to a marina up the East River. We were two excited nuts, on our way to somewhere else. We found the marina and then the Yacht, *Jill's Mermaid*, the most beautiful Yacht I had ever seen, let alone was going to live on for some time. Rusty showed up and was a red headed dude ready to get going. When he saw my friend was Sherry, he suggested we take the owners cabin, as it was larger. He didn't need all that room. I knew from then on he was going to be ok.

As it turned out he knew I was a novice and wanted it that way, as he would rather teach than unteach, which made a great relationship. I learned so much from Rusty it was incredible. I found out after we were underway that he had been a test Captain for most of the Bertram Yachts that were built. And I knew he had to have plenty of experience to get near that job. Everything I did on board he did with me, once. Then I was on my own to do as I had learned. It was great as I was immediately trusted and counted on. I caught on fast to everything including how to handle the lines, fix everyone breakfast, and to what they drank and when.

I am in awe as we split the water off the bow and there off the starboard are the skyscrapers of downtown Manhattan and Wall Street. I kissed it goodbye and waved to my Dad up there on the 53rd floor of the First Boston Building. It's been great, but that was his thing in his time. I was finally finding mine. After cruising down the filthy East River, past the First Lady of America, the Statue of

Liberty, and under the Verranzano Bridge we were into the open sea. I shouted my primal scream, "Yahoo!"

Rusty gave me the controls and I was in fat city, so to speak. I was bursting with joy not only with what I was leaving behind, but where I was now and where I was going. If I died at that moment I would have died happy, not saved, but happy. The joy reminded me of what Peter Van Ness's parents said after his death at sea, "At least he died doing something he loved." I now understood in full what they were saying. Little did I think how close I was to that fateful moment.

Letting Go Through the Mist

The weather was perfect, visibility crystal clear, and the horizon never looked better. Was it because I had given up everything my privileged life had offered, and now I had everything I had ever wanted? Here I was on a 63-foot yacht with teak decks, highly polished brass fittings and varnished mahogany rails, the surroundings of a multimillionaire. And I had my girl friend with me to enjoy the days to come.

There was a very profound principle at work here, but I only knew that I had never felt better about anything. I was starting a new life with absolutely nothing, and as always without the financial support of my parents. They just thought I was still nuts. And yet I was now able to enjoy life in a new way. Who said one has to own something to enjoy it. The owner of *Jill's Mermaid* was not able to make the voyage down to Miami because he had to be home making a living to pay for my enjoyment.

We cruised at almost full speed over the ocean blue, with calm seas and cloudless skies. I had almost forgotten that it is not always like this at sea. But hey, why think about anything but the present. The future is not in my hands anymore. I am just going with the natural flow of events. I don't have to make a list and call thirty people to get three appointments to make the day happen. When we wanted to eat, we ate. When we wanted to have a beer, or a swim, or chart a course to a great restaurant, we did it.

And it was with that thought that Sherry, on our third day of cruising stated that she had to be back to work in her garment district selling designer clothes on Monday. What was a Monday? Finally days of the week had become meaningless until she popped the bubble. We had been cruising down Barnegat Bay past our beloved Bay Head, the beginning of the Intracoastal Waterway, past the house in Mantaloking where I had grown up, all the way down to Barnegat Light Inlet where we overnighted on the pier of one of Jersey's great seafood restaurants. We decided to cut outside there and make better time to get Sherry to Norfolk so she could catch a flight back to New

York. I told her to quit her job, but of course, like most people she couldn't even consider it. She was really tempted for a while.

It was a bit choppier outside than in the northern Intracoastal Waterway that we had been leisurely enjoying. We had to make sure everything was battened down and secured down below as well as on deck. Now this was getting exciting again, as we entered a new experience. Clouds started to scud into our sky and I had to learn to hold a helm in a heavier sea. It is like a dance on the waters as you get the sea and your yacht into harmony. The bow rises up and tries to spin left or right, and the good dancer at the helm will subdue her into submission and she will go on down the giant swell off the bow without swerving and getting broached sideways by a rolling crest.

I was getting ready to get back to the calmer waters when we decided that was where we wanted to head. The only problem was that the closer we came to land the shallower the water and therefore the steeper the swells. It got to be really hairy and Rusty had to take the helm after complimenting me on my three-hour watch. But he wanted me to stay above to help him if needed. We were trying to beat the darkness to land, and it was just barely in sight. The swells were much higher than the bridge and we were having to tack into the inlet even though the sea and the wind were behind us.

This was Rusty's call and I trusted him with the situation. I had never been at sea when the rain was blowing sideways, it was dark and the spotlight didn't show the cause of the roar of the sea that was trying to devour us. Sherry was below and somehow slept through the whole nightmare. After hours of wrestling with the helm, Rusty proclaimed us safe; we had made it inside a reef where the calm was greeted with a mutual Yahoo! We followed a myriad of channel lights into the depths of Norfolk where we finally found a dock and after securing all the lines and other chores I wasn't anxious to do, we crashed for the night in our cozy bunks down below.

The next morning, just walking around the deck as the sun rose, was a beautiful feeling. Hearing the halyards rattling against the masts of neighboring sailboats became my theme song. I awoke Sherry so we could share these last few moments together, for she had to catch a taxi and plane back to New York. She promised she would come down to Miami and visit. I really didn't think I'd see her again as we sat there sipping coffee on the bow seat. We discussed little as we were feeling a lot. It was just the time to be quiet and together. The scene couldn't have been more us if we tried. The salt air was in our veins.

Finally, it was time, and Rusty carried her bags so we could hang on each other. I felt awful sending her back to the Big Apple, but I had paid my dues and she was just catching on. I wished her well as she waved out the rear cab window, tears in our eyes.

I looked at Rusty and he looked at me and we knew we were ready. We had the engines roaring and the lines off in a heartbeat. I could smell the southern breezes beckoning as he headed out of the port toward the mouth of the rest of the Intracostal Waterway. I stood there on the foredeck, coiling the lines and stowing the bumpers, and just thinking, I am where I belong, right here and now. I wish I had known our God to thank Him for this, then and there. It would have been even sweeter.

I fired up some bacon and eggs, English muffins and OJ and we went up to the bridge and chowed down as the Chesapeake Bay birds flew alongside catching our left overs. One lone cloud hung off our southern horizon as if to guide us.

The next few days we cranked down into the Carolina Waterway which was so unspoiled and beautiful. I thought maybe someday I could live here when I'm too old to do much else. There were hundreds of deserted islands to explore and then there were those seafood restaurants. We docked for the night and went ashore to phone in to the owner.

After putting down some great local samplings from the sea and several beers we went back aboard the *Jill's Mermaid*, like it was mine. Rusty even let me stay in the owners cabin, as he was plenty comfortable in one of the forward cabins. I was just about asleep when I heard a crackling sound with loud snaps. My God, I thought, the ships on fire. I ran up to the main salon to listen and there was Rusty also listening. He thought it was my cabin on fire. It took awhile but I finally got a light and shined it over the hull and then I saw it. Giant shrimp were working over the bottom of the boat, and the loud snaps were the shrimp tearing off the barnacles on the underbelly of the ship. Whew, what a relief. Rusty and I got a throw net and in one throw we had enough shrimp to fire up for several meals on the way down the waterway. We slept good that night.

The weather was predicted to kick up again the next morning so we decided to stay inside rather than fight the swells offshore. We wanted to make it to Charleston, South Carolina for the next night and it would have been a quick trip by sea, but the inland coarse took us further inland through a meandering cut between miles of marshes. I was awestruck by the lonesome beauty that existed here. I don't know the history of the area, just the moment, but I don't think anything I saw had changed in a hundred years or more. Rusty was on watch and so I went forward to check out the scenery when I just knelt down on the teak deck and while the blue water shot below me I let the wind caress past my hair and face for what Rusty told me later was for over three hours.

I was being transformed by the elements of nature that were around me. I felt alive for the first time in a long time. I was heading to a new world, a new future and I was excited while I was at peace. I felt every fiber of my mind, body, and soul was in harmony with this incredible exposure to God's nature surrounding and caressing me. I lost all relation to time. As I said, for over three hours I let the wind peel off of me the barnacles of my past life. I felt almost purified by the blue waters rushing under the bow and skitting out from under me, and rushing backwards in a white foam, as I relaxed into the future.

I felt like Tarzan did going thru the mist into another world. Or a crustacean that had just shed its shell and was new and pure, but still vulnerable. I had many mixed emotions as I went through this metamorphosis. I knew I hadn't arrived anywhere, but I seemed to have a new clean beginning.

I always knew that I was on a search for the ultimate truth, and that I was possibly now on the right track to finding it. Little did I know how right this was, and how many times I would jump the track to fulfill my more carnal interests. If only some one had just told me about the Good News which I wouldn't discover until it was almost too late. It would have spared me a lot of pain and given me many more years of real blessings. But as it was, God loved me before I loved Him. And to continue from here will be to continue His story.

For as it was in the beginning, is now, and always shall be, He is with us. I just didn't know how to love Him._

That night we had another awesome sunset for us to admire and be thankful for, when darkness fell. Then we had to watch the charts for timed blinkers as channel markers. That seemed fairly simple until suddenly the waterway we were on seemed to merge with three or four other channels and bays and inlets, and ships! Wow, I wasn't used to all this at one time, and then the city lights of Charleston lit up behind our markers and played all kinds of tricks on my eyes and mind. Fortunately Rusty was standing by and correcting me as I would head for a wrong marker, or chase a ship thinking it was going my way and finding out otherwise. It was pretty scary for a city boy, but we finally came into an area where we could see an inviting dock and restaurant to tie up to for the night. We feasted on shrimp and clams and oysters and fish steaks and beer. We slept good that night too.

The morning brought me new treats of the south including hush puppies, grits and biscuits in a sultry humid atmosphere. It wasn't heaven, but I knew I was getting closer. Rusty had the engines idling and was ready for me to throw off the lines. We had it down to a teamwork science. After I had the lines coiled and stowed, the bumpers in their lockers and a big cup of coffee for us each, Rusty handed over the helm to me and we headed for the nearest inlet. We were going to go the rest of the voyage on the outside. Why not, it was just beautiful in every way and the seas were easy.

We got out our charts and put the *Jill* on autopilot and just did what ever we wanted. We were traveling too fast for any serious fishing, but lying on the forward bow cushions was one spot that looked good to me. I even did some writing of letters to the folks and friends, which got me thinking. We had three square meals out there that day and took watches during the night as we continued to cruise. I walked the deck alone at night and looked at the sky and knew only a Great God could have done all that. I had never seen so many stars in my life. I could see a falling star within any minute. Some seemed to go right into the sea. My main concern was to be on the watch for lights from other ships. I only spotted two different boats, but they were not on a collision course and soon disappeared. I finally got

Rusty up for the sunrise watch from 4am to 8am. I knew it was going to be beautiful so I stayed and had a little brandy in a cup of coffee and got rid of the morning chill and got ready for a nice nap down below. I tried dreaming of what the rich people were doing that day. I went out with a smile.

Moon Over Miami

Rusty and I were having coffee on the aft deck when a fishing boat came in. I wandered over there after a nice breakfast on board and asked the skipper if he had any fish for sale. He went down in the hold and came up with a ten-pound chunk and asked if that was enough. I told him I didn't want to start a shark frenzy. I just needed enough for a couple of sailors that might get hungry down the coastline. He cut up the fish into steaks and I found out later it was swordfish. I had never had that before and I am here to tell you that it is one of the best the ocean has to offer. That was a welcome treat we enjoyed a few times on our way down to Miami.

After topping off our water and fuel, I held the spring line while Rusty let the current back us off the dock and then we were free, heading south again. I hope you can feel the exhilaration that has filled me every day of this new life. I had no idea what the future held for me, but the present could go on forever as far as I was concerned.

We were heading out an inlet and off the coast of South Carolina when I realized how big the ocean felt when all there was to see was water. We were able to cruise at full cruising speed on autopilot for most of our next leg, which was all the way down the Florida coast to Francis Langford's Restaurant. In case you didn't know either, she was the widow of Mr. Evenrude. Her yacht was so big there that it carried a dozen Evenrude outboards of all sizes just for the lifeboats and dinghies. The restaurant had a Polynesian atmosphere with the thatch roofs and Samoan drinks and menu. All the girls were dressed in formal luau attire, which was similar to a long handkerchief. I wanted to be buried there someday. I had a Mai Tai and a few other Polynesian treats as we were waited on by this staff of angels on board our Yacht. Rusty had been here several times as many knew him by name. We were getting into Rusty country for sure.

We spent an extra night here to get a few things straight before our final run to Miami. It was probably another two days down the coast. I was wondering if I would be looking for a place to stay as soon as I got this 'job' finished. I didn't have to wait too long as

143

Rusty had called the owner and while he had said he might meet us here or there, he never did. But *the man* asked how I was doing and Rusty told him I was a big help and doing great and would like me to stay on as permanent crew. The owner didn't buy the idea, but told Rusty that if he wanted me to help with the refitting and maintenance on board that I could live on board at no cost. That seemed like a fair deal and Rusty said he would pay me enough out of his pay to cover any expenses. I learned all this as we were on our southern course skipping over the ocean like a song. I had a home. I loved this boat and it would just be a pleasure to just work on her. Rusty said we could charter her also. The only time I would have to disappear would be if the owner wanted to come down from wherever and go cruising. In that case only Rusty would be on board and I would stay with Rusty's family at their home in Hialeah.

While we were still a couple hundred miles from Miami I called Rusty up on deck to see the big city skyline dead ahead of us. He said, "No way." But as he looked up off our starboard bow there was the distinct Miami skyline. He recognized it for sure.

But then he explained that the skyscrapers reflected down into the sea and back up into the atmosphere, and that was what I was seeing. Sure enough the mirage disappeared and it wasn't until late the next day that I saw the real Miami skyline and it was much lower than the day before. But at least it was the real thing. We cut into the inlet and cruised into the Biscayne Bay. It was not that I didn't notice we were going by Pompano Beach and Fort Lauderdale and Hollywood before the big city. I was very observant of my new adopted home on the ocean chart spread out on the navigating table by the cabin controls. Rusty took us into the dock slip at the Racquet Club where we had a permanent berth arranged.

We were not the biggest yacht here at this twenty-yacht marina. I was humbled. But we weren't too shabby. Actually nearby was the yacht *Miss Budweiser* and she was a sister to *Jill's Mermaid*. I was in good company and suds.

I was real thankful for a safe passage and yet I had no one to thank except Rusty and Mother Nature. I sure had a lot to learn. I might have come a little closer to reality when on my first night aboard alone I laid up on the foredeck. Rusty had gone on home to Hialeah to be with his family. It was a clear warm night when the biggest moon came up over me, the moon over Miami. I wasn't alone anymore.

The Racquet Club was the typical home of elitists. I knew I was as 'good' as any of them, but they didn't and treated me as low life. Actually they were the members and I wasn't. That may have just been the difference, but the gap seemed wider. Well, their loss, not mine, I thought. I watched them play their tennis from the control deck and then sit around inside their club drinking and snacking on boiled peanuts, the local rage at the time. Yuk.

So I made friends with some of the other boat people at our tiny marina. One of the largest yachts was run by a black guy who seemed pretty normal compared to our elitist members. He and I would have a beer on his yacht and I got to meet some of the people he had come to know. One was a fairly attractive brunette. She showed up the next day and needed a ride home, and El Capitan wasn't around. I was chosen to borrow a car and take her home. She had a very humble apartment, but she invited me up and I was ready for some company. It was later I found out that this was El Capitan's girl friend of the day. He told me later that it was no big deal and no hard feelings, but I had a feeling I was set up and the results could have been different. I began to be careful.

It was then I got a letter from Sherry. Remember she started the cruise with me and had gotten off to fly back to New York to sell her dresses for *Leslie Fay*. She wanted to take me up on my promise that she could come down to Miami after I got there. She wanted to fly down and spend a weekend with me. I got the clear sign from Rusty and down she came. We had a fabulous reunion and took our yacht over to the Fountainblu Hotel and docked on the Intracoastal. Sherry and I went over to the hotel and pretended to be guest tourists and were lying around the pool. The Activities Director tried to get the crowd there active and with her microphone announced a diving contest. She was going to throw 12 large dinner plates into the pool and the winner would bring up the most. Sherry made sure I finally got into the contest. I was the last reluctant diver, and after searching all over the pool, I brought up all 12 of the plates. But so did six other guys of the 25 that gave it a try. So there had to be a run off. I suggested an underwater distance race down to the far end of the Olympic size pool. This was my favorite game, and I was ready. After doing my deep breathing on a cigarette she said, "GO!"

None of my fellow divers made it down to the far end, but I was in rare form and did the turn and made it all the way back down to the starting line. By this time all the guests were up on their feet and cheering as I slowly emerged. The applause was unreal, and Sherry was just beaming. I had to talk on the microphone and give my humble speech. Later guests were asking me how I could do that. Answers were varied including that my father was a pearl diver. We were treated like royalty for the rest of the day. Later as Sherry and I were having a toddy back on board across from the hotel, many of the guests recognized us. Soon we were dancing up on the foredeck to the stereo we had rocking while we were rolling. We slowly cruised back to the Racquet Club under the real Moon over Miami. What a day, what a night.

Unfortunately Sherry still wanted me to be like her father, and if there was one thing I couldn't do it was be somebody else. I was sad to see her return home after a few days of this kind of fun, but I knew it was over as we each went to our own different worlds. She went back to the highly competitive, wealth seeking machine of New York's fashion world, and me to my bare feet and shorts lifestyle. I was the original "I'm homeless, will work for food" guy you may have driven past. Except I never begged for anything, I did it the old fashioned way. This was lot more fun and much better for the ole ego system. The moon disappeared for a while after Sherry disappeared from my scene.

Rusty and I had a few charters on which I made some extra money. One was a bunch of Democrat Politicians from Washington. I was not too happy about the way I was being treated by these braggarts, for while I was serving drinks and delicacies I was being treated like a bathroom attendant. After listening to their scheming and scamming dialogs, I just had to ask some of them, "Why do you feel you have to lie and deceive the American public. Why don't you just tell the truth?" They laughed at me and only offered that I didn't understand the definition of politics. Was I really so naive to believe that truth had any place in our national leaders? Boy, did they ever wake me up. Who could I trust? My search would have to continue elsewhere.

I had some free time here that let me write home and to some of my other friends. I only heard back from one friend and that was when Barbara replied, and included music on tape that she had written. She asked me to listen and tell her what I thought of it. I was able to just write lyrics to what the music said to me, and it was as if my soul opened up to her music. I didn't realize it, but the words that came to me and that I sent back to her were to be sung around the world. I called it *Bring a Soul*, and she called me on the phone.

Barb said it was incredible and was going to drive to Florida and sing it for me. She did just that, and within ten days she was sitting up on the bow singing a song still known as *Bring a Soul*. I still can't believe I had written this song, even after hearing it sung all over the oceans coastlines. Oh sorry, didn't mean to get ahead of my story, but watch as I bring this Soul mate to incredible places singing:

Do you know where you are?

Have you ever been there?
Or are you some place new to you?

Let's go find the beauty in this land
Bring a soul and gently hold their hand.

Do you know who that is with you?
Have you met their soul?
Or is it someone new to you?

Let's go find the beauty in this land
Bring a soul and gently hold their hand.

Find out who's inside of him,
For it's you that you've never met before.

147

Now go find the beauty in this land
Bring a Soul and gently hold their hand.

Barbara stayed with me a few nights on the yacht, and was
awaiting her friend and the two girls were going to get an apartment
down here in Miami. They had left home to come be near me. Sure.
But as it turned out, that was sort of the case. After the girls got their
apartment it was a convenient place for me to visit when not on board.
Sometimes when the *Jill's Mermaid* was in dry-dock, I would stay
with Rusty and his family in Hialeah, near the racetrack. That was
pretty far away, so not much happened there except to listen to their
family squabbles. So I wanted to get back to the yacht as soon as
possible.

On board I sometimes would get a $100 for just making the yacht
available to some people I had met there at the Racquet Club. They
would have some really good looking hookers meet them on the dock
and then I was to pretend the men owned the yacht and they would
take the ladies down below and impress them. I was to keep watch in
case a wife or two arrived looking for them. That actually happened. I
was sitting up on the bridge when I saw the Mrs. looking for him. I
turned on the intercom to give warning down below, but they were
making such loud moaning noises back over the speakers all over the
yacht I had to shut the intercom down. I still wonder if that is what
drew the Mrs. to come along side and beckon me to come down to her
on the dock. She gave me another $25 to tell her if her husband was
on board. I told her I didn't know her husband and no, she could not
come on board as I had a private charter on board. She was feisty, but
I held my ground and probably saved his rotten neck.

Shortly after this incident Rusty had arranged a charter to go back
up to Francis Langford's to be able to watch the Super Bowl which
was going to be blacked out in Miami. Guess who the charter was.
Yep. The Mr. and Mrs. We had a great time and neither of us let on
about the aforementioned tale.

It was just a week after this charter when Rusty said he was going
to put *Jill's Mermaid* up in dry-dock for a major overhaul, and then
she was going to be sold. But that someone wanted me to negotiate

with them about being Captain of their yacht when they bought it. Meanwhile I could live at their Frank Lloyd Wright house on Key Biscayne with pool and private quarters until their ship came in. If I agreed to help out with some minor chores for the Mrs. and jitney their kids to the beach, they would pay me $150 a week.

So my lot had temporarily changed from being 1st Mate to Houseboy. It was just going from one millionaire's lifestyle to another's. The Mr. had a three-car garage with a Mazeratti, Caddy Eldorado, and Lincoln Town Car. The red Eldorado convertible was mine and the Mr. and Mrs. used the others. I had such fun taking their teen-age daughter and her younger brother to the beach, surfboards sticking up out to the sky and the stereo playing the latest Beach Boys hits. Oh, did I mention that the Mr. and Mrs. were one and the same, as I had kept separated that fateful night at the Racket Club. The situation was never discussed again with me, but I knew they both guessed the truth. She tried to get it out of me subtly, and it would have been easy for her and I to have reversed the roles on him, but it never happened.

I was welcome to have Barbara over anytime and while they were away traveling, she was asked to help out around the house. It was as if we owned it. The beautiful screened pool area overlooked the Biscayne Bay, as did the master bedroom, which even had a remote control for the curtains, lights and TV. The black marble foyer with marble columns just made us feel at home. Sure.

But one night, Barbara started getting abdominal pains, and by 2am they became so severe I finally took her to emergency at Mt Sinai Hospital across the bridge by the beach. She was a hurting puppy, and the doctors said her blood count was so high that they finally had to combine two very serious antibiotics which could have very serious side affects. It was that or die. I was not sure how to pray, but I tried with all earnestness. Barb was going in and out of consciousness for two more days and finally the doctors and I saw an improvement. Finally she was coming back to life. That was the night when I met a girl on the elevator who had been visiting a relative. She was from up north and needed some company. We went to the beach and there was that full moon over Miami. So we sat just under the boardwalk and talked and it was an unforgettable night. She wanted me to come up to her hotel room, but I just couldn't do that and expect prayers to be answered that Barbara get well. Besides, I always have been and always will be monogamous, that is, loyal to my friends. This was no time for exceptions.

After Barbara got better, the Mr. asked her to do an errand of picking up some artwork for his real estate scam. He was selling lots out in Arizona and New Mexico. Anyway, the artist turned out becoming our best friend. We were invited over to his home, which was just across the causeway from the Racquet Club. He had his office in the back overlooking the pool area, which he had designed like a jungle. The Tiki shed and waterfalls and bamboo gave an atmosphere that even his legally blind wife could enjoy. They were just so real and fun to be with. He could talk smut and make it funny.

He would draw obscene pictures just to warm up for some important project he had to do that day. He really was creative, and he hired Barbara to do freelance paste up work and that started a new career for Barbara. She was able to use that talent in most any place we went and make over $60 and hour.

This couple, Bob and Lee, had two sons who were also artists and musicians. So many a night we would have concerts around the pool with some incredible talent that had not been discovered. I was the professional audience, and whoever wasn't playing at the time would be in the pool. Bob was almost always naked, and he had no problem with anyone else being naked there, and that often caused everyone to just get naked in the pool and then spend the rest of the day like that. His wife, Leah, couldn't see so what did he care. Some of their kid's girlfriends were shocked at first, but if they stuck around, they too were trolling the waters au natural. And for this, Barbara was making money.

I lasted about six months at the Big House when it was getting pretty obvious that the Mr. was going to lose everything and maybe end up in jail on some real estate illegalities. It was going to be a rags to riches to rags story for these nice folks. I was told, therefore, that my services would not be needed soon, as he was not going to be buying that yacht for me to Captain. All things happen for good to those who believe. I had heard that somewhere and made it my motto.

Bob asked me what I was going to do now, and all I could say was, "I don't know, but something better."

Barbara said I could come and stay at her apartment with her and her friend that came down from New Jersey to escape the jungle up there. Her name was also Barbara, but she was a real dip. As a matter of fact she would start dipping about dawn and be really sloshed by noon. She got a job baby-sitting someone's parakeet and put it near the couch I slept on. All of a sudden I had bugs running around on me. That damn bird gave me the crabs and so I gave the bird the bird. It took the major treatment and combing to get all the critters. I never have, and hope I never will be a host to such a mini zoo again. Needless to say Bird Girl Barbara was on my bad list and won't be mentioned again.

Have I mentioned that my Barbara had the best singing voice and creative talent on a guitar I ever knew or heard? She could sing for hours all the hits but even more impressive were the songs that she wrote herself about life. All this was not nearly as appreciated by club managers as by me, and that became almost life threatening for them. They would want her to audition for a week or two without pay, and then dump her and do their scam to some other poor artist. Finally we landed a job at the *Jungle Lounge* where it seemed we were playing to the inmates of one of Miami's most serious asylums. And the owner turns out to be their leader. She had me running every 20 minutes to the Jai Lai courts two blocks away to make bets for her and she tipped me for the efforts. We wondered how low we would go. But we did it anyway and wrote it up to experience.

Barbara somehow heard of a group that met in Coral Gables that was some kind of a growing experience, and talked me into going with her. I had been through the Fritz Purls stuff in New York and found it to be kind of cool. So I went with her. This turned out to be a group of people about our age, but I never realized how different we each are. This became obvious as we each divulged the most intimate details of some part of our lives that seemed to be a stumbling block to our growth. I knew I was carrying some garbage that had not been handled. I had just pushed them off and tried to ignore them. But each weekly meeting I just sat and listened as our group leaders, a married couple Alan and Betsy, worked the people through their usually difficult problems that they had not faced before. One was Carl, a dentist and his wife, finding he totally hid his feelings and never showed any emotions. Their friends, Mickey and Susan, owned a flower boutique near us and found they had no problems.

But one night our leader asked me how I was doing. I said, "Oh, ok." He said, "What's that I hear? Did you hear Peter? Would you like to work on it?" "Well, it's nothing," I tried to cop out. He had me and I knew it. But I didn't know what it was I could work on. To make a two-hour session down to a few moments, it turned out to be my recent conversation with my parents. As he led me it came out that my problem was not my mother as I thought. It was my father who I had always thought was perfect, but who didn't really care about me. He had me finally stand awkwardly and hold out my hands to my imaginary father and call him.

"Dad!"

"What did he do"?

"Nothing."

"Call him again, louder."

"DAD!" He still just stood there in my minds eye. He had me call him louder and louder each time until it became a primal scream for help and my father just stood there. I was spent and reduced to sobbing. It took all that to let me see that no matter what I said to my Dad it wouldn't change anything, and I could finally quit trying. What a burden off me. I became an adult right then and there. Interestingly I was totally unaware of all the other people in the room until they gave some feed back and congratulations after my work out. It was neat.

On one other week I told of my experience of seeing my ex-wife on TV with her new fiancée Chevy Chase. On a show called *Saturday Night Live* they did some skits, on my furniture, about me. I could tell the cutting humor was aimed at my old life style of selling insurance. I had been taken by surprise when I saw them and had to call Barbara to make sure I wasn't seeing things through the fuma. But it was a new show called *Saturday Night Live* and there they were. Jackie was pretty bad, but this Chevy guy was very funny. So when Alan saw me he asked "How's it going Peter?" "Oh, Ok." I heard it immediately and knew I was elected to work out something that night. I told them of my chance encounter on TV with my ex wife, and my future ex-husband-to-be, Chevy. Everyone in the room seemed to disappear as Alan threw me a pillow on the floor and said, "Tell her." I was familiar with this procedure, as I had watched many others come through their relationship problems. The pillow became Jackie, and I couldn't talk to her. Alan told me to just make some small talk. "Ask her how she's doing." I finally got that out and then he signaled me to move to the side of the pillow and become Jackie and answer, "OK, how are you?" A discourse evolved where things that were never said when we broke up finally came out, until sobbing, I told her I loved her and goodbye. She said goodbye and it was over. It was finished.

Everyone hugged me and Barb and I went back to Mickey and Susan's house with the dentist couple and celebrated with some wine and fuma. It was intense and therefore incredibly relieving. It was also the beginning of a wonderful friendship with these two Jewish couples. Barbara and I were even invited to their family religious holiday dinners. No gentile had ever experienced this privilege, delicious food and fellowship.

With Barbara making big bucks, she leased her own apartment up in Bar Harbor, the ritzy part of North Miami. We had a great time there as Barb was an excellent cook and she could raid the fridge and make up a platter of all sorts of food. Then she'd get me blindfolded and laid back on the floor. She would make up different combinations of food and condiments, feed me teasingly, and I would try to guess what was on the Ritz cracker. I was treated to all kinds of Polish delights there. It was a happy time, but it was also time for me to move on. I thought I would go down to the islands and see if there were any boat jobs there as I was not having much luck this time of year in Miami. They had a big going away party for me at Bob and Leah's and I charged my ticket on a long cancelled Diners Club Card and flew on down to Puerto Rico and then over to St Thomas.

Peter B. Cannon

Come to De Islands Mon

Oh this felt so right to be back down here, and how it had grown. On my first visit you could count the houses up on the hill overlooking the Charlotte Amalie harbor, but now there were dozens and dozens. I went to Morning Star Beach Club and thought I would stay on the beach there again, but it wasn't the same without Erla. I met a native guy and he wanted to meet me in town later that night and show me around. He gave me a ride on his motorbike to my Casa and I said I'd see him later. I wasn't sure I would meet him, but he found me and it seemed to have saved me from getting mugged by some toughs. We went over to the boat marina and walked the docks and met some folks. Then my friend said he would pick me up in the morning and drive me out to Red Hook where you catch the ferry to St John. We did that, and I remember him waving as I went on over the Straits to that beautiful Island that Erla and I camped on. That was the visit at Cinnamon Bay Campground that was cut short because Cotty and his wife showed up full of bad vibes, so we had to leave. I had not seen Cotty in a couple of years, but I had heard he and Marin were going to get a divorce. She was dating Huntington Hartford, the A&P multimillionaire, just to hurt Cotty some more.

Can you imagine my surprise when I caught a ride out to Trunk Bay, the beach just before Cinnamon Bay Camp Ground? I went out to look at the incredible blue water and remembered the snorkeling here and the little fish I had revisited. I asked if there was any food available nearby as I was starving by this time. Someone pointed up the steep hill to a white house sticking out on a precipice overlooking the sea. I walked up the rocky steep hill and found a way to get in. No one was around so I started snooping and saw a gift shop and a bar and so I sat down and found a menu on the wall. As I was reading the menu a bartender stood up right in my way. "What are YOU doing here!?"? Cotty said. I couldn't believe it. We had been through so much growing up, and then ending up at the same high school in Lake Placid, New York, and then both of us marrying models and now both divorced and now here in Paradise. Then he said, "Want a job?"

154

"Sure." I said. "What is it?"

"I hear they're looking for a Beach Director at Caneel Bay, and you're the man. I was just getting ready to close and I have to take my money in for the day. C'mon mon, I give you a ride and we get you a job."

Caneel Bay is the Rockefeller Resort that is the place to be on the Island. I guess old man Rockefeller bought most of the Island and gave most of it back to the US Park Service with the promise that no other hotel can open in the park, and then took a giant tax deduction. The resort was a refurbished sugar mill plantation on the most beautiful beaches in the world. I fell in love with the place when I first saw it, but knew this was a place for the rich and famous and I would never be staying here. Well, 'never say never' someone once told me.

I had my job interview the next day with the head of security and staff personnel. He hired me on the spot as Executive Beach Director and explained the what, when and where. He told me I would have a staff of natives that would keep the seven beaches clean, the ripe coconuts picked, and I would make sure everything was done. I would have a private house, maid service and dine with the guests, but I would breakfast with the rest of the staff, just to speed up the mealtime, so I could get to the beach and start my Directing. I also rented out mats, snorkel gear and small Sailfish sailboats. I had a week to go back to Florida and get all my gear and be back to the door of paradise.

I took the Caneel ferry back to St Thomas from the dock on MY beach and flew back to Miami. I was ready to get out of the big town, but Barbara wasn't ready to let me go, especially alone, back to who knows where. But Bob and Leah gave me another big going away party and it was a night that was hard to remember, if you get my drift.

Barbara took me to the airport in tears, and I said to her it wasn't goodbye, just the beginning of a new beginning. Don't worry. Actually, I had been with her everyday now for quite awhile, and I was looking forward to being single, free, unencumbered, even though I know I'd miss her. But it was time, and the big bird took off and I followed my beckoning to de Islands, Mon!

I flew non-stop onto the Harry Truman airport, which begins its runway out in the blue Caribbean waters and ends abruptly at the base of a mountain. With full brakes on and engines screaming in reverse the pilot gave us a safe landing in Paradise. I shared a cab into Charlotte Amalie, and couldn't wait to get over to peaceful, beautiful St John. So I continued on in my cab out to Red Hook where the Caneel Bay Ferry was awaiting me. I introduced myself to Beaver, the native first mate, and the rest of the native crew with whom I was to work closely. I was to be on the dock for each guest ferry arrival and departure from then on.

When I arrived a porter took my gear to my house and Cotty saw me as he was just closing out his bank for the night before going to party. He told me I could get oriented later and to jump in a jeep and off we went to a place called Gallows Point. We had more than a few drinks there while we caught up on war stories since we had seen each other and to reminisce about the good times we've had over the years. I met Charlie the bartender from Antigua, and some of the Continentals (Whites) who now resided and 'worked' here on St John. One man named Forrest was a surgeon back home but was told by his Physician that to live another year he had to eliminate all stress in his life. So he was here. He had bought hunks of land that was available and built rental houses on them. He had a car rental business there by the dock, and he gave me one to use until I got settled. It was a mini mote, a little open square looking rig like a small jeep. It would handle all the steep rutty 'roads' the island had to offer. The manager of Cinnamon Bay Camp Ground was there and remembered my first visit to St John many moons ago with Erla when they put up a new tent for me.

And the big surprise was that Bevy, the young sister of one of our friends back in Jersey was also working at Caneel. I had not seen her since she was at big sisters wedding to our friend Bob Henry. She was probably 15 then and now was a beautiful 25. She was just a bubbly personality that added joy to every minute. There were several others that I met here that night and on the successive nights as this was where all the Continentals would congregate after the days end to wallow in some rum and watch the sun set on the sea.

The only trouble was that no food was served here, and some nights we wouldn't make it back to Caneel before dinner ended and the locals would say, "Come to de Brown House, dey have fish tonight." Or goat, or rooster. That was never my first choice but sometimes it was the only choice. But then we made friends with the chef at Caneel, and now we had contacts in the kitchen, the boats, (me) and the Trunk Bay bar and restaurant (Cotty), and Bevy in the front desk. Then John joined us from motor pool, so we had keys to about anything that moved. Then we would party all over the island, including Cinnamon Bay.

My house was not quite private as two other guys were there. One was Gary, the former Beach Director who actually stepped down for me as he was going to go back to school in the states soon. He taught me the ropes on the job and calmed me of any new job jitters I might have. We had a good time working together. He became real interested in my 'magic' that I had picked up through a combination of my exploring what I now know of as occults. But I was able to get people to do many strange things there in this peaceful setting. The 'Magic' which I taught him, emanated from a picture in the mind out through the back of the neck. It would make me shudder sometimes. Gary would tell me to get a guest sleeping on the beach to get up and straighten the surfboards. I would do my thing, which we called zapping someone, and the guy would jump up and just go over and straighten the surfboards and then just walk off unaware. Gary would laugh and wanted to know how to do it. I told him it was a process of exercising the knowledge and having faith in the results, and that the end was never to hurt anyone. I made him promise and he tried learning. It was funny to watch him strain to get it out the back of his neck. But finally he started to catch on and was able to do it sometimes, but not to the extent that I did yet. So he would say, "Pete, get that girl to look over here." I would and he'd be there smiling like a Cheshire cat when she turned around.

Speaking of girls, Caneel had so many good-looking girls sent down to us daily by their rich daddies who were too busy to take time off. So Gary and Cotty and I had our hands full, so to speak. Many nights after our R&R at the Gallows Point Rumeria, we would head back to Caneel for the sumptuous buffet dinner, complete with ice carvings and gourmet delights. Then we would retire to the roofless lounge where a steel band would be playing and the bartender would know our favorite drinks. All the girls would be there and it was so much fun to teach them how to dance to the steel band, native style. We had more fun than any man should be allowed to have. There under the full moon and stars and the smell of jasmine and gardenia and whatever else she was wearing, we would dance ourselves right down onto the beach some 50 feet away into my 'Office'. There I learned the secrets of high level living back on the mainland and taught the simpler pleasures for the week or so that they were visiting.

One day I saw a name on the incoming guest list that sounded very familiar and I thought I recognized him as he and his wife disembarked onto my dock. Later he came up to me on the beach and wanted to take out one of my Sailfish. I asked him if he had any experience sailing and he said he hadn't, but he had seen lots of people do it. I said that I couldn't let him take one out alone. He got all excited, and gruffed that he had been to the moon and back. I said, "I know Colonel, but this is dangerous out here." Whoa, I hit a nerve and he stomped off to find the manager and report me. I said I'd help him. But the manager was not to be found at that time. He must have run into my friend Ivan, the front desk clerk, who sometimes would pretend to be the manager. Because, later he came up to me all cooled down and asked, "Pete, would you take me out on the sailfish and get me checked out on it?" I said sure Colonel Borman, and we shoved off with me at the helm and on the main sheet.

I explained to him how the direction of the wind and the tiller and the amount of sail to the wind all worked together. He seemed to catch on pretty quickly so I changed places with him and moved up near the bow. He screwed up some, but was getting the hang of it. Then he saw a big 35-foot sailboat coming in with guests for dinner. They were safely outside the ropes from where we were allowed to sail, but Borman said I better let them go by. I told him to hold steady, as they had to stay out side the buoys. He didn't hold the course and let out the sail all the way. Well the full sail caught the wind whipping around the mountain and we headed straight for the sailboat coming in to anchor. I jumped up on the bow and pushed off with all my might, as we would have put a gaping hole in the side of that yacht. I was just able to push off and was breathing hard as I sat back down and glared at the Colonel. He seemed like nothing had happened. He was weird.

That night I told this funny story at our Gallows Point 'waterhole' and one of the guests there hearing me happened to be a NASA engineer. He asked me a bunch of questions, like his reactions to stuff and any marks on his body. I said he never looked me in the eyes, and his eyes were weird. He also had a scar that looked like a corrugated tube across his abdomen.

Then the engineer wanted me to ask Borman some questions when I got the chance. But meanwhile, he explained that these astronauts are so trained or briefed to remember every detail in an emergency crisis that they become weird. They can virtually recite the readings off their entire control panels at a given time. But when they debrief them, the lack of emotion this calls for doesn't return to normal. They act like nothing has happened. And while Borman was up, a Pulsar seemed to pass through his space ship. I asked what a pulsar was. He said it was top secret, that they are not sure yet, but that it is a star, a black star, larger than any star in the universe. It is so huge that it gives off this pulse of X-ray and the equal and opposite reaction is that it absorbs its own light. It also eats stars for dessert. This black hole in the sky is so dense that a teaspoon of sugar at the entrance would weigh about the same as three million elephants. And he thought Borman was up there and was hit by this X-ray, and that was why he had the scar on him, from tubing in his spacesuit. Whew, this was scary stuff, and I asked some questions, like is this God? He said, "Not quite, but it sure shows us a whole new side of the universe." I asked, "If the black hole absorbs its own light, the speed of light would be reversed in effect, does that mean that time would be reversed?" He had not thought of that one yet, and said he wasn't sure. I had to hold onto this top-secret info for years before it became public knowledge. They were afraid if the people knew about it before they had more answers that they might panic and worry. Jeez.

At the end of Colonel Borman's second week with us, he was a new man. He seemed relaxed and in tune with the naturalness of the island. The engineer wanted me to ask him one more question. My opportunity came as he was waiting in line to board our ferry back to

St. Thomas. I walked over to him and said, "Colonel, can I ask you a personal question?" He said, "Sure, what is it?" I asked, "Have you ever seen any UFO's?" He looked me in the eyes for the first time and said, "No" and bolted to the front of the line and pre boarded the boat. I could see him pacing back and forth there as the rest of the guests awaited permission to board. You see, the engineer had heard Borman say over the speakers at NASA from space, "What the hell are those things out there?" The rest of the message was scrambled so the general population at Cape Kennedy could not receive the rest of the transmission. That's why he had me ask, and that was the reaction.

Colonel Borman returned to Washington where he was President Nixon's advisor to NASA. I often wondered if he ever sailed again. Somehow I knew I'd find out.

But back to normal again as my routine became more typical. I would get up around 7:45am so I could get a shower, buffet breakfast over looking my 'office' and show up in uniform, (a swimsuit) with a T-shirt that said Executive Beach Director, and be on the dock for the first boat of arriving guests at 8:15. Beaver would throw me a line and I would hitch it onto the piling. Then the bow and stern lines. This was just like the ole days with Rusty and I.

Then the guests would start showing up at my 'office' where I would sign out snorkel gear and floating mats and, if they could sail, a sailfish, and if not, a floating surf mattress. I was very popular guy there in St. John. Then at lunchtime I would join my guests for the chefs' buffet lunch, which was always quite elaborate, but after a few weeks, very boring. The only things different at the meals were the guests, and I didn't eat guests. They would ask the stupidest questions and I got my jollys giving them stupid answers. For example one lady asked why the water was so blue. I answered with a sincerity of caring that it was because the fish made sex in it. That lady did not go in the water again during her remaining six days of 'paradise'.

So I began to look for alternatives. Especially after work, when Cotty and I would go to new homes on the island and be guests for dinner. Eventually we were asked to 'house sit' peoples' cliffhanging homes that looked down over a secret cove and were just exquisite. We would have a party most every night for our continental friends and have a demijohn of wine, or two. These are four foot high glass bottles wrapped in a tight braid of straw, and we would pump air into the bottle through the two-inch wide cork with a needle. This would force the wine out through the long needle, sort of like taping a keg of beer. Well one time Cotty pumped too hard and the massive glass bottle broke and I don't know how many gallons of wine just spread all over the first floor of this house. Luckily we had a back up that didn't have a weak spot in the glass.

Drinking was a way of life on the islands, and I was right at home with that concept. Also, my cigarettes could be bought tax free at one dollar per carton for Pall Mall, no filter. My beach was my ashtray, and the island was my party. It was unending. I am amazed that I am here to tell this story for this reason alone, let alone all the previous and future tortures I put my body through. We had fun, but we paid for it until past noon everyday and until it was time to party again after work. We were unstoppable and so was the fun. I would wake up just in time to get to the beach and that was all I really had to be concerned about.

But then there was the party that all we Plainfield people working there couldn't have avoided, Bevy's birthday. We went out to a far point of the Island where there was a deserted sugar plantation. The bare walls of the ruins were witnesses to a new life here. We were all a little too aware, and it was quite spooky meandering in and out of deserted buildings when suddenly we were surrounded by a resident herd of bulls and cows that didn't appreciate our intrusion. They knew their way around the maze better than we did, and we couldn't get away from them. We would turn a corner and there would be this humongous bull turning toward me and bringing a few thousand pounds of hamburger behind him. I finally slid off a short cliff to a path that took us out to a high point behind the plantation. Scrambling up the path I saw a huge statue, of Jesus Christ. I didn't know whether I was safe here or in more danger. I looked in awe up at the statue and then back at the herd following me. I swung around the statue where I was safe, and stood on the two feet of the Christ statue. Then all I remember was the feeling of just being shoved from head to toe off the feet and down a cliff toward the ocean, tumbling head over everything else. When I finally stopped at a level spot short of the water, I looked up and it sure seemed the statue was looking right at me and intimating never to step on those feet again. I scrambled to my feet and found my way through the beaches and bushes to the road where I was picked up by Bevy and taken home to Caneel Bay Plantation.

But I was ten minutes late to the beach that morning and Beaver had to jump onto the dock and tie his own spring line to the dock. The head of security had a meeting with me that afternoon warning me of one more late day to the beach and I would be packing. I remember thinking that would be unfortunate as there was not much else I could do there on the island. We had been running the only game in town. So I was extra careful to be at the beach on time, no matter what the night before had beheld.

I became friends with the owners of that sailboat that Colonel Borman tried to sink. And one day I was out on their anchored yacht and looking in at my beach there at Caneel, and I just started thinking:

> Peace is here upon my boat
> Surrounded by ripples that seem as
> A moat, between me and land and
> The people I see
> Pretending they love whatever they be.
>
> They run and scurry from door to door
> With a frown on their face to show
> It's a boor. But they must find a trinket or two,
> To show their neighbor that they have one too.
>
> And in their rush to prove what they are
> They forget to look up at a star. Or down
> At an animal or ere to a tree, which
> Try to prove nothing to themselves or to me,
> For just as God made them so shall they be.
> If man could but stop for a second to see,
> The peace from nature that's in a tree,
> He might find himself whoever he be
> And live in harmony with life and with me

And then it was that Barbara showed up right there on St. John with no place to stay. I stowed her away in my house without the other guys there knowing, for almost a week. I'd bring food back to her from the buffet and other sources, and slowly most everyone knew she was there, except for the head of security. Bevy was quite put out as she had started thinking that maybe we were becoming a thing, which would have been very possible. But Barbara changed everything. It was not too long, therefore, that I was once again 5 minutes late to the beach. That was the 'doomsday' I had been awaiting. I had a week to get my things together and move off the Plantation. And it was Christmas time to boot.

Everyone wanted to know what we were going to do, and as usual I would say, "I don't know, but something better." That first night that we were 'out in the cold,' a sweet old lady who had broke her arm asked if we would come and stay at her house and help her with her life. We cooked for her, and us, and she even invited all our friends to her house for Christmas and had presents for us all. Not only had she invited all our friends from the Caneel Plantation, but also Charlie (native of Trinidad,) the bartender at Gallows Point. She was a refreshing change from the Rockefeller mentality as demonstrated through that head of security.

Within a week, because word was all over the island about our situation, we were asked to be managers of the second largest hotel on the island. It was Estate Beth Cruise, a rather run down resort on top of a mountain overlooking the Pillsbury Sound and St. Thomas. It was beautiful. We had partied up there a few times, but the access road to a novice was very intimidating. We went up there to check it out and decide if this was where we were to be. What we saw was not the present condition, but the potential. There was definitely room for improvement. We decided to take the position, mainly because the owner was out of the country in Canada. We'd have free reign to do our thing. Barbara and I made some heavy demands that we would expect and they were all met. We had the best of the apartments overlooking the main buildings and the sea, and we had our own car, which was part of a fleet of mini-motes that we rented out to guests (and loaned to friends.) We had a decent budget with which to repair the guest cottages, replace carpets and decks, redo the pool and deck, and have a staff of four to help us do the work. After we did all that we had the owners son open the dining room. He was a bit strange, but we thought it better to have him busy than to just walk around stoned in his white robes thinking he was Jesus of Bethany.

His mother loved cats, and had about twenty pet cats and about twenty wild cats joined them. They were the dining room's main clientele. I learned to hate cats. One of our first guests was dining in our open-air dining room when a black cat named Jumbie (native for ghost or spook), pounced up on their table to the screams of our first guest's wife. The other cats came running to see if Jumbie had scored some food. Our first guests checked out the next morning, a week ahead of schedule. It was time to take action. Barb and I were being served lunch when Jumbie arrived in the middle of our table. In a split second I had Jumbie spinning overhead by the tail, and you could hear that D___ cat screeching all the way down the cliff. Then silence.

The next day, Barb and I were just finishing up our breakfast when who should appear on our table again. I grabbed a laundry bag and in went the Jumbie. We took a long ride to the far side of the Island and left the bag opened in the woods.

We had a great day discovering some new beaches and celebrating the good life. We needed a day off as we had been working hard everyday for almost two weeks. When we went past Trunk Bay we visited Cotty and his new girl friend Bevy. Then we just partied and collected folks all the way back to our resort where we opened the bar and just had a blast. Barbara sang and played her sweet sounds and those that had never heard her sing were amazed and in love with her. We decided to have one night a week when she would entertain all the continentals, and then Wednesday nights would be native night.

These two nights turned out to be the big events on the island. They were really fun, and my native dancing became an attraction of itself. The steel bands would change each week, but many of the native girls would always be there, and could they ever dance. Once I had a bit of the rum in me, I became native myself. And all de native girls, dey want to dance wid me. I loved it, and we had so much fun just letting go and being as free a spirit as these wonderful people were here on St. John.

My buddy Sturge was my main guy on the payroll. He and his wife had never been any farther than St. Thomas from home. Yet he was as capable of repairing and fixing up things as anyone could ask for. And all I had to do was mention something that could be fixed up and he would tell me with a smile 'not to worry, Mon, it's almost finished. No problem.'

But one time we had a photographer sent to us by the owner. He was from Screw Magazine and his model was here to make our hotel look pretty. Sturge did not take to his New York ways. I had been that route with my ex, and so I was able to handle the jerk. They were with us for a free week as his pay to take pictures for a brochure. One evening I didn't see him at our usual happy hour around the bar by the dining room, so with rum in hand I went looking. There I found him and his model trying not to fall off the ridgeline of the roof over the dining area, in the nude. Then he started saying shhhhh, as if the setting sun would be disturbed if some one said something. Then as I watched, the model grabbed his butt just as the moment he had been waiting for happened. He freaked, pushing her off the roof onto the deck in front of the bar. He had been waiting for the moment when the setting sun just dipped below the ocean horizon and a blue streak came off the top of the sun. This only occurs in the Caribbean and our roof was the perfect spot to photograph this phenomenon. But all we saw was her bare moon in front of our eyes at the bar.

They packed up and left the next day. We said good riddance to New Yorkers and were glad we were not a part of that scene anymore. We hoped that the owner, who we had never met, would also stay away, as we were still trying to get rid of a few cats also.

We actually started having some real guests that came to us by referral that really enjoyed themselves there. It wasn't for everyone, we understood that. But for those who were between the luxury resort and camping, we were unique. We actually started showing a profit and had funds to finish some projects. Barbara and I felt like we owned the place and therefore gave it our all. We were naive in that respect.

Meanwhile, we had the idea to open our own restaurant at Gallows Point. We went there every night anyway to hang out with our fellow Continentals and swap the day's stories and let Charlie bartend us to oblivion. The owner of Gallows Point was also not residing here and our friend, ex doctor Forrest, was the manager. He more than welcomed the idea that Barb and I do our thing there. So we bought all our supplies including plates, silverware and other supplies from a restaurant in St. Thomas that was going out of business. We made our contacts for some gourmet food. And we took orders in advance for the opening night from the gang there. They filled out their name and number in their party and their order on our tie-dye pad that Charlie kept at his booze shack. So for a week people signed up and decided between Pork Chops, Shish Kabob or Filet Mignon char grilled with all the baked potatoes, garlic French bread and salad they could eat. That first night we made enough to cover all our opening expenses. From then on our only overhead was the cost of food and the umbrella in the palm tree we had over our homemade char grill. We became so popular that we had to open a second night and then a third. We really busted hump during this time as we also were running the resort too. But we were really making some money. Our little savings account started to go up instead of just down.

Nothing goes smoothly in de Islands tho Mon. There is a book called, "Don't Stop the Carnival" that captured the mysterious life here in paradise and the sense of humor necessary to survive it. Often our food would not show up on the ferry on time. So I would have to drive all the way back up the mountain from the docks. Then we would get a call that our filet mignons are sitting out in the hot sun on the dock and back I'd go to rescue the evening's dinners.

Then, just as everyone was getting fat and happy, the owners of both resorts came back to St. John. The owner of Estate Beth Cruise reinstated her alcoholic accountant and let all her cats loose that I had enclosed in the jungle where all were happy. The cats again were the main guests in the dining room. The owner was also upset that we were making a profit, as she would not have a write off. Duh. We were on the outs and couldn't wait, but we didn't want to leave our restaurant or St. John and all our friends. But the owner of Gallows

Point wanted his friend to take over our dinners as we were making more than she was at her gourmet eatery at her house.

We gave up the restaurant and took a break. Barb and I deserved some free time, and we would just go sailing to deserted beaches and picnic. One time we were having fun frolicking in the water off Francis Bay. This is named after an old lady who still lives on the island here in her house that she built with the help of some wild donkeys. She had been on a cruise ship decades ago when she saw St. John and said to her husband, "That is where I want to live!" He didn't and so she jumped overboard and the rest is history. We would see her once a week going to St. Thomas to shop with a hibiscus flower behind her ear, in memory of her husband I presume.

While Barb and I were swimming there, the wild donkeys wouldn't let us out of the water, and were eating our food. An older couple came rowing their dingy toward us and wondered if we would like to come to their boat for a drink. Well it sure was a better option than having to fight those crazy donkeys for our picnic. And so we went with them and found their hospitality was a little more than we wanted to enjoy. So we had to swim ashore anyway and rescue our belongings and sail back home in our total sunburn.

Charlie also quit his bartending job and surprised us with the news that he was getting married. Turns out he had a date with one of New York's richest heiresses to be. She was the daughter of Cotty's old nemesis that dated his ex-wife-to-be in the limo. Her name was Kathy Hartford, daughter of Huntington Hartford, owner of all the A&P supermarkets on the east coast. And we were going to see his daughter marry this good friend who had never seen anything but Trinidad and St. John. She was going to take him back to New York and dress him up and make him famous. The wedding was on the beach between Trunk Bay and Cinnamon Bay; a beach I didn't even know existed. Ivan, Cotty and Bevy were there as well as a couple dozen other friends. We all had to wade out into the water around a big point and there was this pristine beach awaiting the nuptials. I had tried to talk sense to Kathy, but she convinced me she was really in love with Charlie, it wasn't just that he had been supplying her with all the drugs she desired. In case I forget, they made it to NYC and nothing worked. We saw Charlie two weeks later, back from New

York, out of work, and out of money and out of a marriage. Kathy, I believe, may have done this just to show her father she could screw up also. Unequally yoked came to mind.

It was time for Barb and I to leave. We had done St. John, and there was much more to go see. I had remembered a guest we had befriended at Caneel Bay who was the manager of another Rockefeller Resort on Little Dix Bay. He loved Barb and I as we had met him as an equal manager of a Caribbean resort. He had said if we could ever come and visit him to just show up and he would take care of us.

Well, funny how things work together. Barb and I packed up our gear, after many going away parties, and moved to St. Thomas where we left our excess stuff with some friends at the Yacht Haven marina. We then went to the airport and coincidentally there was a plane going to Little Dix Bay Resort on Tortola. We charged the plane ride to Tortola on our room tab as suggested by the stewardess, and then when we arrived, there was our General Manager friend. He was so glad to see us, and told us how the Duke and Duchess had this guesthouse reserved on the beach, but that he had moved them to make room for us. We were treated like royalty, fruit basket and all. Not bad for a couple of peons we thought. He spent every free moment with us for a week, and when he could not be with us he made sure were taken care of.

He had horses brought to us at dawn so we could ride the beaches before a sumptuous breakfast on our verandah. He had Barbara sing at nightclubs around the island and just beamed like he had taught her all this talent. He showed us off as if we were his long lost family. I really didn't know why, we just let things like this happen. When it was time to leave, we were celebrities all over this little English island. He was not able to take us to the airport where we caught a plane to St. Maartin to see an old friend there while we were between scenes. As we were departing our hospitable host, he said that the room and meals were on him. He would have the hotel pick up the expenses. This was done often for VIPs and of course, that was us. What I forgot to tell him was that our plane tickets were also on that tab. But I'm sure he knew that too. We were on vacation from our vacation. Wow, how much better can it get?

It was the Christmas season again, and St. Maartin was celebrating with all the colors of your favorite tree. We stayed on a houseboat with some friends for a few nights, and then we started meeting other people who lived here. We really enjoyed the new life here and everyday was again a new adventure. New Years eve was really an evening of contrasts. As you may know, St. Maarten is part Dutch and part French. It was decided way back when that the two countries should stake out the island separately for themselves. So a very scrubby Dutchman and a very French Frenchman started back to back at dawn, just like a duel. Except they would continue walking around the island away from each other until they met somewhere on the other side. Then they would draw a line from that point back to the starting point and that would be the dividing line between the French side and the Dutch. The Frenchman, being French, stopped at all the taverns, and wherever there was food and had a merry time during his hike. The Dutchman, being Dutch, quite efficiently navigated around the island and when the line was drawn, the Dutch had over three quarters of the island.

Viva le differance. The Dutch are clean and quite sober folks. They had Christian symbols of the three wise men and Jesus portrayed for the holidays. The French were not sober but rather quite wrapped up in their love of wine, women and song. We got to experience both cultures on New Years Eve, and suffice it to say we enjoyed both. One acquaintance asked us to sail over to St. Bart the next day. We met him down by the waterfront with all we owned, a duffle bag and a guitar case. And we helped him sail his charter over to St. Bart's. They paid, we didn't.

Now St. Bart's is just so quiet and peaceful there's no way to know the day let alone the year. We had lunch at a small restaurant high over a pristine beach. Everywhere we went Barb would bring out her guitar and just strum and hum. People would gather and soon she was singing "Beautiful People" or one of the dozens of songs she had written. We were then invited to go down to see this guy's beach. He had a commune of people, living in individually made caves. They had their own printing press and newspaper. He said he seldom asked people to stay with them, but that we were welcome to stay with them as long as we wanted. He hoped we would become part of the working commune. It was definitely hippieville, and very enticing, but not for us. We had some skipping over the ocean to do, and off we went to sail back to St. Maarten. There we were greeted like old friends, and several others had their instruments with them around a hotel pool where an awesome jam session took place. I, being the professional audience was right at home in my poolside lounge chair.

But soon it was time to move on, back to St. Thomas where we might find a yacht delivery, which was our mission this whole time. But either the yachts had already left and were already up to St. Thomas, or not ready to go north yet. So we mounted the Golden Goose and took off from the bay there, waving out to the window to several of our old and new friends. Watching the water blow off our pontoons we settled back and thought that was the best. What next?

Instead of landing at the island airport, the goose lands just as she passes over Morningstar Beach and banks around and through the inlet touching down in the harbor of Charlotte Amalie. What a thrill and view of what was to become our new home for a while, as it turned out. The goose taxied over to the waterfront docks and we 'debarked'. We no sooner started walking the dock when we hear our names called out. And there was Cotty. He had quit Caneel Bay and decided to move here a couple weeks ago. Bevy stayed on St. John and was engaged to some guy who lived on a far side of the island I had never seen. [16]

Cotts was living on Hassle Island, which was just to our left as we flew in. That was a civilization all of its own. We will visit there later. Meanwhile we had to find a place to stay and find some work. So we jumped in Cotty's outboard and skipped over the water to the marina/bar.

There we saw some old friends and were introduced to a few new ones. It was one of these new ones that said we would be welcome to stay at his house up on the hill and share the rent and he would pay the bills. We said that might just be the ticket if we could see the house. He drove us up there in a cab and it was perfect. We overlooked the harbor and marina and could walk straight down to the

---

[16] Bevy is still there married to the guy.

waterfront and catch a ride either way. We gave him, Bruce, the rent and rode back to the marina/bar and partied the night away. Then it was time to head back to a much needed sleep. We got a ride to the waterfront and then found the stairs up to the house. Little did we know the stairs counted one hundred seventeen. I thought I'd die, but Barbara wanted to go first. After many rests, moans and groans we made it. We were sore for a week until we finally got in shape and could stride up there without stopping.

Now there was another resident here at the house. Bruce had adopted Beauregard, the smartest ugliest dog ever born. Beau is a Basset Hound who knew how to get around St Thomas better than any tourist. One time I was heading over to Yacht Haven marina on the far side of the harbor and I left Beau at the house. Dang if that dog didn't beat me there. I found he could get rides by cars, cabs, buses and boats. Everyone knew where that dog was headed and he'd get rides there. It was uncanny especially since he needed a bath worse than any other body on the island. Don't tell me being ugly is a disadvantage. It's character that counts. Hmmm.

Barbara went on a job interview and was hired at a small advertising agency by Michael, the Art Director. She was to be paid about $30 an hour as a paste up artist. Unheard of wages down in de Islands. I was hanging out at Yacht Haven where it was possible to have a rum and tonic for breakfast and keep 'eating' until the day ended. One day the principal of a nearby school came to me and said, "Peter, we hear you speak Spanish. "I said "Wee" thinking that would end the conversation.

She said, "Oui? great! We're looking for a Spanish teacher, would you consider teaching, at least for a few weeks? If it doesn't work out that will give us time to find some one else." I figured if she didn't know the difference between *oui* and *sí,* then I could do it, especially when I heard how much they paid. It is a private school for children of boat owners and other sailors around the marina. The kids thought they were privileged and because they had little home supervision, that job seemed to be up to us at the school. These kids were all a constant source of 'let's aggravate anyone older than us.'

The day before I actually started, I went to a local grocery store and bought some Peanuts comic books in Spanish. Nothing like

Charlie Brown to bring the word to these children thirsting for knowledge. I was surprised that I could actually read most of these cartoons as I had really had trouble with Spanish when I was in school. Some of my classmates were Catholic and knew Latin and found Spanish to be a cakewalk.

But it was all foreign to me. My grades were always borderline passing. I won't say which side of the border I was on, but here I was teaching Español in de Islands.

I decided I would finally teach school the way I had always imagined would be really fun. So I promised the students the first day, that if they could control themselves instead of me wasting time controlling them, we could really have fun in this class. Some were skeptics and got to stay behind in a detention class. The rest of my class followed me like I was the pied piper and we went to the great outdoors and I would stop and point at a tree and say, "*arbol.*" They would repeat the word and no '*Ingles*' was spoken. We went down the *calle to la playa* under the *cielo azul*. After we had about 30 words, we would march back into the class and they would have a contest to see who could put the most new words into sentences. The winners got to go to the front of the line on the next days outing.

Then I would read them a Charlie Brown comic in Español, and we'd all get a good laugh. Pretty soon my whole class was going on the outings, unless they misbehaved in the other classes. Then their teachers would threaten them that they couldn't come to my class unless they did well in their class first. I learned more Spanish in these six weeks than I did in all three years of high school and college Spanish together. It finally all came to make sense. I also came to love these kids and we learned together. Viva Español!

Several of the kids lived on Hassle Island, the recluse island to the port side (left side), as a ship would come into Charlotte Amalie Harbor. Cotty was now living there as well as his younger sister Pam and her POME [17] boyfriend Brian. He's the Captain of the 70' yawl *Spartan* and when he wasn't out on a charter we would all sail out to a deserted island and frolic for days. There was much left over gourmet food from the charter and Pammy was as good a cook as Brian. We

---

[17] **Prisoner Of Mother England**

had greenies (Heineken Bottles of Beer) by the cases, and of course the rum. We would sometimes play games on the island, running around nude while on a Whelk hunt. These snail like creatures would hang onto the rocks and be really hard to pull off. But we would get a dozen or so and stir fry them up in garlic butter and have another greenie.

Then we might stand up on the bow sprint and with the main halyard in hand, swing out overboard like Tarzan on a vine and see who would be the last to let go and splash before crashing into the side of the hull. The bottom of the rope was an extra threat as it could snap like a whip when letting go and catch us on the bare butt, or worse. What fun we would have just laughing and lying around the deck as sun set and Barbara and Monte Negro would take turns playing guitar and singing. Even Brian dared a few numbers of British ballads. Bloody good they were. Then we'd swing the charcoal cooker out from the stern over the bluest water and cook fresh caught lobster and filet mignons, and have another greenie. Moose[18] was even with us on a visit from the Yukon Territory. He too had a huge beard. Some of us would sleep up on the deck under the stars and others would go down below. It was hard to escape paradise. The moon had a rainbow around it and we took that as a special sign.

Sunday night we'd sail back into the harbor, all at peace, and as we passed Hassle Island where friends were waving to us, we all jumped up and gave them a big moon.

But as we were leaning on the lifeline for stability, it gave way and Barbara fell overboard into the dark polluted shark infested harbor. I don't think I hesitated, and just jumped in with her so she wouldn't be alone and maybe help her. I said let's swim over to the island, about 100+ yards away. But fortunately someone had the sense to cut the dingy loose behind Spartan and we swam nice and slowly and cool towards its safety. I wanted to make sure Barbara didn't show any fear, as I was sure that was a vibration the sharks would be attracted to in a second. As it was, I was getting bumped on the legs

---

[18] Moose: aka Henry Foster, my boyhood neighbor and soldier buddy who was with me in my fatal car crash 10 years earlier.

just as we were getting to the dingy. I got Barb on one side and as I held the other I told her to jump over and in the boat. Well, she started to panic and started kicking and splashing to get in, and was having a hard time. It was then a big hit on my right leg told me I either was just dinner or was about to be. I couldn't wait any longer and was over the side in one leap from the water. I figured I must still have my legs to have shot out of the water like that. Then I grabbed her hand and pulled her in. Whew! We rowed ashore and everyone was glad to see us ok and we had another Greenie.

We got to meet all the other folks there on this little island, which was a very closed microcosm of our island society. They liked us and we were accepted by most right away. Some made jewelry, or were yacht surveyors and sail makers or some trade in the yachting world. Even Joshua Slocum's daughter lived here with her husband. Her famous father was lost at sea attempting a round the world cruise by himself in a thirty-five foot sailboat. About six weeks after our meeting her, her husband became lost at sea doing the same thing. Lightning hit her twice in the same place. But she had her sailing buddies here to help her through another of life's dole. Death seemed to have less sting as long as one died fulfilling their life's dream. Another Don Quixote story unfolded. And so I related that to my class so they too could "Dream the Impossible Dream" and chase it if it were worthwhile. I only wish I could have taught them what the truth of life really is, of which I was yet to discover.

New Horizons

The season was winding down for the tourist and charter businesses in Saint Thomas which allowed us more free time. Often Barbara and I would go out to Morningstar Beach and party all day with her Ad agency 'boss', Michael Haley and his girl friend Anne Roberts. They were fun in that they had nothing to do with our sailing and boating world and therefore were a refreshing change. We were still able to also lay back and just be us and they felt the same. We took them over to St John and showed them our trail of history there. We went snorkeling and bar hopping, but while everyone was glad to see us again, it just wasn't the same. So we felt it was time to move on, but to where.

Back in Yacht Haven, a few days later, I was strolling out on the pier when I saw a longhaired hippie freak with a long black beard sitting on the edge of the dock. Just as if I were pushed to do something I wouldn't usually do, I went over and sat near him and stared into the water below. I saw my reflection and realized I too was a longhaired bearded freak. But I felt the same as always under all that mess. Then I asked some obvious question, like "Just sail in?" I needed to see if he could talk. He could and we did. I found out he had just sailed up the islands with his buddy Richard in their boat. They were looking to sell it and do something else. His name is Frank and he was from Virginia Beach. I asked if he knew of any yacht deliveries that may be coming up. He said he was waiting to hear of one to Spain. Wow! I had never thought of doing that, but what the heck. I told him to keep me in mind, and that I was teaching Spanish over at the local school. He said that would be a big help and he would let me know.

Later I introduced him to Barbara, and Barb introduced me to a lady named Anne who was living on a motor yacht, and was a nurse at a Nutritionists office. Her doctor was big on natural cures rather than manufactured medicines. I learned, for example, that many autistic children that began taking more zinc in their diet and less copper suddenly would come out of their shell. Anne was also into the occult and was teaching gullible Barbara about how to throw tarot cards. I showed my card tricks and I became "Magic Man;" more proof of the occult.

I saw a gorgeous old sailboat tied up at the transient dock and went over to check it out. I met one of the owners, Neal, and found he was having it delivered up to Newport, Rhode Island. I asked if he was looking for crew, and he said that he wasn't, but his captain probably was. That meant the owner wouldn't be on board, which means my kind of delivery!

I found the captain over at the bar, supposedly rounding up crew. I told him I was trying to get to New Jersey and am available to go up to Newport and that Neal recommended me. He said I'm on, be ready to sail in three days. He added, when I volunteered Barbara to cook, that they had a cook. Well this was rough news for Barbara. We had not been separated for a day for over a year. Part of my wages for the delivery was a plane ticket back to St Thomas. If she needed it I would mail her the money to fly back up, or I would fly back down myself. But I wanted the experience of sailing the grand old lady *Cotton Blossom*. She understood and said Anne had invited her to stay on her yacht until she decided which to do.

The next few days were non stop parties, on Hassle Island, at Morning Star Beach with Michael and Anne, and on board *Spartan* for a goodbye cruise with Brian, Pam, and Cotty, and of course at the Yacht Haven bar, *Fearless Fred's*, with Crazy Carl bartending, and many others we eventually crossed paths with again.

We sold our outboard dingy that had so trustily carried us across the harbor from Yacht Haven to town to Hassle Island and even out to Morning Star Beach. I picture the time we went to town and just got loaded. On our return to Hassle Island, Cotty jumped in his dingy and Barb and I in ours. Cotty stood on the rear seat and pulled the starter rope but the engine was in forward. Cotty did a full one and a half gainer with a full twist into the harbor and his dingy was singing its way to Hassle Island. We had to chase it down and while Barb steered I had to jump from our dingy to his at near full speed. I felt like Tom Mix or for you in Rio Linda, John Wayne, jumping from one horse to another at a full gallop. Then we had to go back and find Cotty in the dark. He was still sputtering water from deep down back into the harbor. Yuck! He was alive and it was just another day in De Islands. We had bought the dingy for $300 and now sold her for$400, and it was time to move on.

No one at Fearless Fred's knew or even cared that it is Thursday, May 3rd except the captain and crew of Cotton Blossom IV. For we were reefing sails, stowing gear and food, and biding our time with old friends over 'the usual' rum and tonics.

By 2:30pm the captain, Charlie Gee, and his crew of eight are ripped enough not to think twice about shipping out on our 10-15 day crossing from St Thomas to Newport. A fond and happy farewell wave to loved ones as they watch the crew up the sails and reach out of the Charlotte Amalie harbor. No one on board felt the tugging in the heart as I did leaving Barbara behind, but also having the faith that all will be well. This was hard for both of us but we had been here before when I left Florida, and since then neither of us would have changed a moment.

Now I was looking at some serious seas, which are heavy, and driving us at 10 knots out of the Caribbean into the Atlantic. By the time our first dinner is served by our sea sick Swiss Miss, everyone is feeling a bit queasy. Teams of two are set up for round the clock watches. One experienced sailor paired with a less or no experienced sailor. Bill Parr with Chuck, Doug and Tom, Stuart and myself. Stu had never sailed before so that left me in charge of our watch. The watches start at 6pm the first night with 3 hours on and six off. Our duties are outlined and every hour we enter in the log down below the time, Gaff Rail log reading, speed, course, wind and sea speed and direction, and the barometer reading. We also mark if we pumped the bilge, which is necessary, every hour or two on this ole lady.

Stu and I had our first watch from 9pm till midnight during which we were both scared poopless (for three days), but we get into it even though it's dark and rough and very windy on our starboard beam. We have a real good rap about life, probably because we think it might end any second. He is fresh out of the Marines as a Captain in Nam. He has left that life to go on scuba diving, skydiving and mountain climbing instead of going to law school and sitting behind a desk.

177

Our next watch at 0600 is still nervous and the cook, Fran, is puking and can't get out of bed. Bob Parr, our navigator, whips up sausage and fried eggs. It's a beautiful day and we average 9 knots. We could make it in 8 days!

But at noon, as if our Swiss Miss had zapped the wind, we were becalmed enough to make 0 knots while she whipped up her first meal- bologna and American cheese on wonder bread. She ate saltines. Nevertheless, two hours later we found some wind and she was hanging over the rail again. I really felt for her, but I knew better than to watch her get sick or even think about it. The 0300-0600 watch was beautiful. The 10 knots, the sunset and the moody ocean let me know I didn't have to worry about losing my lunch. This was sailing.

Again for dinner, Swiss Miss Fran is out for the count. I almost joined her this time as the fumes from the alcohol stove woke me from a sound sleep. With clothes off, side nets up and from the top bunk in the forward stateroom, it took me 7 seconds to reach the deck for a gasp of fresh air. Alcohol stoves and I have never, and will never, be able to get along on the same boat.

Tonight we have the mid watch. Stu asks me if this is an average sea. I said, "Being an average day, I would guess this is an average sea. But what is an average day?"

We whipped along at 10 knots (quite fast for a sailboat), seeing one distant cruise ship, and a billion stars being matched by the phosphorus rushing down the deck, over the leeward rail and back out into the rushing sea. There is no moon, but we can make out the wind clouds against the stars. I have a cold beer and wake up Bill and Chuck for the next watch. I am asleep in minutes. I awake hearing the boat being torn apart. It's raining, cold, big seas and mucho gusto winds.

I take the helm without breakfast again as we're seeing if Swiss Miss can make the scene. She couldn't. At 0910 a big wave comes over our side and fills all my foul weather gear, including my boots which I haven't even gotten on yet. This was a long watch, and I wished I had brought some Contact.

After the watch, just as I was going below, a bird flew into the starboard side of the hull. I watched him float away in our wake and disappear. Suddenly he was flying towards us again and missed our landing platform and socked into the hull again. I sat shivering and wet on our spare diesel fuel drum feeling for myself and this poor bird. Next thing I'm told, "don't move!" Next to me on the barrel was this shivering patch of wet feathers, the wind wetting his half closed eyes. He wouldn't eat the bread or fresh water, but didn't fight sitting in Bob's hat in the warmest corner of the Captains quarters. We both slept, but the bird never woke up. The crew was quite upset, but Bob said that he was sure the bird died happy. We all nodded. Bob said that before the little tern had passed away it had pooped in his hat.

Bobbie Parr is our navigator on clear days. Other days he's our naviguesser. There was no other navigation available except by the stars or the sun. His way of toilet training the new crew was to refer how he's had girls on board who would try and flush the worst things down the head. He solved the problem with his little sign posted in front of you where you sat, "Don't put anything in this bowl you haven't already eaten!" He had a full charter season without having to dig out hairnets, bobby pins or those other things.

During my 1900-2200 watch we put up the storm trisail. Obviously someone knew something about the weather I didn't. The North east wind and high seas put us way off our mark of 355 degrees so with a storm and night coming we made very little headway east, and drifted considerably south. Both wrong directions but we couldn't tack west or we'd be right on top of Cape Hatteras. The same course prevailed during the 0300-0600 watch. At noon we put back up a double-reefed main and then tacked west. The crew's anxious to make headway, but next came the calm.

We sat all night drifting and banging around. The next morning I awoke with the boat again sounding like it was being torn apart. Bill Parr is in the salon and I ask, "What's wrong?" "Nothing's wrong" he replies turning the page in his book. No one else is down below and up above I find everyone edgy. The wind is blowing hard, we're heading dead south, three crew are holding the main down so Bob can sew on three carriages that tore off the main sail, the smoke pouring from the engine room filled the cabins, the bilge pump is broken and we're leaking. Back down below I see Bill and say you're right, nothings wrong," and I crawl back into my bunk.

After the bad comes the good. The wind shifted around to the southwest and we were off with four big sails and a fisherman. This type of sailing is what sailors go sailing for, calm seas, and 15 to 20 knot winds on blue waters. The dolphins arrived by the hundreds and swam with the wind, staying with us for about 40 minutes. They seemed as happy about the day as we were and wanted to touch us as we hung down our hands off the bow. But after they left so did our wind, and for a day and a half we rigged under power. What with 360 miles of our 1400 mile crossing yet to cover, a storm, fog, rain, and a crossing sea from our stern had us screaming on a full run towards Newport. Each watch that night had close calls with trawlers and one freighter. Appearing suddenly out of the fog, these monsters of the deep make your wet hair stand on end. The trawlers were Russian and probably just passing time harassing us. And on a full run, with preventers on the booms, there aren't too many places we can go if they want to cross our bow. Fortunately each gave way to us, some so close we could see them walking and hear them talking on their deck even in the fog.

With about 50 yards visibility, rain, 40 degrees, 15-18 foot following sea and on a dead run, we naviguess our way into Newport and arrive happy as a tern in a hat. Our log reads 1492 nautical miles. I had guessed 10 days 24 hours when we left St Thomas. Actual time was 10 days 22 hours.

After ship shaping we had a private celebration. Neil showed up and after a big greeting he gave me a telegram he received in Boston from Barbara: "Saving berth for you at Bermuda on yacht *Star Song*. Probably arrive May 20th. Can wait until 24th. Love always, Barbara." I had a feeling while sailing up that all this was happening and had told the crew this was my plan, so they weren't surprised. But the mental communication Barbara and I have never seems to amaze me. So now my schedule is tight, but with a good purpose. I know all I have to do in New Jersey will get done, no matter what obstacles arise.

After a festive night of drinking everything and anything, and having two dozen steamed clams and real lobsters at the Black Pearl, the crew collapsed on board. Early the next morning, I think it's Tuesday, I grabbed my four of twenty suitcases and two for the Swiss Miss Fran who had finally come through with a meal or two. We loaded up Neil's car and off we went to catch the 12:30 bus to New York after fond farewells to the rest of the crew, who then went to get loaded again at the Black Pearl.

The bus ride was a mind blower, what with driving on the right side except for expressways where they drive in any of three lanes and at 60-70 miles per hour, with hundreds of cars per mile. It's spring and the new leaves, grass and flowers are just in full bloom. It is a beautiful ride until we hit the Bronx, co-op city, Harlem, New York City and Port Authority. Ugh! I called a red cap, gave Miss Swiss a goodbye kiss and headed for the suburbs in New Jersey. Again the culture shock was still overwhelming as I saw some of the earth's ugliest trash heaps man could create. But finally I was home, or at least at my parents home in Plainfield, which was always cozy and very comfortable. They were glad to see me, but not my beard. I had to explain how difficult it is to shave with salt water, as if I had just grown this mess in ten days.

This was a great couple of days of reunion with the family and friends. I even went into my old insurance agency and there everyone was exactly where I had left them, except now they were fatter and balder, but just as pale. I was very thankful it was my desk chair that was empty. I was now 33 years old and as good shape as ever. I didn't take my good health for granted, but I didn't want to waste it behind a desk either. I may not have any money, but I had everything I needed, or so I thought.

Peter B. Cannon

Bermuda Buggy Ride

I surrendered my plane ticket back to St Thomas and cashed it in for a one-way ticket to Bermuda. Bermuda! I had always wanted to go the land of pink coral and bicycles, of pubs and roast beef, of the Bermuda Triangle??

The airlines would not sell me a one-way ticket. The only way to get into Bermuda was to be a citizen there or buy a round trip ticket. They had not considered that I might be sailing out and don't have, need or want a round trip ticket. So I called my 'friend' (whom I have never met) at Eastern Airlines, and the airlines called me back and said I could pick my ticket up at the airport. I asked if it was a one way, and after checking they said it was. "Hmm, quite unusual," they said. But they left it at that.

I had a few days to visit with my folks, which seemed a bit embarrassing to them what with my beard and all. "It's still me under all this mess" I wanted to say. They reluctantly took me up to the Country Club for dinner and once again they were not really interested in anything I might have added to the conversation. I recalled my encountering this situation in the Miami encounter group and found I had no problem with it anymore. I just accepted that Dad was never going to hear whatever I had to say. So I enjoyed the meal, no problem. The staff at the Country Club were glad to see me anyway. I managed to get a few other details done and visit some friends that were still doing what they were doing years before, and doing it very well.

But my excitement of getting to Bermuda and seeing Barbara and then sailing to Spain was mounting, and nobody wanted to hear about it. Can't blame them. I felt at home and yet I just wanted to get back out of town before it enveloped me, as it had all these poor creatures, and I'd be here for the rest of my life.

Tom and Carol Pearce took me to the airport. I could see Carol was ready to move to Florida tomorrow if she could. But it too would have to wait until another tomorrow. And another. But I could see it in her eyes that she would make it some morrow day.

I said my goodbyes and headed for my gate there at Newark Airport, the site of many of my joyous departures. But this was the grandest of them all. I was finally going to Bermuda on a one-way ticket, and then to Mallorca, Spain! Of course the trip was going to be getting there. So let's get started.

The engines were roaring as the Captain revved them up and the brakes were finally let go. The stewardess explained our over water procedures, and then, as soon as the nasty oil tanks and chemical plants disappeared below, the cockpit was playing the Talbot Brothers favorite theme song, *Bermuda Buggy Ride*. The Brothers used to come from Bermuda to do a concert at our Yacht Club every summer, and then usually play at someone's house on the Jersey Beach for an all night party. They were great sports and became quite a famous group. And now here they were singing my way up into the skies of the Bermuda Triangle as we sailed over the ocean like a cloud.

My parents had honeymooned in Bermuda waay back when, but from what I guessed, it hadn't changed much. It is still as charming as ever. So when I arrived I was just beaming with excitement and anticipation. Of course you have to go through customs, but everyone was breezing right through, till they got to me. "Sir, would you please take your bags and just step over there." I was now in detention until everyone else was processed and then taken into the interrogation room where they demanded to know why and how I had obtained a one-way ticket into Bermuda. Whoa, I had no proof of anything. But then I remembered a love letter I had received from Barbara saying they were saving me a berth to Spain if I arrived before a week from now. I finally found the crumpled paper and after three agents read my note, they made the decision whether I went to jail until I paid for the next flight home to the USA, or whether I was free to visit their Island Paradise. I tried my sense of humor, but they had none. I fell quiet, and they decided I was going to leave the island for real and could go to my boat and tell Barbara she writes a good love note. No humor intended I'm sure. I yes sired my way out of there and have no idea how I got to the docks and found "Starsong" and Frank and Barbara. We partied. The pubs abounded and so did the roast beef and popovers and ale. I slept like a rock that night, up in the forward quarters where the moon shone through the open hatch and the stars surrounded it like I had seldom seen before. Barb had the bunk below mine and could see it too, and she said, "Welcome home, Magic man." Now she was good for my ego, but you and I know that I have no control over the stars. But it was strange how the Controller kept giving me signs of His presence in a special way. He was definitely getting my attention.

The next morning I had a chance to really size up *Starsong*. She was a beautiful fifty-foot yawl with a steel double-ended hull. She looked very seaworthy, but then nothing is seaworthy unless the Controller of the stars wants it to be. But she had a very roomy galley and that is where Barbara shines. She can crank out the best food, but she has never cooked at sea until she made this voyage up from St Thomas. Bar none that I have ever met, she is the best cook. That is why our restaurant at Gallows Point was so successful. It wasn't all because of my superb steaks and chops. She was famous amongst all our friends, and most of them were excellent cooks also. The galley and storage space was very important for a crossing and we all had a lot to learn about our ship and her capabilities. So Barbara and I were in charge of that department, and then we were to help out with all the other details as well.

Captain Frank, who looked the same as when I met him, as did I, was in charge of getting more crew. Some continentals who had sailed up from St Thomas were not about to cross the 'pond' with us. They had been bred on a 'Chicken Farm'. So we, or I should say Frank, had to find more crew here on Bermuda. The 'sad' thing was that it took him two weeks to do his part, and that meant Barb and I had to go boogying all over the island while he looked for some sailors. It is amazing how many people that live on islands are afraid of the sea and many don't even know how to swim. Tell me about it.

I recalled when I was back in Plainfield last week that I heard that Crosby and Pete (my skiing buddy) were going to Bermuda about the same time as I was, but they had to buy round trip tickets. I never expected to see them, but because it was taking Frank so long to find good crew, our times overlapped. They too never expected to see me. So when Barb and I were out near the end of a pier looking at other boats, who shows up but Crosby and Pete. Do I need this? Cros can't believe he sees me, as he rides his moped out on the pier and sees us and gets so wacked that he just keeps riding off the end of the pier with his moped like it was a horse off the Silver Pier. Kaploosh! No sweat, Crosby was ok. The bike was gone. Was he going to have as hard a time getting off the island as I had getting on?

It was so much fun biking all over this land, visiting the Empress Hotel, the Royal Yacht Club and the Queen's Pubs. Of course Crosby mimicked the Bobbies and Peter egged him on until I thought we all might be leaving the island early. Laughter never stopped. The ugly Americans had landed on British soil and were reveling in it.

And then Frank told us he had found three new crew and that would make seven of us counting Barbara. We were approaching our Bon Voyage. We had been here about three weeks, and were ready. I was in charge of finances and stocking supplies, so off Barbara and I went to the local market. We bought whole shopping carts full of cheese and candy as well as many filled with legs of lamb, rib roasts, and sirloin steaks just to name a few of the entrees that Barb would prepare at sea. Before we got finished we had shopping carts lined up from the store on down the hill to our yacht. We used them all. It is so much fun to spend others money so we could survive. We had fruit for the first days out, twenty-four dozen eggs which we coated with Vaseline and stowed the cartons under bunks and cubbies throughout the boat, and another cart of just coffee and hot chocolate. We stocked the freezer carefully so the next days meals would all be on top as we worked our way down toward the last supper in the bottom. We bought for six weeks, and then a little extra just in case. We had cases of beer, brandy, rum and some other stuff we then considered fun. We were ready for anything. I remembered Pete Van Ness, and how he, as his parents stated, died happy. Well, we were going to make it happy if we died here too. (Would you say that our values were askew?) I did feel a renewed closeness to Peter as we sailed out of Bermuda, possibly just where Peter and the good sail yacht *Windfall* had gone down. I said hi to him just in case.

Our new crewmembers were a mixed bag. At the last minute one of our regulars decided to jump ship and left Frank with a last minute replacement for us. This could have been our undoing as the newbie was just a drug addict with no experience or morals. The other three guys were young, but ok. The real test would be at sea. We were about ready when I heard the engine starting up early in the dawn, and I jumped up to see the dock disappear as we headed out through the rainy channel.

Skipping Over the Ocean

Three days after the Duke's demise, two days after the Count's relapse, one day after the Queens Ball and the day before Her Majesty's birthday, Star Song II set sail from Bermuda for Spain at 0800, Sunday June 4th, 1972 Bermuda time.

"We're going where the sun keeps shinning" as Bermuda's weather has been cloudy and rainy for most of the two weeks we've been here trying to get crew together. Barbara sang our theme as we motor sailed out of the west end of the island 'in the pouring rain'. And we got a bit ripped after watching Ralph Meehan in his dingy while he spun it in tight circles scaring our ex-crew member, "Spider," to near death. I was glad ole "Spider" had jumped ship after seeing this circus. Ralph told us he would see us on the other side of the pond as he was going to sail his 40 foot sloop single handed over to see us and get another of Barbara's famous dinners. We'd see if he makes it.

Sam's parents and sister in their outboard escorted us after they dropped him off to us. Sam was the best of the new crew and was going to be my watch mate. His buddy Scott, piloted us through the channels and reefs until 1100 when Sam and I took the helm for the last hour of the watch. She feels so fine. This, remember, is my first sail on Starsong, and I was already impressed. Eight miles off shore I waved to several natives in fishing boats. They eagerly waved us on our voyage and Bermuda disappeared at 10 miles offshore at high noon.

Sam and I took the 2000 to 2400 hour watches after a beautiful tuna noodle casserole dinner by Barbara. She then came and sat with us and enjoyed some really perfect sailing before she turned in for the night. I was real proud of her. This Polish girl from Somerville, New Jersey had become quite a salty sailor. We enjoyed this night at sea so much we even stayed up on watch an extra half hour. We briefly sighted a cruise ship off our starboard beam. Apparently it is very rare to see another ship during a crossing. I saw a bird fly by our stern light but had a non-believer on watch with me. So when he saw green lights in the water or heard a motorcycle or saw a cow, he didn't have a sympathetic ear with me. I'd just say "Sure Sam." When I went down below to wake up the next watch Sam yelled, "Pete, I think we have some trouble here!" When I get on deck he is 50 degrees off course and climbing. "I don't know if we've lost our rudder, or some strange current is…" he starts mumbling. "Sam, you're steering the helm in the wrong direction." He went to bed feeling like jelly between the ears. The night can play those tricks on one.

I didn't sleep too good the first night, nor did anyone else. My stomach and brain felt like they were just bobbing around in me as *Star Song* did her climbs and dives. But after a super breakfast I felt fine on the helm. The skipper cooked up his catch of two flying fish he found on the deck and he was soo happy! "Look what the Lord brought me," he'd claim. What was he talking about?

We sailed 22 miles in four hours through the pouring rain. But it was real nice. On the pm watch we passed the 200-mile mark. Beautiful. But we awoke with a start at 4am (0400) when the jib halyard snapped. It was jury rigged till dawn and we all got back to our dreams.

Barb opened our eyes with French toast and bacon and oranges, coffee and the trimmings. I don't know how she did it in the heavy 3/4 seas. On watch Sam tried a new fishing lure way off the stern. Whap! There went the new lure, leader and all. A container ship passed us well astern as the sun finally decided not to come out. The cloudy weather was getting to us, but Scott treated us to some candy from the 'shoplifting bag' that hung by the helm and was occasionally refreshed by Barbara. She also warmed our tummies with Stuffed Peppers, rice and salad. We wallowed nicely through the evening giving us 118 miles for the day.

Wednesday, June 7th brought a beautiful sky, and after a delicious eggs and bacon breakfast, everybody's happy! At noon we set the drifter, a red and white striped foresail, and the black and white striped mizzen staysail after we dropped the jib and main. This stopped the rolling and pitching and made sailing about perfect, and sleeping so peaceful, that by dinner everyone was feeling real fine. T-shirts on deck, it was our first day without foul weather gear. Barbara served up a roasted chicken, mashed potatoes, gravy, cranberry sauce, and salad dinner, which 'greased' everyone. Ah so fine! A little fuma after dinner and Sam and I put in the most perfect night watch ever. All we could say is, "This is nice, real nice. This sure is nice." Barb even sat up with us till 2230 (10:30 pm). We didn't want to give up our watch at midnight, but did, and I broke out a bottle of red wine, which Sam, Charlie and I knocked off. "I'm so happy!"

Thursday, June 8th

Woke up suddenly with the Captain yelling, "Clear the halyard!" and Barb answering "The what?" The noise of the big drifter luffing as we headed into the wind and waves sounded like the bow was being torn apart. I jumped up half naked through the hatch and the whole world was a gross out. Barb in bare feet on a heaving deck with high seas and rain, the sausage burning and it was colder than a clams behind. This was destined to be a long day. The mizzen staysail had just blown out, everything was being tossed and spilled in the galley, I had Barb upset and I felt like I had been on an all night binge.

The morning watch was a super workout on the helm, with each following 10' wave soaring us up wind so that it took brute strength to bring *Star Song* back down to 70o from 120o. We made 28 miles, tied the record, but Kenny made 29 on the next watch so that was no consolation. As the day went on the winds and seas got higher. We had to reef the jib and drop the mizzen and get into some real heavy weather sailing. No one slept too well or felt too great all day, but the helm took your mind off that as it needed constant attention. By midnight Sam and I were aching all over and were in the rack by 12:05. I had beautiful dreams of dinner: spaghetti and clam sauce that was delicious but wouldn't look too good the second time around.

Friday, June 9th

The wind had all but subsided even with gray skies, but the waves kept coming. So we rolled and rolled through our French toast breakfast. Barb still had to use a harness in the galley to keep from being thrown across the salon into a table. The sun made a super effort to come out prompting a sky game of Blues vs the Grays. The Grays walked away with it today. Game was almost called due to rain, but just before noon Sam and I set the drifter as Barb had noted in the log after spilling tea on her white pants. We found a sign in the galley: "Barbara off duty forever! I'm going on strike." Well the drifter stopped the rolling and our 'Mother' gave out with another super lunch. So good a little nap was enjoyed to the rush of the sea. Then Barb and I were brought back to reality to a high-pitched 'Wahoo! Oh that feels so good!" Our glorious Captain Frank was bathing on the deck with buckets of seawater. We lay in our bunks listening, "Woooo oo! This is heaven! When I was back in Virginia we used to do this every three weeks! Wahoooo! This Johnson's Baby Shampoo is beautiful! No tears! Wahooo!"

Well we laughed till we cried, and then we went on deck in our bathing suits and took our first 'shower' under the first sun we had seen. "WAHOO!" I yelled. "Back in New Jersey we do this every three months! Wahoo! Johnson's Shampoo! No tears. Makes you ball! Wahoo!" Did that ever feel nice. Clean hair, bod and mind. And a hot fresh water rinse too. Wahoo!

We set our watches ahead one hour in the AM so it was strange to go on the pm watch and it be still light out. We were taking two-hour watches on and six hours off. It was the ideal schedule. Dinner was even an hour late, but that's beautiful too. We motor sailed through the night, and while it wasn't sailing it had no one complaining. Barb did it again: Roast leg of lamb, roasted potatoes, homemade bread, salad, mint jelly and brownies. Best grease on the Atlantic. What a day! Wahoo!

The blues and the grays were tied today. The sun peeked out at noon and Frank got a reading which put us 120 miles ahead of our DR (Dead Reckoning). Turned out we were way ahead of ourselves. We motor sailed most of the day. A huge freighter passed us about two miles off. It only took it a half hour to go from horizon to horizon. Had to be going 22 knots. They can get on you real fast. We had a red sunset at night, usually a good sign -tomorrow will tell.

Sunday, June 11th

Finally a spectacular sunrise. [19]A beautiful blue sky, a wonderful day of rest, a day of relaxing and reflecting. By 0800 Captain Frank Mullen had completely washed down the decks and topsides. With the 1st blue morning sky, the red and white drifter, main and mizzen set perfectly for self-steering, *Star Song* looked like a beehive. Heads, bunks, quarters, laundry, clean sheets, all standing tall. The washed and vacuumed *Star Song II* made her crew very proud and happy. She self steered all day in calm seas while Charlie went for a swim dragging behind us like live bait, Sam hung from the boom out over the water, Barb sang her sweet songs and Frank said he was "So happy! Praise the Lord!'

The luncheon feast of crabmeat cocktail potato salad, olives, lamb, mint jelly, Spam, etc etc was too much. At 1400 Ken called, 'There she blows! Whale on starboard!" We all got to see her jump and dive. At 1930 the sunset was at its glorious peak when Frank happened to pull out a dolphin whistle. I saw and called "Porpoise!" He tooted a couple times and the smiling mammals made a right angle turn and came right for us. Barbara, Scott, Frank and I serenaded them with the whistle and three harmonicas on the bow for half an hour. The porpoises loved it, but the rest of the crew never could really get into it like we did. We were so happy! What a day!

Under a mackerel sky and red sun set we had a 15-mile watch, and we never touched the helm. We just put the spotlight on the water and freaked out over the nightlife here in the middle of the Atlantic. Sam saw something big fly by our stern light. Frank said it might have been a Pico Bat, but didn't think it would be this far out from the Azores. As we got closer though, we would have to watch out for them. Sam asked some questions and Frank explained that they nest up in the craters of the volcanoes, and yes they get pretty big, and yes sometimes someone disappears off a boat at night and many natives have seen the bats carry somebody away. Well Sam's short hairs were standing on end. I told him not to go up forward on the bow without his safety harness hooked on. Later, on this calm night, Sam

---

[19] Red sun at night, sailors delight.

was standing on the bow with his harness hooked to the cockpit stanchion looking out to sea searching for Pico bats. I quietly came from the helm around the far side of him and laid a claw on his left shoulder and gave a tug. If his harness weren't hooked on we would have lost Sam overboard. Glory be to the "Highest!"

Monday June 12th

Frank woke us to see another spectacular sun rise. Yellow clouds trimmed in gold, covered the east from north to south. And what a way to start the day- hot cream of wheat with raisins, brown sugar and milk topped the morning menu. Wow! Being a gorgeous day, out on the line went the laundry to dry, and up on the sun deck we lay and fry. Star Song II was still doing her thing, just skipping over the ocean at 110o (east is 90o). It was our 8th day out, and our noon sightings showed us to be over half way to the Azores. I was tired today after yesterdays 'Day of Rest,' so I went forward after lunch and did some thinking. I was feeling uptight and I wanted to listen why. A lot of stupid things went through my head as I searched for the reason, but none of them relieved the tenseness in my gut. Barb came in and I was almost so uptight I didn't even want to rap with her. This let me know that whatever it was, was hot, and had to come out. So I just started saying garbage and finally out came the big lump. I was putting myself in Barb's bag even though I thought I was staying out of it. I was getting mad at things that I know wouldn't ordinarily bother me, but which I felt from past experiences would bother Barb. These were things which weren't in my bag and therefore not in my sphere of control. So they were eating my insides up making me uncomfortable, tired and irritable. With Barb to reflect this on, it became clear so I told her (the fantasy her I had created inside me) to f--- off. Just fu-- off and let me be. And I felt fine. We hugged and went up above where I played poker with the antagonists and Barb cooked dinner. Everything cool again.

The evening watch was so beautiful. Sam did the dinner dishes and Barb stood watch with me. Every star in the heavens was shinning so bright that they were truly innumerable. The heavens were a 360o dome of stars covering the sky all the way down to the horizon all around us. Again, the Creator's works were indescribable. Venus came up and over the horizon and freaked Sam out. (He freaks out easily.)

While we were all sitting in the salon listening to Barb sing and *Star Song* was sailing herself, Sam saw Venus and he thought it was a masthead light of a boat right on top of us. He got nervous and jerky, but didn't want to say anything while Barb was singing. He'd rather die than be impolite, especially while she was singing. Sam slept on the deck in his mummy- with his harness on. I told him to just keep tossing around so the bats wouldn't think he was dead. Sam didn't sleep too good this night either.

Tuesday June 13th: DR 39o 36' 2"N - 42o 35' 0"W

After sleeping like a babe, Frank called down the hatch, "Good morning y'all. It's 7 o'clock and God loves you." Barb said it's only 6:00 am but Frank said we'd gone through another time change so he set his watch an hour ahead. Barb said that's not fair and that she had taken Sam's watch the night before and was too tired to get up. (It's called Mutiny on some ships) But Frank said he'd cook and so he did. He cooked and cooked until we had the most delicious omelet at 10:30 I've ever had up to that date. And to perk up our appetites, at 0930, about thirty feet off the starboard beam we heard a whoosh A 90+ foot whale giving us the eye. The crew got a bit pale. Just for laughs I got out the life rafts, but hoped that we'd get some breakfast before we needed them. Moby Dick then crossed our bow so that we just missed him. We thought he was gone when he whooshed us again on the starboard side. Then his friend came up and they invited all their friends over. I guess they had about 10 or 15 friends, most of them distant relatives who didn't think Moby had picked out a very good crew for a meal. So the party didn't last more than a half hour and instead of being a meal we had one. Skipper Omelet!

When the sun hit high noon she was warm and beautiful, as if we were seeing an old friend. I came below to ask Barb to go on a picnic with me. I led her up on the sun deck for two hours of solitude. Off with the bathing suits, up with the pate de fois and down with the wine. But even out here, we heard an alarm, "Freighter off the starboard bow!" We looked abeam and there we saw that the good ship *Egon Wesch* (Hamburg) had come off course and about a mile out of her way to see what crazy people were out here in a little 50' sailboat. We got on our PA system and said, "How y'all doing? Do you have any ice cream?" Convinced we were crazy she turned and went on her way.

At about 1600 Frank cut the engine and everyone went overboard for a swim. It was the bluest calmest, clearest water I've seen at sea. Barb and I managed a shampoo and a fresh water rinse and felt great! Cleanliness is next to Godliness they say. Sure felt like it.

We motored the rest of the day while chasing turtles and shooting the 30.30 at empty bottles we'd chuck off the bow. Barb whipped up a super dinner and we sailed under a blanket of stars.

Wednesday, June 14th

Still motoring we awoke to a beautiful golden and yellow sunrise with a school of 25 + porpoises off the starboard. They were so incredible to watch. I always felt close to them, as if I knew them and they knew me. A small freighter passed across our bow –Norwegian we think - as we were all finishing up our sunbathing for the day. Then we motored all night with head winds and seas.

Thursday June 15th - Noon Position: [39o37'4"N-37o32'0"W]

This was another glorious morning as we still motored at about 5 knots. We saw a whale do a 20-25 foot jump and dive just before Barbara treated us to a breakfast of wheat cakes, sausage, juice and hot coffee. Barbara has been working her tail off constantly with little or no help from most of the crew. She really appreciated a little help and gets really irritated at those who are here for a free ride and treat her like their coolie. It came to a head at dinner, but it was poorly timed, and the cause of her being ticked off was obscure to most of the crew. It was a long night, but it would find its resolve.

Friday, June 16th: [38¦51.1N - 35¦18.5W]

A heavy overcast- you might call it gloom- stayed over us all
night as we motor sailed. I had a discussion early with Frank
concerning the foul up on the night watch. The motor was revving at
12000+rpm into a head sea (off course) while the head of the watch
sleeps in his bunk and a non-sailor co watch was in the galley eating.
Sounded like the bow was being beat with anchors. I had gotten no
sleep and became rightly pissed. We were now in the middle of major
shipping lanes and these two guys that do nothing anyway, now didn't
even do their watch. They needed to stop that BS before we are in real
trouble. By noon all this was off our chest and it was 'real nice out.' A
red sun and then a yellow moon both set on our 0800 to 1200 watch.

Saturday, June 17

Again we motored all day over seas of glass with occasional haze.
After lunch we enjoyed a long nap and then up through the hatch to
sun bathe for an hour or two before dinner was served by the famous
Boo. She put on a feast fit for a king, with roast pork, mashed
potatoes and gravy, with chocolate pudding and coffee. It was a fat
watch, but Boo kept Sam and I in hysterics till 2300, and that's the
truth. We also were kept company for three hours by sea gulls and 20
porpoises off the bow. These 'best friends of men at sea' played
games racing around the boat, jumping and talking and looking like
green torpedoes shooting through the dark jelly fish laden waters.
They enjoyed our company as much as we did. They were still
singing when I went to bed and I fell into a beautiful sleep to their
song. Oh to be a porpoise.

Sunday, June 18 [30¦28.0 - 30¦ 43.5W]

During the past week I had been working with Frank on
navigation. It's so simple! It's just a few logarithmic formulas. I took
the results and put a dot on the corresponding longitude and latitude
and voila, there we were. This morning we finally cut the engine and
put up the drifter and mizzen. That made the day fine already. We

were past the first island of Flores in the Azores with another 300 miles until we reach our destination of San Miguel. Our course of 120o should bring us right on the mark by Tuesday or Wednesday. The following wind and sea we expected to find here has finally arrived and was picking up.

The porpoises were out on maneuvers early in the day. We always wondered what they did all day until 1800 when they would join us under the bow and squeak that they were so happy, and we'd laugh and whistle back the same to them. But this day we saw hundreds of them heading towards us off the port side. We whistled and they came toward our bow with a perfectly executed flank movement, but then turned and went away from us on our same course, all in a wide line, feeding on every fish that got in their way. They looked like an army with perfect discipline as none broke ranks to come and play. But after their day of 'bringing home the bacon' they joined us again at 1800 hours laughing and squeaking. We also had sea gulls now for the third day as well as the sea terns. This must be the breeding ground for Portuguese man-of-war jellyfish as we've been seeing babies with sails the size of a half dollar. At night with the spotlight on the green blue water, we could see blankets of jellyfish all over the surface of the ocean. I'd hate to take a bath here.

After Barb treated us to a chicken tetrazini dinner with peas, homemade bread and chocolate cake, which again was so delicious, we sailed under jib, main and mizzen with the moon off our stern giving us a golden wake. Barb sang to Sam and I until she dropped of exhaustion. She's been going from 0700 till 2100 everyday, all day with little or no help from the crew. I'm afraid she'd never sign on as cook again unless it were with friends that were all together. I wouldn't blame her. She must feel like a gourmet chefess serving and waiting on the derelict ward at Sing Sing.

Just before the moon set, looking like an orange and black Halloween poster, I saw a light on the horizon just under it. We signaled with our spotlight and we freaked out when she signaled back. Then she changed course and came up on our port side about a mile off. Probably a local fishing boat saying goodnight. And it was.

Monday June 19th

Our sixteenth day at sea and at 0745 I awoke to Frank's yell, "Land Ho!" It was cloudy and had just finished raining when he brought the direction finder up on deck. The LORAN signal we received was right off our port beam and as we looked the mist broke and there was Fayel! Pico Peak was barely visible, but Sam and I got a good look at this 7000-foot volcanic island during our watch. Sure was an impressive sight. Most everyone was over anxious to reach land except Frank and I. We were digging the sail now and would dig land when we get there.

The mountains were causing some freaky wind changes as the wind had come from three different directions doing a 180-degree each time. The top of Pico Peak finally became visible and as Kenny put it, "It has a nipple on it." I took a picture of it and just as I clicked a whale leaped out of the water about 200 yards away. Probably neither will show up in the picture, I thought.

Frank gave me a story to read, which his previous cook, Mona, had hand written about their first charter in Spain on *Altair* (as *Star Song* was previously named. Frank had done a crossing on her a year ago.) The story was about their charter, a mysterious German couple: he beats the crap out of her, blood all over the cabin, suitcases filled with money and diamonds. Strange these Germans. And I thought our crew was weird.

This night we had a mini party as we sailed along with these incredible peaks to watch. We had in the cockpit smoked oysters and clams, cheese and wine, which preceded a fried shrimp dinner as we trucked along at six knots heading for San Miguel.

Tuesday June 20th

The sun arose behind the clouds and even as Sam and I strained our eyes through Polaroid glasses we still couldn't see San Miguel. But what looked like clouds slowly turned into land and at 10:15am Sam declared, "Land Ho!"

I wasn't sure I wanted to stop this timelessness of nature's beauty that surrounded us from sunset to sunset. But I also was unaware of what I might find here on this Portuguese paradise. It was 36 miles later at 6:50pm when the Portuguese Pilot came aboard. This was after thousands of members of the Portuguese air force (known elsewhere as sea gulls) surrounded us, and their Navy (whales) blew us a greeting. The myriad of peaks on this volcano are manicured from summit to valley with beautiful farms and fields of wild flowers. A camera could not do the scene justice, so we sat on the rail with our mouths open, transfixed by the ever-closer beauty and mumbling "Wow."

Starsong looked proud sailing into the harbor as we had been washing her down since 0600. As we nudged into the dock at Ponta del Gado, a crowd was waiting to greet us. "Do you know Mr. so and so in Bermuda?" or "Hey my friend, how have you been?" We had never seen these hawkers before naturally, but we felt we couldn't trust all of them. They apparently hang around the docks for yachts to hire them as watchdogs, runners, or guides. No price is set for their services.   We hired Joe, and adopted Eddie who was watching *Giavanti,* a yacht we met in Bermuda.

After clearing customs and getting into the rum, gin, wine and other spirits, Joe took Barb and I to a little cafe restaurant. It was less than special except to Barb who finally got a night off from cooking. I had a pork chop and Barb a steak, and neither were worth writing about, except you'd think that on an island of farms you would get great meat. But the folks here can't afford to buy good meat, so it is all exported and 4th grade meat from Argentina is imported. The two bottles of Mateuse (3.50 escudos each) cheered us up and then we went out to a hang out for a brandy. We stood out quite plainly in our Yellow foul weather gear. Barbara was the only girl in the place, which led me to make friends with the toughest guy in the place in case the other 30 guys wanted trouble. We got weird stares, but soon they were all sitting around our table and buying us brandies. After more than enough Boo and I went back to our cabin on the sea and enjoyed a night with no mid night watch.

Wednesday June 21st- everyone felt rightfully rotten the morning after. By noon we were able to walk, and went into town. Needless to say it was siesta time so all we did was walk and walk. We got strange vibes from the people as they would stare at us for blocks away. We were noticeable for miles in our orange foul weather gear, as black and gray seems to be the National color. The buildings, streets, sidewalks, sky, cars, rocks, clothes and even the beaches were gray and black. White lines are embedded in the sidewalks so people don't think they are blind. There are so many creepy looking old ladies wearing black shawls, black sweaters, dresses, stockings and shoes. We figured that it was some sort of a religious sect the Pope was running. But we found out from Eddie that they are mourning. If a husband or wife dies, the survivor wears black for the rest of their life unless they remarry. If a relative kicks, the fashion statement is only for a year. The beaches are black because of the volcanic ash and of course everything made out of sand is a similar color, black.

Barb and I walked back to the boat feeling kind of depressed under a gray black sky. The rest of the crew were back on board thoroughly pissed to the gills. I love drunken sailors. They had been picked up while hitchhiking by a lawyer, Paul, and taken to his house where they were royally entertained. Frank went out with him around 6:00pm and said he'd be back soon so wait for him. At 10:30 he wasn't back. The gallon of wine we consumed had us all pissed, so off we wobbled into the black night to find food. Barb and I ordered steak sandwiches. It would have made a White Castle hamburger look like a feast. We ordered a chicken dinner to round out our still empty tummies.

While we were in Bermuda loading up stores for the voyage, we had met many other sailors. One was Ralph Meehan, who we had hoped to see again as he was going to sail across the big pond single-handedly. After what we had been through, we realized how foolish this would be to attempt. We still haven't seen Ralph, but another ship and crew we met in Bermuda came sailing into our harbor. *Bel Espoir II,* which was a French drug rehabilitation center.

She came and docked near us, and her crew of Jean, Claude and the Doc joined us on *Starsong* for dinner. We were really glad to see them, but the floating asylum they were running was a threat to mother nature. Earlier in the day Barb and I heard on our ship's radio of a rescue of two Frenchmen on a life raft out in the ocean by the Portuguese Navy. It was officially called an accident, but Barb and I knew' differently. Our belief was reconfirmed when we saw the big brigantine sail into Ponte del Gado harbor and Claude told us the missing addicts had even used his personal life raft for their 'accident'. He had found them missing in the morning when they had cigarette roll call and there were two no shows. They always showed for a cigarette. He called San Miguel Radio and after much confusion he found that the Navy Police had them in custody. So they had to sail 10 hours back to here which cancelled their planned trip to Gibraltar, and instead will go right back to France and end the 6 month nightmare on this floating Ward 8.

After dinner and many laughs, we sauntered back to the docks. It was midnight and also visiting hours at the Ward 8. All the addicts were sitting on a bench on the port side of *Bel Espoir* staring into space. One French girl and I had a complete conversation without either of us understanding a word of it. She liked my French laugh I guess. She had bad breath.

Thursday June 22nd

Joe arrived early, but politely waited until 8:30 to take Barb and I shopping for stores. We could hardly wait and we could hardly walk. My hips were seizing up from yesterdays walking and my brain was seized up by the vino. But off we went, to twenty different stores to buy twenty things. Prices were ridiculously high in the 'supermarket' A small jar of Hellmann's Mayo - 52 escudos=$2.08. So we were carrying 18 different bags and finally got a taxi for the last two stops - the bakery and the ice cream factory. Fine. Back to the boat, stowed the stores and collapsed, exhausted.

Meanwhile the rest of the crew had rented cars and were off tooting around the island. Frank was having a rough time getting himself into gear to change the oil, fix the generator etc. So I said, "Mañana, do it mañana." He was hoping someone would say that for he was really in no mood for all that greasiness. On board popped the guy who fueled us up earlier in the day and his buddy Jose, a cab driver. What better way to spend the afternoon than be driven around the island in an antique Mercedes Town Car.

We gathered our tourist gear together: bathing suits, towels, cameras, a gallon of red rose wine, and stereo tapes. Off we screeched wearing our new berets into the country. Whew! A whole new world opened up to us as we drove in this convertible over mountains and through villages. The roads are all smooth cobblestones and lined continuously with wild flowers that would make any front page of Better Homes and Gardens.

We waved to everyone, tipped our berets and smiled, and the world smiled back. The wine was cracked open and we toasted everything we saw, it was SO beautiful. Cliffs of flowers overlooking farms above the sea. Peaks of lush trees reaching behind us to the sky. Kat Stevens, Paul Simon and Handel let us hear what we smelled and saw. We're so happy!!

We toot tooted at women and kids, cows and horses, cars and wagons. We stopped at a cafe for brandy and potato chips. By the time we walked out we had met half the townspeople, the other half lined the streets staring at us and waving. Now we knew how celebrities feel: rather undeservedly flattered, but flattered just the same. So to fulfill the role we smiled and nodded and waved and shook hands. "Bon dia, Bon Dia."

On we went up to the town of Furnas and parked in front of a rather non-descript hotel. But then walking to the rear of this only hotel on the island high up here on this volcano, a garden of Eden opened to us. We all walked up a path lined with hedges of flowers to a bathtub 100 yards long. The light brown water didn't look too tempting, but we change into our suits and walk down into the most beautiful bath we've ever had together. The water was about 100o and within ten minutes this hot sulphur spring had completely loosened up all the joints from my hips down which had almost seized up from yesterdays walking. We couldn't believe what bad condition we were in from just snoozing and cruising. Floating on my back, and paddling around in circles I looked upon grassy mountain peaks being a backdrop to huge maples, oaks, willows, pines and palms. Then I saw the caretaker's house, a 20-room mansion on a knoll overlooking the pool in front and a paradise to the rear. Then I heard Boo scream,

"It feels so good!" There she was under a foot wide spout that's gushing the hot mineral water right out of the mountain and into our tub. I too let it pour down over my head, shoulders and back even though it pounded harder than a Swedish masseuse and was twice as hot. Oh what a feeling. I wondered why I was being treated to such a magnificent satisfaction of all the senses. Here were Frank, Barb and I taking a shower bath together and alone on top of God's country. We didn't want to leave this rusher gusher, but the Lord wanted us to see some more of His miracles.

While feeling higher than the mountain peaks, we dressed and started walking down the paths of righteousness for His Name's sake. Here past the caretaker's home we came into another part of this garden of Eden, God's big acre. He had really done a number here.

There were trees that weaved or soared to heights beyond our sight, flowers of every kind some big as beach balls, others only visible because of their multitudes. Tea grew behind rows of bamboo, orange trees offering their fruit over azaleas, lilies forming snow white fields, swamp leaves bigger than an elephants ear. Streams rippled over gems of all colors, through caverns and over falls and through valleys. It was 360o of beauty, 365 days of the year and so it was impossible to capture the vibrations with a photograph. Only a polygraph and a soul could get a reading of the peace, serenity, care, love, majesty, completeness, perfumery and harmony that nature had manifested here. After tasting the perfect fruit, hugging the ideal tree, and drinking in the essence of the earth we went on down the road to smell the boiling sulphur springs and taste one of mother earth's Alka-Seltzer's. Two springs came out of a rock on a cliff and one was hot and the other was cool effervesant water.

With wine back in hand, we tooted the winding roads of the north shore, each bend bringing a whole new panorama of mountain and sea and wheat and flower and then a red ball of fire that set in the western waters. Jose stopped to call his mother and when we arrived at his house she came out to the car with a bouquet of lilies that three hands couldn't hold. Barbara was almost in tears, because this Portuguese woman had planted, grown, cut and gave these magnificent flowers to her with love and hope that our journey to Europe would be more pleasant. (The flowers lasted all the way to Gibraltar even though we were always sniffing on them to get high again.)

After receiving her gracious gift, which wafted sweetness throughout the cab, we toot tooted past children at play and men returning from their fields, into Ponta del Gado for a typical no luster meal at Sargo's. (Not exactly Sardis in America, although there were pictures of fishermen on the walls.)

On the verge of blissful collapse, we five went back to *Star Song* where Frank coaxed Barb into singing "Beautiful People", and beautiful it was. Jose recorded five more songs to play in his taxi from now on. And that was another day. In retrospect it was a day when God showed His love to us in a very unexpected way. He had not only looked over our safety at sea, but had brought us into His Garden and showed what He can do with natures finest flora. There were no formal man made gardens, so it truly was as I would imagine the original Garden, and we were the unoriginal Adams and Eves

Friday June 23rd

This early morning reflection was awakened when Joe arrived at 0730 as it was time for the fish market to open. Frank poked his head down the hatch and said, "Good morning Y'all, God loves you." Sure Frank sure," we thought, and rolled out of our bunks and hit the deck. Off Barb and I went to watch 3000 fish being cut up. I was already on the critical list from another day of hiking, and this really helped.

Frank started fixing the engine, generator, water pump, sump pump and electrical shorts that had developed. I was on the critical list from another day.

After sending Joe on last minute errands, topping off the water and ship-shaping *Star Song*, at 7:00pm we pulled our tar coated lines and fenders from the dock. Joe and Eddie and other San Miguelians waved us off and even cried while Barbara sang our theme song over the PA system, "I'm Going Where The Sun Keeps Shinning, through the pouring rain, goin where the weather suits my soul..." They really dug us and we were all kind of choked up too.

The rest of the night we motor sailed past and out of sight from this unique piece of real estate in the middle of the Atlantic, where people were real, simple, earthy and proud. Where man has labored for over 2000 years, and the same fields and church are still the main reason of their lives.

Saturday June 24th

Sam and I are now on the midwatch- 12:00-4:00am and pm. This will take a few days to adjust to, but we have seven to nine days before we reach Gibraltar some 980 miles from here. We see many fishing boats on the horizon all lined up like streetlights on Interstate 95. The sea is like glass except where dolphin fins are cruising up and down under a full moon. The day was also calm and gray. As a matter of fact, the next three days we motored on calm seas in cold damp air under gray or black skies while everyone did their watch and then went back to sleep. It was a drag except for surprises from Barbara in the galley where you never knew what to expect, but couldn't wait. On Sam's birthday, June 25th, we had roast pork, red cabbage, applesauce, and corn and raspberry cheese birthday cake under ice cream. Whew!

Wednesday, June 27th

Sam started the day by freaking out and preparing to abandon ship. Again. At 0100 a white light was spotted coming over the horizon astern. At 0115 Sam said get the life rafts out as an ocean liner was about 1/2 mile off our stern and coming right up our tail wake. Our spreader lights were broken, and by mistake Sam pulled the button for the spotlight, which just happened to be aimed directly at their bridge. Suddenly this floating city seemed to rear up and swerved so as to pass us less than a half mile to our port side. We could see the passengers in the large portals looking out, probably expecting a titanic iceberg or whatever that could cause their great ship to go full astern on her engines and turn on its haunches like a horse pulling a roped calf. She was so big we had to look off our bow and the stern to see all of her. Sam was in shock till 4:00 am, but then he freaks out easy anyway.

Noon Position 38o 10"N - 15" 45'W

At 1400 Sam and I set the beautiful red and white drifter and finally we were sailing. We turned off the kicker and went with the wind.

June 29th, Thursday

The midnight watch was wet, windy and wobbly. As the day wore on the wind and seas came on. We estimated force 12 winds, (30-50 mph) with blue and breaking white seas running 8-15 feet under sunny skies. Reaching under the reefed main, we averaged 9+ knots. We were really trucking. By 10:00pm we saw the first lights of Europe - San Vincente, Portugal. And then ships all around us bashing through the seas. Oh happy night!

June 30th, Friday
0001 - The seas are calm and we're sailing at 6 knots. It is really so beautiful. And what a feeling - across the big pond! The sun rose in its spectacular fashion and stayed with us all day. At night we sighted the lights of Cadiz and changed our course from 115 to 155o and headed for Trafalgar.

July 1st, Saturday

The early morning fog lifted and 'God's Glory' lit up the east. With Spain to the North, Africa to our south, we sailed ahead to Gibraltar. What a spectacular sight as fishing boats from Algecerias and Gibraltar came from all over to greet us. And finally at 1230, the big rock appeared! We motored into the North Mole through oil slick polluted waters and smog filled sky and tied lines port side to a dock along a jet landing field. Not pretty, but we had made it, and we were Happy!

Peter B. Cannon

Planet of the Apes

As soon as we had cleared customs and all the scary searching of our boat and our papers, the crew split up and each went their own way. The derelict member of the crew went and found the drug dealers so he could set up a deal. Frank stayed on board as the yacht service brokers were all vying for our business. Barb and I went to an open-air restaurant and had cold beers, burgers and chips. This was great, and everyone spoke English and the girls of Gibraltar were something to see. What was this place we had come upon? We were about to find out.

We were happy to find that the heavy military jets and commercial flights seemed to stop during the night, because we really needed the sleep to shake off our 'ocean lag.' We had started getting our land legs, but we knew tomorrow would be the real work out. And then trying to sleep with no noise and no motion was also pretty hard. But we suffered through it.

The first morning I awoke to the smell of coffee and bacon and homemade sweet buns a la Barb. As we sat up on the open deck enjoying our good fortune, a young Arab boy came up and smiled and said, "Psst, Captain, you want some smoke?" Barb and I waved him off, but he hung around and as we were disembarking, he came up again and volunteered his services as a guide, no charge. He just wanted to be around us. His name is Abdel (That's like John at home) and he turned out to be very entertaining and knowledgeable. [20] He told us the history of Gib, which has been under many flags, and even now there is still a dispute as to whether Spain or UK should be the ruling power. Definitely many languages are spoken here but English is what's really happening.

Abdel wanted to take Barb and I up into the caves of Gib. I never realized the importance the Rock has played as a military keystone. Within the Rock are over 60 miles of tunnels and caves that housed

---

[20] When I think back on many other places I have been, a young guide seemed to appear and take care of my every need. Were these Angels put here to look after me?

206

hundreds of cannons which guarded the Straits of Gibraltar, the critical passageway from the Mediterranean Sea to the Atlantic Ocean. Whoever controls this piece of watery real estate has power over much of the coming and going of commerce and Naval shipping.

Abdel took us on a killer uphill hike and then through many miles of tunnels with cannons overlooking every angle of the Straits. What caught me by surprise was the incredible society that lives within this fortress. The apes of Gibraltar have lived here for centuries and have formed families which have as many problems as your own local society. The Peyton Place scandal news of each ape is related in the London papers on the same pages as those at the Palace. These apes are named and watched by ape reporters which tattle their every sin to the anxiously awaiting soap opera loyalists back on the shores of the Motherland. It made me wonder if some people would be happier on another planet.

There were many restaurants on the rock that Barb and I enjoyed discovering, but not much else of real interest. Meanwhile the derelict crewmember had taken our zodiac dingy without permission and went to Morocco and came back with bales of hash he was going to sneak onboard. He threw them overboard short of our boat and sank them with balloons that floated just underwater. He was to sneak out later and get them aboard, but now he needed to clear customs again, as he had to get his passport stamped in Tangier. When he started bragging about his coup the word spread and we panicked. They throw you in jail over here and throw away the key if you get caught smuggling drugs. One thing life has taught me was not to get involved with the wrong crowd, and this did not sit well with me. I told Abdel and he knew it could be real trouble. We told our derelict that he could not use our dingy again, but he borrowed a row boat the next day and looked and looked all day for his fortune, but I believe maybe angels caused the oil pollution to dissolve his balloons and he couldn't find his expensive stash. He was so determined to find it that when we shipped out a week later he stayed, looking like an ape all dressed like an Arab ready to do business. What a relief to all of us to see him gone. I would wager his butt is still in jail over there somewhere. Unless he found what I was yet to find, Bermuda will be well served without his return.

So at dawn, after two full weeks of fun and frolic and restocking our stores with the help of a ships chandler named Gonzalez, we sailed out of the sleeping harbor and went our way into the Med to make our short sail over to southern Spain to check out the Costa del Sol. I had been there before with fond memories with ex-wife Jackie as a side trip when we were in Mallorca with Hunter and Joan. I'm looking forward to the fun of Malaga and Torremolinos. This is the major hangout of the happy wanderers and vacationers of Europe, second only to Mallorca as far as I could tell. And here I am heading for two of my ten favorite places on earth.

We had a chance to reminisce on the way across the Straits about our recent visit to the Rock. We had all seemed to go our own way, and Frank seemed to stay close to the yacht most of the time. But he had gone to the Seamen's Mission there on the dock not 100 yards from our ship. He said it was really fun. But now I wonder if it weren't for his prayers there we all might have ended up in the Brig, or the Paddy or what ever they call jail.

As we pulled into Malaga Harbor, we heard cheers from the Marina as the Spanish Pilot motored us up to the dock. By God, there was Wally and his girl, two of the last people I had said goodbye to when leaving St Thomas and the two of them had made the crossing in an open cockpit 29 footer with a tiller rather than a wheel. This was a wholly different way of sailing compared to the comfort we had. But they too had made it. Must have been his stubborn German upbringing.

We had a great visit that night with him, but the highlight of the night was when this little sailboat came sailing into the harbor, saw us and started blowing his horn like it was New Years eve. Here was Ralph Meehan, who since we left him in Bermuda had single handedly sailed his little sloop all the way to Malaga. He's a funny guy and had us laughing for hours about the ordeal of his crossing. He told how one midnight, a storm came up and he needed to lower his mainsail so he could reef it down onto the boom. But his halyard was jammed at the top of the mast. With a gale blowing up, he had no choice but to climb to the top of the mast above the spreaders and loosen the jammed rope so he could get that big sail down. It was a struggle to have one hand for the boat and one hand for the rope, but finally it loosed and then a big wave hit the boat abeam and shook Ralph like spit on the end of a whip. He free fell down from the top, and by a miracle only he can describe, he ended up in the ocean with one leg caught by a jib sheet. He seemed to awake in that position, head bobbing overboard and his yacht protecting him from the raging sea. He pulled himself aboard, not knowing where all the pain was coming from, and dragged himself below where he passed out. When he awoke, his mainsail was lying on the deck, the lifeline was broken where his neck had hit on the way to his demise. He had a goiter on his neck that was bigger than his fist. Ralph promised me he would never sail alone again (He kept his word. On his sail back to California he took on a Nun as crew. She drove him so nuts he put her off in the Canary Islands and continued on himself. Haven't heard from Ralph since.) Ralph was not a down and outer type, but rather a handsome successful business man, with a screw loose. I think he would have fit in at that special society in the tunnels of Gib. We had fun in any case.

After a few days in Malaga, we set sail for our destination, Palma de Mallorca, Northern Europe's answer to a Caribbean Paradise. I couldn't wait to see it again. This time I was single (well almost) and would see this Iberian island from a different perspective.

Peter B. Cannon

After the Crossing

After we celebrated with our old friends here in the Costa del Sol, the good ship *Starsong* headed for our final destination Palma de Mallorca, España. We made a circle around the harbor singing our song over our PA speakers and waving goodbye to some tear-filled eyes. Some of these friends we will never see again, and some will surprise us again.

Our five days of sailing around the horn was a time of reflection and thanks, as we all felt that we had been looked over by at least our guardian angels. Frank had visited the Seamen's Mission there at Gibraltar and seemed recharged in his spirit of Jesus and was glad to share it with us pagans. I had to think of the times during our crossing when all we had was air and water and stars to guide us. And during the gales and smashing waves upon us, Frank was whistling and singing hymns, while I had knots in my stomach wondering if this was the wave that was going to take us out. He seemed to have something I didn't know or have, but I knew I wanted it. Unfortunately, I just didn't want to ask for it.

Frank took the derelict's watch and sometimes I would sit up with him and chat about God and the universe. It was always very interesting, until he would say something like, "Look what the Lord brought me." And he would hold up another flying fish which he would cook for himself while I was on watch. It did smell pretty good, but I would not eat of it even when he offered. You see, I could not accept the gift of God, not even a fish. Had Frank been more mature in his faith he would have shared it with me, but now was not the time. Now was just not the time.

We had a real pleasant sail around and up to Mallorca, relishing the zillion stars and the stellar sunrises and sunsets. We wondered if we could ever accept any other way of life than just being with the Creators beauty rather than man's feeble attempts at re-creation which paled in comparison. We passed more fishing vessels, some surrounding pods of small whales. I wanted to just run through their nets, but Frank told us they are in their turf and God has it all under control. Who can argue with God?

Reading the Palma

After five days more of snoozing and cruising, we approached Palma. We didn't need to actually go through customs as we had already done that in Spain. So we were able to cruise around and scan the island some before we decided to pull into the Palma de Mallorca Royal Yacht Club, where I saw more beautiful yachts than I ever thought I would see outside of the States. I was really impressed, but I hadn't yet realized that this was one of the Europeans' favorite playgrounds. And the play was just getting under way. Welcome to the land of anything goes.

I was never real ready for the 'anything goes' stuff, but I am sure that my lifestyle seemed so to my parents. They were very tolerant though, and I guess they had to be after buying me Playboy subscriptions for Christmas since I was 16. Not that that had any influence on my life. Sure. I used to hang out at the Playboy Club in New York and in Miami, visited them in Chicago, Wisconsin and Jamaica. I was always looking for that lifestyle, but always figured it was just beyond me. Actually I think I was better off in many ways, though I think it was the liberal thinking that screwed my head on crooked when I was married. Now that I was not married, it seemed more appropriate. But I still had my friendship with Barbara and I would be monogamistic with this and any relationship as long as they were so with me.

And so Barbara and I were a pair, a couple, and friends together. We therefore found friends that were couples either married or not. In Palma we met lots of people, but the town was a bit large for our tastes. After Frank flew back to Virginia and we had been paid for our crossing, we cashed in our plane tickets and were quite 'well off' as bilge bums go. So we rented a car and tooted around. One of our first encounters was to visit an old monastery in Valldemossa. Earlier it had been the Royal Palace before the 1400's. We seemed drawn there and found it quite creepy. The most famous visitors were Frederick

Chopin and his cigar-smoking mistress George Sand.[21] She had arranged for their rendezvous here for his health. But either her cigar smoke, or the chill he and I got in these breezy halls caused his death by consumption. (Dere's just too much consumtion goin on around here.) We much preferred the warm beaches to the bone chilllin castles. So we split, and meandered around the island.

We went to the far side of Mallorca from Palma and found a real quaint old town called Puerta Pollensia. We liked it so much we decided to get an apartment. The soonest one was to become available was in about six weeks. So we leased one from August till November. It had a balcony overlooking the ocean, and was real quaint what with its fireplace and all. There was a small garden in back where we could dine under a grape arbor. While living there, we met some new friends at a cafe that were sailors and had lived in the Caribbean. I think they had hit big money doing a hemp run, and then retired over here. They had bought an old finca and were fixing it up by putting in 'running water' and 'electric' and stables and other niceties. Larry and Betsy made us promise to let them know when we came back to town.

Meanwhile, we went back to Palma, and while we weren't looking, the height of the tourist season was upon us. We spent a night or two on *Starsong*, but found the owner was coming from Canada and we were persona non-gratis. So a bartender, who I had met when Jacqui and I were here at the *Africa Bar*, invited us to stay at his place. We did and then found out he was queer and also not getting along with his boyfriend. Gag. But we stuck it out until we could get our act together to tour the mainland.

Meanwhile in Palma we had a great time with the Spaniards as well as some American sailors. One of them invited us to visit his ship in the harbor. The next day we boarded one of the lifeboats, which was tossed about quite readily by the very choppy seas, and as soon as we got to the mother ship it was like the rock of Gibraltar. It had no motion at all in the heavy seas. We were amazed, but this ship was the nuclear aircraft carrier *USS Kennedy*. Our friend gave us the royal tour and after being at sea for two months on a 50 footer, it was

---

[21] I always thought George Sand was a guy. Duh! She wrote "A Winter in Mallorca."

hard to relate to this floating city. As a matter of interest, our friend's brother was also on board for six months before they met each other, and that was because of a letter from their mom telling them that they were on the same ship. We met him and we saw stuff that is still classified. Sorry, that means I can't tell what I saw or I'd have to kill you. But it was an awesome experience. Back on shore we were grilled by people at the Royal Palma Yacht Club about our Naval experience. We just told them that they were a lot safer than they could imagine. But if they wanted to buy us another drink, we might start talking. I don't think we ever told.

We went to some beach parties with some of the locals we had met, and the beaches were as beautiful as the people. One girl was named Mercedes. [22] She was the organizer of food and drinks and took especially good care of Barb and I, making sure we met everyone. I seldom felt so at home as at this new place in such a short time as we did this day in Mallorca.

But soon it was time to go to the mainland as things were getting too busy for us here, and there was no room at the inn. We caught a ferry to Barcelona where we stayed with some guys that we met at the zoo that day. They just wanted to get us drunk and who knows what. But they passed out just before we did, and we were gone the next morning just before they awoke. We wandered the Ramblas, the main boulevard, lined with floods of flowers, and shopped at the market for some food to eat on the run. The European fast food: a loaf of bread, fruit, cheese and a bottle of wine. The people here spoke Castillian, the very formal Spanish that I had studied in school and College. We spent a few nights here and on the third night I was dreaming in Spanish. It seemed like English to me compared to the Spanish in Mexico or Puerto Rico. A Spanish couple we met there teamed up with us. We all went to what they call discos and had drinks and tapas. These were not Playboy Clubs, but everyone had fun. Then they got serious and wanted a different drink at every club in town, ending up in a Flamenco Club where some feathered beast clomps her heels to the beat of your headache.

---

[22] Mercedes=Mercy

The next morning we wondered whose home we were sleeping in this night. One night we ended up in the home of a Colonel of the Spanish Army. His new bride was not sure what he had brought home this time, but we were surprised that they had only been married a couple weeks and yet were so hospitable. She spoke no English which was very handy for us. We were able to communicate that we could not stay a week, that we had to be leaving in two days. She was glad to hear that. But the Colonel wanted us to stay on so he would have someone to escort to the rest of the clubs in Barcelona. These people are nuts. They drink to die every night. Then by 2 am they want you to try a mixture of the brandy, champagne, beer and whatever else we've had for a nightcap. We kept up with him, but it wasn't healthy.

Finally, the Colonel's wife had him take us, and our bags which she had already packed, to the train station. We got on and with a smile to each other we slept until whatever. But everyone else was already off the train when we opened our eyes. Our car was just sitting on a track in Seville, and not knowing where we were, we grabbed our duffle bags and checked it out. This looked like souvenir town what with its little swords and trinkets. We were not in the mood for a history lesson, so we missed much of the message here. I felt like Don Quixote just looking for my next windmill so I could conquer it and rest on a real pillow. Barcelona had done me in.

Following the Sun

We checked a map and saw the Costa Del Sol, the old fun stops we had sailed to after Gibraltar. We decided to hitch our way down there to Malaga or Torremolinos and get a room until our apartment became available. Were we ever naive? We had no problem catching a ride, but when we arrived in this seething mass of international tourism, we became aware there was not a room available for two months. Anywhere. We went to a campground and found the origin of the word. They rented out a space on the dirt ground for as much as our apartment per night. But finding a piece of dirt big enough for two was very difficult. It was just body next to body next to mosquito eaten body. I have been miserable, but this night sticks out in my mind. Some of the French thought dirt meant bathroom. Others thought it meant talk all night. We were first up and first out in the morning. I had to go dirt.

We went to a beach and bathed in the peace of Mother Ocean. By the time we turned around to get out the beach was full of bodies, and they were not a pleasant sight. We looked all day for a room to no avail. As sun set we staked out a park bench with two sides to it. We put our stuff on it, but had to watch it so no one would steal our 'bed.' Our bench had blue Spanish tiles all over it, very pretty and very hard. It also held the nights cold right in it so we could know we weren't in a nice warm bed anywhere. When we awoke to the sunrise, I said to Barb over the back of the bench, "Who won the war?" "Why," she asked. Because I heard Germans and Japs on either side of us talking. And the sunrise was a perfect Japanese symbol, with the rays just shooting out of its rising orb. And then I saw the Germans and the Japs playing Frisbee right over our heads. Somehow I knew we were doomed. We had to get out of Dodge. We had crepe suzettes for breakfast on the boardwalk at Torremolinos. Yum. But finding no rooms again we decided to take a ferry to Africa, and stay in Ciuta until the rush was over. Surely no one would vacation there.

We took a ferry across the straits and slept on the forward deck. This seemed almost as good as *Starsong* except for the smells. Upon arriving in Ciuta, a cabbie said he could find us a room. He drove us all over and then had to drop us off at the bus station until after his siesta or prayer time. Now bus stations in America can get seedy, but this was like an all nighter on death row. These were the meanest looking sub humans I had ever seen. And they were taking particular notice of Barbara's naked face and shorts. They grew horns right in front of us. One guy offered to get us coffee. I accepted and wondered which camel he brewed it in. Finally our cabbie came for us at midnight and said he found us a room. He had, but it had no bed or anything. Two burlap bags to snuggle down onto, and a one holer down at the end of the hall. He said he would come and get us in the morning and get us a better room. I pleaded with him to forget it.

The next day we took a bus to Tangier where there had to be room for us. When we arrived, same same. No room at the mosque. Finally a guide took us to a small hotel and we got a room right over the 'road' where everyone walked to and from the Kasbah. We could hear their voices as they passed. We looked out our window and saw the sea in the distance and the sea of faces coming toward us, and the faceless robes and hoods after they passed us. This was a mysterious land indeed. A strong feeling of dejavu crept over me as well.

Barb and I got prepped and decided to join the rush hour of walkers. We were blitzed, but that seemed not out of the norm here. First stop was to be pulled into a shop where they make you try on Jalabas so we can look like the rest of the boys in the 'hood'. We decide on one each, but they won't let us buy until we sit down on a dead camel seat and smoke something in a pipe. Then they have hot mint tea brought in. Then we can't just buy our new outfits, we have to bargain for them. So they got me for some dollars, some escudos and some cigarettes, and we had a deal. No one had any idea of the actual deal and I'm sure I still don't. But everyone was happy, and that is what it is all about here in the Kasbah. [23]

After getting used to our new culture where we had to bargain to just buy grapes, because we also *needed* to get figs, or not just milk, we had to also get bread for just a little more, we also had to get blitzed just to close the deal. We finally got away from the merchants

---

[23] Apparently we even bought the camel ottoman some how in the deal, because it was shipped home some months later.

and found our way back to Mother Ocean. The beaches were so wide that it was a five-minute walk just to get to the water. We laid our clothes and towel down and headed for the salt of the water. As soon as we got used to the temperature we saw a man by our clothes motioning for us to come out of the water. He was a policeman and we thought it was all over, but he just wanted to warn us that our clothes were not safe there on the beach by themselves. We thanked him and put our clothes on and went back into the ocean. It was beautiful.

That night we decided to hit the nightlife and spend a bit of our small budget. That was a thrill I'll always try to forget. The Coos Coos and belly dancers were my biggest 'treat.' Somehow we had pigeon for dinner and the belly dancers were the most unattractive males with little cymbals on their fingers, that I wanted to leave my grits there on the floor and cancel the rest of my life. Barbara got me out of there before the Royal Guards took me away. They looked like the Royal Guards that had machine guns pointed at me when Jackie and I were here some ten years earlier. They were at least as ugly. All in all we had a great time, but were more than ready to go, anywhere. We decided no one would be in Madrid this time of year, they're all at the beaches. Let's go!

We got our gear together, and headed for the ferry docks. We went through customs with a breeze, especially when the custom agent saw Barb's guitar and then the Bible Frank had given me on top of my clothes in my duffle bag. He looked no further and tried to put the make on Barb. She just smiled and pinched his cheek till it hurt. But just before boarding, we noticed a major scuffle in the crowd that had arrived and the customs window was closed and the ferry was canceled. With three hours to kill. we went back into the Kasbah and upstairs to a place we had had hot mint tea. We were just about to leave when I heard, "Pssst, Captain, you want to smoke?" I looked over and there is Abdel, our friend from Gibraltar. "What are you doing here?" I asked. He said something about Allah and can we take him back to America. We still knew better and told him he would be miserable there, and that we were going to Madrid now, not America. He said there was some kind of trouble brewing at the docks, but that we would be safe to go to the ferry now. We hugged and were really glad to have seen him, and sad to say goodbye.

"¿Habla Español?"

We finally got to the ferry, but as we leaned on the rail we noticed heavy suitcases being transferred on board, and some Arabs climbing up ropes to get on the ship from little boats below. We let it ride, and then we got to Spain where we got a comfortable compartment on a train to Madrid. The first stop was Rhonda, but by then we had noticed Arabs running along the moving train pushing heavy suitcases through the windows into the hallway, About ten minutes later five of the ugliest Arabs crammed into our compartment and after taking off their sandals, sat like the end of the world was happening. I was sure it was, as the whole aura became similar to the odor in a camel-tanning factory. They had eyes missing, and their body odor matched their foot odors. But nothing matched how mean they looked. There was nothing cordial about them. The hairs on the back of my neck were doing that panic thing. But the train was so full there was no place else for Barb and I to go.

At one point one of them, the youngest, went out into the hall and I joined him for a smoke. He offered me a cigarette and I then to him. He got the better deal. I asked, "¿Habla Español?" I found out by using three different languages and signs, that this bunch were going to Munich for the Olympics. I asked where they were from and what they were going to do in Munich. They were coming from Syria and they were going to be janitors at the Olympics there. That struck me strange later, for how is it economical to travel from Syria to Munich, Germany to be a janitor?

Finally I cornered a conductor that would come get us as soon as there was room to move us to a sleeper car. By the time we were gagging and terminally not happy with life next to these shoeless Arabs, a conductor came and moved us discreetly to a sleeper with curtains and a pillow much like a marble slab. We were happy-er.

The rest of the ride to Madrid was fairly quiet except in my nightmares. So I felt that the night before with these Arabs was just a fig of my imagination. When we arrived in Madrid we had the town to ourselves. Almost. Most of the Spaniards were on their vacations somewhere else. But we found an old style Spanish lady who rented out her old style Spanish rooms and we had the best nights sleep that we had had in weeks. We awoke to the smell of olive oil and burned huevos. She was our Madre Madrid. She put up with us as we visited parks and museums and restaurants and nightclubs and stumbled in late at night. But one morning I noticed the words Olympics and Munchin in the newspapers, and it reminded me of the Arabs and that awful train ride.

We had another week before our apartment would be ready in Puerta Pollensa, so we headed for Barcelona to catch our Castillian breath. There we met some more juvenile Spaniard men just wanting to be hospitable. We couldn't wait to get back 'home' to Mallorca. So after spending another night as a guest of the great society, we boarded the ferry back to our little island in the sun.

As our ferry arrived, we noticed some of our favorite beaches, and then the marina where we left *Star Song*. We wondered if she was still there. We grabbed our bags and got ready to make the long walk around the harbor, but as we did, we saw her familiar hull at a marina right where the ferry came in. A fella named Tor was taking care of her until the owners arrived to sail around the island. He remembered us and let us stay on board until our apartment was ready. And as we were therefore guests at the Royal Mallorca Yacht Club, we enjoyed all the perks and privileges of the other wealthy yacht owners there. After ditching our bags onboard, we headed for one of our favorite outdoor cafes for some brandy and coffee. As we sat there I noticed a newspaper headline someone was reading at a nearby table. It said, "Terrorists Murder Jewish Olympic Team." My heart went into my stomach. My God, those were terrorists on that train. We knew they were up to no good, but murder. It could have been us as well. We were expendable if we had interfered with their bloody mission. But I like to think I would have gladly taken a hit to stop what I saw in those headlines. These were cowards killing some of the world's greatest athletes for some stupid political statement.

We were still in shock when a guy came over near us and smiled. We smiled back and he came nearer and in his Norwegian accent asked what we thought of eternal life. I told him I didn't think short term, but asked why he was asking. He asked to sit down. He very politely told us some of the things that Frank and I had talked about while sailing. How we could be assured of eternal life just by accepting what Jesus had done for us. It was all very interesting as I had never quite heard the old story so clearly. But I asked some stupid questions to show how smart I was, like what about all the other people on earth that never hear the story at all? What about all those Jewish athletes that were just killed? He admitted he did not have all the answers, but that if we liked we could come to a chapel up the road and meet with his pastor who may have answers to our questions. After we finished our third coffee and brandy, we strolled up toward that chapel but something kept us from going in. I believe we were not ready and so we were actually conned into not going in by Satan himself. Don't laugh, these were powerful forces keeping us away and making us just keep on walking away. But I will never forget the assurance that that young Norwegian showed by coming over and sharing something so personal with us. I will always hope I see him again to thank him. He had planted a seed that will grow forever. Maybe even in eternity. Can you believe we were with those terrorists, and then with possibly an angel? At the least a Saint. What a contrast we have here on earth.

Sitting on *Star Song*'s deck, we mused over these events until we finally went below and fell asleep to the familiar slapping of the halyards on her mast. "God it's good to be alive. *Gracias por Dios.*"

The Good Life

The next day we had a big reunion with our Spanish friends and went to the beach for a mega party. We frolicked with Mercedes and her Majorcan friends, Alan, from the African Bar and his patrons, and several couples from foreign yachts that we had met. What a great time we had all mixing with each other and sharing our food and drinks. The weather was just perfect for swimming and for frolicking in the sea. What more can be said? Even the calamari tasted good. "Viva la vida buena!"

The following day we took our sunburned bodies to the car rental place and retrieved our little car back. We tooted across the island we had come to know pretty well, and found our way to our favorite cafe at the Miramar Hotel in Puerta Pollensa. After a cafe con leche and brandy, we looked up our realtor and got the key to our very own apartment. No more shared hallways and bathrooms. No more moving out the next morning to our next place of rest. Now we could put down some roots and become a part of our environment.

We went to our little five-room pad and swung open the shutters and gazed at our view of the beach across the road and the sea beyond that seemed to go for eternity. It just seems like eternity sometimes. Little did we know how long that could really be for someone out there that night.[24]

It was a cool night, so we built a fire in our fireplace and cooked up a steak and potatoes we had brought from Palma, and toasted our good fortune with some French Champagne. We could see the lights of a mansion out on the end of the point that went out to sea from our shoreline. Little did we know...little did we know. We toasted our '*good fortune*' again.

---

[24] I had a strong sense that a sailboat could be out past that point in trouble. But it was so calm I dismissed it as a bad daydream. A year later I read a book about a family stranded for almost three weeks out there at this time, and they had almost lost hope when the currents took them too far away from the Punto del Cabo which we overlooked.

The next day we had only to enjoy. It was market day in Pollensa, so we drove inland to the square where the surrounding farmers brought their best vegetables and eggs and meats. We brought our straw shoulder baskets we had bought in the Azores and filled them with fresh string beans, and many new *legumbres* we just had to try. The skinned rabbits hanging by their legs were a bit new to us. We passed on the bloody stuff.

While we were there we saw Larry's cousin Ellen, and she took us back to the finca they were still having rebuilt. We had the veggies and they cooked up a leg of lamb for our reunion. They now had running water inside the house, stables for the horses and many heads of sheep baaing outside. We got to know these guys a lot better, and after dinner and swapping stories about our Caribbean adventures, we drove home to our 'home'.

Larry and Betsy said they had some friends that we just had to meet. They didn't tell us much about them, but just arranged for us to be invited to parties where we would meet them. One was Julian. He was single guy in his thirties as we all were. He was born by American parents while in England, which made him a multinational. His main residence was here in Mallorca, but he had a residence in London and New York.

One of his friends owned the house that was out on that point of land from our apartment. And that is where Larry had taken us. Barb always traveled with her guitar, and when the hostess heard that Barbara sang, she insisted that she sing. Even with all that money, they were still starving for real talent here. And when Barbara sang, no one wanted her to stop. She had even picked up on Spanish flamenco styles on her acoustic Martin guitar, which was as good as any native entertainer. But they just loved her songs as well as those made popular worldwide by the likes of Elton John and Donovan and many others. Well this is where we met Julian. He invited us to go out on his boat for lunch the next day with his girlfriend, Larry and his wife, and Ellen and her boyfriend. He would supply all.

We cruised all around the island picnicking here, and beaching there. Smoking here and swimming there. Singing here and laughing there. It was just one of those great days. Julian told us that he and his brother had been building a castle near their large home. He was going to have a grand opening sort of party with all his friends and their friends, and he wanted Barbara and I to be his guests of honor. Could we make it? We would stay at the castle in our own room of our choice. We could make it.

It was so nice to just relax and get into the slow pace of our new town. We would arise with the sun coming over the sea's horizon, and we would have breakfast at *Illa d'Orr*, a local cafe or just cook it up in our apartment. We would hike and swim or go horseback riding out at Larry's. But we finally had to turn in our car and that limited us very little. Everyday it seemed someone would stop by and take us to a new adventure.

Then it was the night of Julian's Grande Festival in his Castle. We arrived by a car that he had sent for us, and upon arriving at the castle we were awestruck. We walked across the moat bridge and in thru the gates onto the open courtyard. Peasant girls and Mallorcan men were dressed for the earlier centuries. There were whole animals being turned on spits over large open fire pits. Huge tables were filled with fruits and others with vegetables.

We were ushered by Julian through the fire lit night, past the torches and up a set of stone steps. There the blue waters of a giant free form swimming pool appeared. On either side of the diving board were full grown stuffed tigers, guarded by suits of armor holding torches. The seating area around the pool were stone bleachers surrounded by flags and torches. On the bottom of the pool was a giant dragon made of very small squares of colored tiles. The turrets were aglow and as we were led into a dark archway, we climbed up circular stairs to come to a circular water bed warmed by colored lights beneath it and soothed by the surround sound coming from the turret walls. All could be quieted and dimmed so as to let the stars brighten the night. We celebrated the night there with a toast, overlooking the pool, courtyards and moat in one glance.

The feast began and I remember having my own personal leg of lamb that I carried around with me to munch on while I picked grapes from here and cheeses from there and bread from everywhere. After everyone was full and their tumblers were full, we all went up to the pool area and listened to Barbara's sweet sounds. She was an instant hit. Everyone was cool about it as well. They just laid back and listened and enjoyed and occasionally made requests of songs they had heard her sing before somewhere.

Later in the night Julian showed us to our rooms. Our clothes had already been hung up there. How embarrassing. But this round room had a theme of an Indian royalty. The surrounding curtains were all silver, and had remote controls so any area of the walls or windows could be opened or closed. The wall between the luxurious bathroom and the four-poster bed contained a very large aquarium with exotic fish and other creatures I had never seen before. The main attractions were the pair of praying mantis fish. They look just like praying mantis, but were probably crustaceans of some rare kind. The female made the male do everything from bringing food, making a nest and once she was fertilized, she ate the male for the nutrition of it, or the hell of it. Don't get any ideas girls. We didn't want to go to sleep, being afraid we would miss something. But finally I was out, dreaming I was King Somebody. This was the Good Life!

We spent a few days here, and Julian was no end of surprises. He had a pet spider monkey that was a real character. He reminded me of the monkey on the yacht across from my apartment in my telescope over looking New York. Was it the same one? You could hold him and he would clean your hair and play real nice unless Julian came back into the room. Then it might bite you to protect her owner. So Jules would call us an early warning before reentering the room. His girl friend, who was a gorgeous brunette from the upper class of London town, was the only other person this monkey would allow near Julian.

Barbara stayed with her while Julian and I went to a cross-country motorbike race that he was sponsoring for young Mallorcan kids. We had a banquet for them all that night, and Julian made me the big deal who awarded the winners their trophies. I had to give a speech of congratulation and motivation in Spanish, something I would have been sure I could not do if I had time to think about it. But the words just flowed and the kids loved my accent and applauded exactly when

I hoped they would. It's amazing what one can do if they just do it. I was a hit in *Español*. Incredible!

The next night we all went to a bullfight to watch Spain's national hero kill a bull in the National sport. I had been a Hemingway reader, so I was prepared for the massacre, but Barbara was only ready to leave. I understood many of the nuances of bullfighting, and the different players on the field. Barbara only knew the bull. She did get to cheer when the bull gored some poor sucker who got too close with his cape. But the matador still hung in there for a very exciting 'moment of truth'.

After the fights we all went up to meet friends of Julian's, Stanley and Helga. They were a very unique couple and they were very hospitable to us. Actually it was like instant friendship, and they wanted to pick Barbara and I up and have us over for dinner and other surprises. These two were also very classy people.

When Stanley's car arrived at our apartment, there were refreshments and music and a note from Helga. We were asked to excuse them for not being there but they had been delayed and would see us at their home. We sat back and enjoyed the champagne and the ride. When we arrived some forty minutes away Helga was waiting for us. She was very excited as Stanley had just smuggled a beautiful white stallion into Spain and it was her birthday present. This Arabian horse had been smuggled from South America thru Mexico into Canada across the ocean into two other countries before its arrival in time for tonight's celebration. And we were the guests they wanted to spend this night with. Stanley was American and Helga from Germany. After greeting this incredibly huge horse, we went inside their mansion they had built in the finca style, but hardly a peasants pad. This place had treasures throughout their home. And then outback was a jungle zoo with all her 'pets'. This was not the average zoo. It had over fifty animals of which only the duckbilled platypus and her cheetah were familiar to me. The waterfall was the beginning of a Chinese waterway that surrounded the zoo and went around the home in small cascading waterfalls. We all sat in their garden and had drinks brought to us by their servants and then we went inside to enjoy the heat of their tiled wood stove. Sitting on cushions around a glass table we had a ten-course fondue dinner. We found Stanley to be most hospitable and he rolled a J in a whole tampax wrapper and we were all laid back to enjoy this celebration. Barbara sang a few numbers between courses and they loved her.

After dinner we were to go for a brandy. Where? Why out on Stanley's yacht. Our driver took us to the top of a cliff where we saw this beautiful old classic yacht moored out in the dark waters of a large lake. We went down to a dock by elevator he had put into the mountain. The dingy took us out to the old lady of the lake. She had been completely restored into high varnish condition, with oriental carpets in the salon. The girls relaxed there while us guys went up to the bridge. The crew served us drinks while I was told to steer a course straight toward another mountain cliff. When we got there Stanley took over and took us into a hidden cave where he had a seaplane anchored and tied to a dock. It was illegal to land planes on water in Spain, but he was about to get that law changed. He just needed to get to court. Tonight, I thought, was not the night to get caught. As we climbed on board, the servant threw off the lines and we putt putted out of the cave and gained speed until we were airborne. What a neat feeling, what an incredible night!

We had several special times with these two 'wild ones' over the next month. I never knew what was Stanley's background until years later when I found out his family owned very big shipbuilding facilities in Philadelphia, and also owned much real estate downtown there as well. I felt like either the Prince or the Pauper. Guess which.

We finally returned to our humble apartment and collapsed in exhausted bliss. Most every night we went to the local sidewalk cafe for a coffee and brandy and did some serious people watching. This I believed is the National Sport in Europe. Little did we know we were being watched as well. Bring on the clowns.

At the market place in Pollensa we would be recognized and always find another place to go for dinner. We would bring the string beans and whatever else we had bought to chip into the meal. The days were getting shorter and we heard that Halloween was called 'All Hallows Eve'. The Spaniards celebrated this by reenacting religious battles between the Christians and the Moors. All the businessmen would pick which side they wanted to be on. They usually tried to get on the opposite side as their enemy or business competitor. Then, dressed in the costumes of that period, they proceeded to get drunk and when a whistle blew they ran at each other and whooped on the 'enemy'. Finally the 'Christians' win and they all end up in a parade of bloody drunk bodies into the Church for a 'high' Mass. This was not very encouraging to my search for the great truth. I still shake my head when I think about it.

On October 28th, Barbara and I had a fantastic dinner that she had cooked up in our apartment. We were relaxed and about to work on some music. We had been also discussing what we were going to do when our lease expired on November 1st. We had pretty much decided to pack up and head back to Palma and see what happened from there. Maybe we could even get a sail back across the pond. The thought gave me a chill. I had not actually thought out whether I would actually have the guts or the desire to go through that life-threatening event again. As I contemplated the chill, I looked at Barbara who was acting really weird. She started making shrill sounds and she wouldn't talk to me. She had fear in her eyes. Was she thinking of the sail home too? Or was she working on some new music. Now she was trying to walk and slamming into the walls, and was she signaling me? This went on for about ten minutes when I started freaking. Should I slap her or was she having a heart attack or what? Finally, long after my total fear set in she suddenly jolted and was able to talk. It took some time for her to explain what had happened and for her to even put words together to talk. What I gathered from her was that a spirit had possessed her and took over her mind and body and it was an old lady with a shrill voice and that the spirit was inescapable. She said she had been under the control of this thing way before I even realized anything was wrong.

"How did you get it to leave you?" I queried.

Barbara said she tried to say but could only think, "In the name of Jesus come out of me!" It was then she could finally talk. She wanted to scream from fear, but tried to stay cool for my sake. I put her to bed to rest from her ordeal and told her we'd talk about it tomorrow.

The next day, Halloween eve, the bitch (bad witch) came into me. Barb kept ignoring me and I couldn't talk. Finally I got the sign language going and she heard the shrill sound from me and it finally dawned for her to say in a powerful prayer of panic: "In the name of

Jesus leave him!" And it did. Now this made a powerful impression on me about the truth of life. Here we were living in sin and unknowingly wide open to Satanic attacks. We were perfect targets for possession by an evil spirit. And this being that overwhelmed me had sealed my lips so that I could not confess my sins if I had wanted to. But the name of Jesus freed me just to show me something I had yet to understand. That God loved <u>me</u> as I was, a sinner. He had a Gift for me and all I had to do was to take it. But I left it under the tree for another time, the last gift to open at the celebration of life.

In other words I had the stuffies scared out of me. And Barbara had too. We spent some quiet time talking about what had happened to us. We didn't change our ways because we didn't think we were doing anything wrong at the time. We just thought this was a supernatural experience and couldn't quite get a handle on it. We discussed the name of Jesus that she told me about which had seemed to save us from the idiot farm. Being Catholic by upbringing and having seen the weird movies like *Rosemary's Baby*, she turned to Jesus for help. This I thought was genius, and left it at that.

We also talked about our lives and where it was going. I saw nothing wrong with our lives, as a matter of fact things were as good as I had ever imagined them to be. What about her?

"Well", she said, "I hope to be famous some day, but I would not trade it for these days for anything."

"What do we do from here?" I queried, mostly for self-introspection. Barbara used my line, "I don't know, but something better." Wow, I thought, 'something better!' Everything had gotten so much better than I had ever imagined I was almost afraid to go on. We started packing up our little things as we were about to go to Palma in a few days and it kept us from thinking that today was Halloween in the states. We had had enough of that stuff. Halloween had taken on a more sinister meaning than the trick or treat days of yore when we were the evil ones.

Barbara and I were having breakfast for the last time at our table and burning the last of the firewood when we heard a beep- beep-beepbeep outside our arched window. We looked out to see what the commotion was, and there was Frank standing by a cab, captain's hat on and same black beard. "Hey y'all, want to go sailing?" His Virginia accent was unchangeable, and his smile undeniable. Barb and I looked at each other and grabbed our already packed bags and the three of us toot tooted back across the island to *Star Song* for a good nights rest. How Frank had found us on the far side of the island, only God knows. He had never been there, and we certainly were not expecting to see him back here from the states. I am sure you can start to see the thin thread that was being woven to change my life. Maybe you have heard of the trial by fire, but mine was to be the trial by water, and the solution by blood.

All we had to do was leave our keys on the table, grab our bags and head out the door and we were off to another adventure. We drove around saying our goodbyes to Larry and family, Julian and family and friends, and Helga and Stanley. It was happy and sad, but just as we thought we were invincible, so we thought were our friendships, and we would just see each other down the road of life again somewhere and somehow. Not always true in this life, and only a thin line to seeing them in eternity. But we sure enjoyed our present time with each of them.

Off we went across the island to Palma where we were able to reboard *Star Song*. This was like seeing an old friend that we never expected to see again, but the cycles of life can come around quickly for reasons beyond me. As before, Barb was in charge of food and I was responsible for finances, planning and shopping for stores and Barb and I would stow the grub away according to a plan with the most recent meals to be finally on top of the freezer unit.

Then we also had to find crew. This was Frank's job and frankly he was too nice a guy to turn anyone down. He just figured the Lord brought them to him and so they were the chosen ones. Well we ended up with Tor, who had been watching *Star Song* and getting paid to live on her, and who was going with us until the last moment when he flaked out. Some girl didn't want him to go away. I was not disappointed even though he was probably a good sailor. That left an old man who was really worthless and Brian, a POME who had some head knowledge and sold Frank on the idea of becoming crew. Frank looked for more crew but after a week of his talent searching we

231

decided to take off and maybe find some able bodies in Gibraltar, you know, on the way home. Home! What and where was that? My home was where I was at that moment, my present was my home. My future was nonexistent other than just having a successful crossing. How many people could exist this way I wondered. Not many I wagered myself, and that is why I was enjoying it so much. Because this was the Good Life!

Homeward Bound

We had spent many days getting *Star Song* ready for her crossing. Every detail is a little more involved than packing a parachute, but just as important. As we sailed out of the Palma harbor we had many friends on the dock waving their goodbyes. This really meant a lot to all of us, except for Brian and the old man. They were looking a little unsure. We had just reached the first sea buoy when I saw both of them hanging over the rail feeding the fish. Oh yuk, and I had to look away as that stuff is contagious.

I quickly had a beer and got life back to normal, for to sit and rock and roll and not be active is the last thing one wants to do. But Brian said he'd be ok soon. The next day, as he was still over the rail and had not eaten anything, we came upon one of the worst storms we had encountered so far. It only lasted one day, but it came on quick and did some serious damage. We had a sail that blew out, sheets that snapped, halyards that jammed and we were taking on water somehow. All I could think of was that Tor had either not maintained our *Star Song* as she needed, or we had been sabotaged. I'll never know the truth, but he did offer to join us later in Gibraltar if we needed him. I swore we wouldn't need him.

But we needed something and somebody, as Brian spent the whole ride to Gibraltar over the rail, and was on deaths doorstep when we got there. I told him he better stop feeding the sharks or they will come to the source. He didn't laugh, but he did move back from the rail a bit. That was no help either. The old man, Stu, finally got his sea legs and proved to be utterly incompetent at anything. So Frank, Barbara and I had to do all the work as well as the watches that seven of us did on the crossing over. Life became tired, tense and irritable, but Frank was always the same. "Everything will work out," he'd say. "The Lord's got it all under control."

I wish I had his optimism, or whatever he had going for him. Don't you? Maybe you already have what I was searching for and are totally satisfied. I wasn't, and if you aren't either, thank you for staying on this journey with me in search of the truth, the meaning to all this.

Somehow we made it through some of the worst weather one can survive at sea. We pulled into Malaga on Spain's Costa del Sol. We were glad for the break and Brian even had a meal that he kept down. The old man slept, while the grace was given to us three to do everything again.

But Barb and I did have some free time and we got to see a few old sailing buddies there and visit some of our favorite cafes. Gypsies would come trying to get us to buy worthless jewelry while looking for the opportunity to pick our pockets or some other scam. I think we beat them. But Gibraltar was our main stop and now that Brian kept a meal down we decided to make a run across the straits. He was sick within the first hour. But he said he would be ok soon. He was ok after we had our pilot boat take us into the Gib harbor and we tied up near the same mooring we had before. At least the oil slicks on top of the water seemed the same.

We had to order engine parts from Britain and get sails resewn, while we topped off our stores. It was going to take two weeks to get our engine parts back from England, so we knew we had time to kill.

The second morning, I was having a hot buttered rum up on the bow with Barb when we hear "Pssst, Captain, you want to smoke?" We look at each other and then knowingly up at the bulkhead and there is Abdel, our Arab boy guide who we haven't seen since Morocco. He comes and stays on board with us, sleeping under the stars on the foredeck. To him this was luxury. He ran errands, showed us some more sights, and became a good friend over the next two weeks.

But he never went into the Seamen's Mission there on the dockside. This is where men from all the different freighters and other ships and from all different countries would congregate. There were Greeks, Iranians, Russians, Italians and many others. Barb brought her guitar at Frank's persuasion and started playing Christmas carols inside. The crewmen stopped drinking and shooting pool and began singing the Christmas songs in their own languages. It was incredible to hear the same familiar tune sang in all languages at once. We all had Jesus as a common reality. Of course we all do and always have, but this was different. So much so that the old man who ran the mission told us he had never seen such a spirit as was there those nights before Christmas. All these men would also sing as a group, some would try speaking their hearts in English, others did their cultural dances. It was an experience that every sailor there would never forget.

Finally our engine parts arrived, but that afternoon hurricane force winds and storms came over us. We had battened down the hatches as Frank tried installing the parts down in the engine room. He almost got seasick down there even though we were tied to the dock. I had to go up on deck a few times to check out crashes and other noises, and I saw that we were actually planing while tied up. The water was going by us so fast that it actually was lifting the hull up as if we were speeding through the seas. I was glad we were not at sea for this one.

For some reason Gib was not as exciting as our first visit, but we did feel more a part of the scene. Soon it was time to ship out. The storm had just left and the sun was about to set. I thought it a bit early after the storm to leave, so Frank said he would get a weather report. He came back on board and said all was clear. Well that was good news, until I found out later that his weather report came from an old man that had said, "Good evening," and Frank thought that meant, well you know.

Just before we let off our tar-covered lines, the old man from the missions came out to dockside to bid us adieu. He had a present he wanted us to have to enjoy on our way back to the states. With much ceremony he unrolled an old yellowed parchment with a drawing of a beautiful square-rigged tall ship. And on each of the square sails was a Bible verse. At the bottom was the name *Gospel Ship*. We never forgot his tears as Frank and I would look up a verse together every night we could on the crossing home.

Abdel wanted so badly to come with us. He had really adopted us and we him, but Frank told him he would not like it in the US and they would either put him in jail or ship him home. He didn't mind, just let him get to America. Frank couldn't and we knew it. We had our hugs and we toot tooted out of the harbor singing our song, side by side.

235

After we got out of the harbor, I had the first watch from 8 till midnight. Everyone hit the sack to get their six hours before they had their four-hour watch. I had my hands full as the winds picked up and we were moving along at a good clip. The seas became choppy along with the wild currents in the straits. I also had several boat lights I was trying to keep track of to make sure we were not on a collision course with any of them. If a ship was too long at one point of the compass that means we are on the collision course. If they slide off the same compass point then we will miss each other.

I now had twelve ships I was trying to keep track of and then there was one suddenly real near us that I somehow had not been tracking. Man, how did that guy get right here. I watched him and he was not moving off the mark on the compass. Damn, I was about to get all hands on deck when it was suddenly no longer there. Did they turn off their running lights? As it turns out it was a submarine that had been thrown into the mix just to see if I might lose my sanity. Spare me ever sailing through the Straits at night ever again, where shipping lanes and military lanes all come together to make real fun for a little Clorox bottle such as we.

But finally the lights of civilization disappeared while the swells of the sea and the increase of the winds let us know where we were. We wondered if we should reduce some sail, if possibly another storm was imminent. Again without any way to contact civil agencies we were on our own as far as managing the weather. Take it as it comes, we'd say. And come it did. We had a course heading for the Canary Islands, which were south of the Azores and owned by Spain rather than Portugal. We were looking forward to our visit there, and then to our crossing the Atlantic riding the currents of the second arc of our great circle.

Not Home For the Holidays

The night sky and the dome of stars that surrounded us during my watch suddenly disappeared. Everything became ominously black, and the wind shifted coming from our course. We had to take a tack up north and it was then we decided to reef our sails. We even trimmed in our self-reefing jib and prepared everything for a rough night. Sure enough, the near hurricane force winds we had experienced in Gibraltar had stalled and we ran right into it again. I was not looking forward to this. Already Barb had complained about us not being home for Christmas because of our delays in Gib. I told her that we would be in mid Atlantic on Christmas and that it would be very special. She almost bought it. But now we were just hoping we wouldn't be swimming across or walking home on the bottom of the ocean.

Frank and I pulled out our *Gospel Ship* scroll and looked up a verse on one of the foresails. It talked about how God would deliver us to a safe haven. I don't know why, but I just believed that would be true. The waves would tower over us and occasionally break sending white water avalanching down at us and bury us in the cockpit. We would be waist deep in ocean and just hope another wave wouldn't break until we had drained this last one overboard. If you have never experienced the wrath of the sea it would be hard for me to describe it any other way than hell broken loose. And this was to go on for two days and nights, with no sleep except for ten minutes on the floor down below in our wet foul weather gear. Then back up to help who ever was on watch. There was one consolation and that was a swig of brandy that seemed to warm us and maybe give us some added courage. Cooked food was a scarcity as Barb had been thrown around in the galley like a bar brawl, and she won and left the premises.

We were on our own to find a piece of something to keep our strength up. A banana would taste real good about now. God must have heard me, as it was shortly decided that we were not heading for the Canary Islands, but rather we were going to go back to San Miguel in the Azores and make our crossing from there. Maybe our lawyer friend will give us another batch of bananas to hang up in the cockpit again. But for now we would grab a piece of bread if it was dry, and forget trying to get peanut butter on it. That takes two hands. We needed one hand for the boat and that just left one for us.

We had put out a big sea anchor off the stern to hold us back from roller coasting down some of the swells and to keep our heading more stable. We were not real interested in making time so much as just maintaining until we ride the storm out.

Again I had to reassure Barb that Christmas would be a special day at sea. She said she was holding me to my word. Finally we saw a patch of blue and within another six hours the storm was history and we were sailing through the still undulating sea. But we were alive and I wanted to read another of the verses on the *Gospel Ship*. We had a prayer of thanks and Barb cooked us all a big dinner. We had buckets of fresh water, so we took turns showering and getting the salt off our bodies that was about to corrode us. Man there is nothing finer than a bucket of fresh water. Don't ever take it for granted. With everyone refreshed we got back on our regular watches and this time I got to take the first watch in my bunk. I slept like a baby and when I awoke Barb had hot coffee, fresh breakfast buns and a bit of brandy awaiting. The stars came out and it was smooth sailing all the way to Pico Peak. It was great to be alive again.

Our arrival into the Azores was an unexpected surprise for us as well as our old friends there. Eddie was at the dockside as usual and was so excited to see us again. What was so incredible was that the whole village was decorated to the nth for Christmas. It was like miracleville. These people were so poor, but they had spared no expense except one. They had every tree wired with light bulbs of different colors. They were beautiful without even being lit, for while they had been decorated for weeks, they are only illuminated on Christmas Eve night. Guess what. We were here for eight days and then we shipped out four days before Christmas. We had to miss this event that people come from all over the world to enjoy and celebrate. Christmas in Madeira was as famous as Macy's Parade.

But we did leave with lots of food goodies and fruits, including a whole batch of bananas hanging up in the cockpit. Barb sang Christmas carols over the PA system as we headed back out to sea. I had to re-reassure Barb that Christmas would be special out in the middle of the Atlantic. Quietly I made a prayer that Christmas would be special again, especially in the middle of the ocean.

Sailing was never better than that day before Christmas. There were wind clouds scattered across the blue skies. The wind was steady and from our perfect direction for an easy reach. We had all our big sails up taking advantage of it all, and we felt prouder than a peacock having all our colors flying. We even had a small Christmas tree on the chart table in the main salon. But there was no one to appreciate our strutting around here, but wait! There on the horizon, is that smoke? And then our watchful eyes began to see a ship, changing its course and coming towards us. Whoa!

As it neared us it seemed as if we could be swallowed up and never seen again, but then her course changed again to pass astern of us. Much to our surprise it was a large Gulf tanker ship and she began to turn to do a 180-degree around our stern and finally came along side our starboard side. We yelled, "Merry Christmas!" and our echo surprised us. We heard voices saying "They're Americans!" We exclaimed, "They speak English!"

It was a miracle in this day and age to find American Merchant Marines on a ship of this size. Barbara sang Christmas carols over the PA system as the great ship idled beside us, but still moving through the sea at several knots past us. The crew of each ship was lined along the lifelines singing along with Barbara. And then several of the guys on the tanker threw what turned out to be Christmas presents overboard as they steamed onto their original course back over the horizon and out of sight. We skimmed the waters in front of us with our nets and boat hooks and picked us goodies that we saved for Christmas Day. Barb was impressed. She said, "OK Peter, What about New Years Eve?" I reassured her that it would be special too.

Christmas came and went as peaceful as any I have known. We had everything it seemed. At the time I couldn't describe it, but from my present spiritual view, we had the gifts from each other and most importantly from above. We all really felt the presence of the Lord here at sea. We read from His word, sang old familiar carols and we sailed under white and blue skies and then the starlit canopy all nite.

We were in harmony with it all. Merry Christmas everyone, everywhere!

On New Years Eve morn, during coffee on deck, we spotted a stick poking above the horizon way to our northwest. It took all day to get together but we realized in stages that the stick was another boat, then another sailboat, then that they were Americans! Barbara reminded me that I had predicted something special for New Years also. Then we came alongside and nestled our boats together for a night of revelry in a Mid Atlantic calm sea under a dome of stars. The crew were three guys heading for California via the Panama Canal. The name of their yacht, *REPETE*. Barbara was impressed. (So was I!) We had another magnificent night in His Sea.

At dawn the wind began coming up, and so after Barb fed us all a New Years breakfast of Bloody Mary's and hot buns and eggs, we separated the lines and let the wind direct our paths. Within six hours they were out of sight again, as if it had never happened. These were holidays we would never forget, and I recommend to everyone.

January 1st, 1972, we started reefing our sails to get ready for a night of heavy weather. The unexpected is what to expect out here, and we were not exactly prepared having all stayed awake most of last night. But we always seemed to have whatever it took to meet the situation at the time. By midnight I was called out of the sack to get up on the foredeck and with foul weather gear and two harnesses attached to the boat I had to clear a jib halyard up on the foredeck so we could reef the jib and cut down our sail exposure to the wind. The waves were breaking over me up there and it would have taken the slightest slipup to find myself overboard. But it had to be done and it was done. I had a shot of brandy back in the cockpit and hit the sack until my watch time in two hours.

Like life, we don't always have it the way we want it. For two more days we had more wind and rough seas than we needed, and then we hit the doldrums. Have you ever seen anyone in the doldrums? It really exists, right here in the Atlantic. The sea is so calm that a ripple a mile away can be seen. Seaweed languishes under the hot sun and there is not a breath of wind under a cloudless sky. Sure we had a motor, but the doldrums can go for hundreds of miles, and we didn't have that kind of fuel. For days we stayed on the deck hearing our main sail straining for any wind, from port side or starboard. It just flapped back and forth and we went nowhere.

This was an unexpected intermission on my part. Frank had done a previous crossing and knew of the doldrums. To me it gave me time to think, as we all just sat around on the deck and stared across the expanse of flat water. It was just days ago we were in a gale wind with seas that would never calm down. But like life the ocean reflects our storms of life and the challenge to overcome them, the doldrums and the power they can have over us, and then the perfect days of sailing through life with good health and a smile. Frank finally told us that back where he had asked me to clear the Jib halyard up forward during that storm was where a crewman had gone overboard on his previous crossing during a similar storm. They couldn't find him. So that was why Frank insisted I have two harnesses clipped onto the boat. I sat there in the doldrums and realized that could have been me. I was glad to be in the doldrums. It seems if we want to not complain about our situation, all we have to do is look around us and we'll see people that really have it rough, and they're not complaining.

On the third day we spotted a small white cloud off to our southern horizon. We decided to go for a chase and turned on the kicker and motored for it, hoping for a breeze under there. After all, altocumulus clouds are known as wind clouds. It took hours and hours of chasing, but finally we actually got enough breeze to keep our main off to the starboard side and we started making headway, and then there were a few clouds and then we could cut our engine and still make some headway. We looked back and saw no clouds and waved goodbye to the doldrums and wondered how many had perished here before engines were invented. Ahha, that's why they invented oars.

Our seas treated us well for the remainder of our sail. I was in sailor heaven. Barbara was cranking out some really special meals with roast beef or leg of lamb with roasted potatoes and veggies, 'salt water bread' and vino. On my watch one morning with my favorite brandy and coffee to counter the early morning chill, I felt a presence off to my right. I looked over not expecting to see anything and there was an eye the size of a nerf football staring at me. The eye was going at the same speed as we were, but after we eyeballed each other and ole Moby realized I recognized him, he swam up and across our bow letting his giant tail just brush us enough so I could feel it nudge us through our helm. I woke Frank and we finally realized that he was a scout and had signaled to his pod to come visit us, and soon we were surrounded by a herd of these giants of the deep. This was definitely a humbling experience. Beside the joy their company gave us, we were also keeping one finger on the starter in case one of them fell in love with our rounded hull. The engine, we hoped, would let them know we were not one of them and crossbreeding was a no no. Anyone of them could have flipped us if they wanted to, but they were peaceful Indians and we were glad.

We were hoping to make land fall in about six days at Grenada, one of the lower islands I had not visited yet. I was really looking forward to seeing this paradise, but how could it be any better than the here and now.

A couple days after our whale visit, I again was sitting at the helm with my special coffee when I thought I saw a dark shadow shoot out from under the port side of the boat. I put *Star Song* on autopilot and leaned out from the spreaders where I could see three or four rainbow dolphins cavorting in our early morning shadow. Now these are the eating kind, and the Lord had brought me a flying fish during my evening watch, which I was going to show Frank and then have for breakfast. But I decided I would up the ante and I found a hand line and hooked that flying fish on there for bait. With *Star Song* on auto pilot, I took it up forward and climbed out on the bowsprit where I swung it overhead and out into the blue waters. A big dolphin shot out to it and saw it was dead, and uninterested swam back under the hull. Hmmm. I quickly pulled the line back in and slung it out there again, and this time when I saw that rainbow streak out there I gave the line a jig to make the bait look alive, and wham. That dolphin hit and ran with it. Unfortunately the hand line was not coiled as I had it the first cast, and as the line was pulled out it suddenly locked around my three fingers and cut straight through to the bone. So there I was, life suddenly changing again, with a tug of war between 3o+ pounds of dolphin and me. I can't explain it, but when I realized the life or death of one of us was imminent I began just pulling the line in, and for some reason that big fish swam straight to me and jumped up and onto the deck. It threw the hook in mid air and I grabbed the winch handle off the mast and tried to konk it on the head. I missed more times than I hit and the racket got everyone up to see me wrestling this bugger trying to keep him from flopping overboard. When it was all over I was shaking like a warrior, our blood all over the deck, the fishing line still wound around my fingers. We ate really well that last few days of our journey as I found that no fish tastes any better than fresh dolphin. And Neosporin healed up my fingers without any infection. My crew was impressed, but so was I. There were miracles there I was sure. Another gift from above and from the sea. And the blood to prove it.

The whole event left me forever grateful. But I really didn't know to whom I was grateful. I believed there was a God, the creator, but I did not believe in Him or on Him. It was not a personal relationship like Frank seemed to have. We had read more of the Bible verses while we sat there in the Doldrums, and it sure gave me time to think about my life and where it was and where it was going. The doldrums are good for that, but so is the Bible for it just seems to be so full of truths that one needs to contemplate. I decided I needed to start examining myself somehow and just be sure I am doing whatever I am. Maybe I should go home for a while to see if that is where I am supposed to be. At least to my hometown of Plainfield, New Jersey which was a far cry from this life style. And what would I do there? I had already done so many different things there, none of which I wanted to return to. I didn't want to sell insurance, didn't want to go back to Wall Street, didn't want to go back into manufacturing, and I didn't want to commute to New York City and see models and other fakers.

And what about Barbara? I like her a lot and we had been through so much together at home and in Florida and St John and now this experience. She wanted to get to her home and see her parents and brothers and sisters. That made me picture my parents and how 'happy' they would be to see me in my beard and long hair. Those were just some of the things that occurred to me in this flicker of time called the doldrums. The beauty of the open sea brought me back to reality and I gave a sigh of relief that I was here and now and not in the future.

We were making good time and sailing under sunny days and starlit nights, enjoying many of life's pleasures, when we finally saw land. It took me back to the future and I didn't want to be there. I just wanted to keep sailing right past our landfall, but in a day or so it was going to be over. I had to get a hold of myself and say it's not the end of time, just the end of this delivery. I had to look forward to whatever was next. My motto when asked what I'm going to do now? I'd answer, "Don't know, but something better."

Well this, once again, was going to be hard to beat. We started getting *Star Song* shipshape so we could lay back and enjoy our landfall in Grenada. We did look sharp coming into the harbor under full sail and did an unnoticed victory lap around the harbor. I was amazed at the beauty I beheld with a very high waterfall cascading straight down to the ocean, the palm trees waving from pristine white beaches and the sounds of steel drums ringing from the forests. Maybe civilization won't be so bad after all.

Return From Paradise

We found the natives here to be quite varied in their response to us. Some were very interested in our crossing. Those were mainly people in charge of customs, immigration and drug trafficking. Others were interested in our money and still other natives didn't care a hoot about us. Now politics was running rampant here and we found ourselves right in the middle of it all. Barbara and I were invited to a white man's home to have lunch. When we arrived he wanted her to sing. We entertained him as if he were some kind of king. Well as it turns out he was running to be Governor and also had just renovated an old building to make it a hotel. As a matter of fact, a freighter was coming in the next day with all the furniture for his hotel.

We had a wonderful lunch and visit and went back to *Star Song* a bit star struck by our new acquaintance. However, we found out that we had been followed and that natives with machine guns were not exactly friendly. Our friend was not at all popular with the incumbent 'Papa Doc' Governor, and now we weren't either. We slept with one eye open that night and a gun near the cabin door.

The next day was declared a national holiday by the Governor, which meant no one worked. So when the freighter came in to port, no one was allowed to help it dock and the goons with the machine guns made sure no one unloaded any furniture. "After all mon, it be a holiday, no?" And so the freighter left Grenada, furniture on board, for points unknown. Had it stayed, another holiday would have been proclaimed ad infinitum. Ah yes, it was so good to be back in civilization. Frank had made friends with a native preacher who had invited him to his church. Frank wanted us to go with him, but I said we'd pray from our boat. Later we found out that Christianity and Voodoo were intermingled at this preacher's service in the name of Christianity. Frank was very distressed at how the Bible was misused and misunderstood by these folks. He was surprised, but somehow I wasn't.

Barb and I were ready to ship out and Frank was going to wait for the owner to arrive. We got our pay and money for plane tickets back to Mallorca, the standard deal for deliveries. We were 'well off' again and we were ready to head north to St Thomas to see where life leads us from there. We had a big good-bye hug from Frank and somehow the feeling was there that we would see Frank again someday, somewhere. I had no idea how real that feeling was to become.

When we arrived in St Thomas, many old friends were there at the marina bar watching the sun go down ever since noon. Many thought we were lost at sea as they hadn't heard from us. We got to surprise many people who kept showing up for days from different parts on the island. Pam and Brian were there, her brother Cotty, all the Hassle Island crowd and the resident boat captains and riggers. This was like a major homecoming. We wondered if we were meant to stay here forever or move on. For some reason we were compelled to move on, and after a few weeks of revelry here and on St John, we decided to head back up to Florida. We seemed to have graduated a notch above where we had been a year ago and didn't have to repeat the grade again. Was that it, or was our life on a track and it had a schedule to keep we didn't even know about? Whatever the plan, we had arrived home as much here as any place. These Islands had been and still are Paradise.

But we were being drawn north and not knowing to where, we booked a flight to Miami and gave Bob and Leigh a call when we got there. They insisted on us coming to their place and just stay as long as we needed. That was really nice as this would give us a chance to reacclimate ourselves with the continent and society before we went home to New Jersey. Bob picked us up at the airport and whisked us back to his backyard paradise, with the pool and waterfall and thatched roofed cabañas and offices. I really enjoyed this again, as just getting naked and swimming in that pool was a reaffirmation of the freedom I was enjoying. Bobby and Kevin would have their girlfriends over and by Bob's laws of his jungle, either they got naked or they at least put up with everyone else au buff. No one complained, and we were all happy campers. Bob was famous for his dinners on the barbe. He would grill out the best steaks and ribs and fish and corn on the cob. Ah, what feasts.

Bob started Barbara working again helping him with some of his commercial artwork that came in. I would go to the beach with the boys...but something was missing here too. I felt that while we loved these folks, we couldn't live their life style. What was happening to us. We got to know our friends better than we wanted to. Everyone has their secrets, and we were getting to know that these sweet folks had their problems and we were in the way. Leigh was legally blind, but she could get around her own home quite well. She even designed and made a line of linen shirts and dresses. But when she went to the department stores her old klepto urges took over, and because she couldn't see she figured no one could see her either. So she got caught pocketing insignificant stuff for her dresses. They could afford whatever, but this urge was overpowering for her. Bob had a standing deal with the police that they would call him whenever she got 'nabbed.' Then he would pay for what ever she took and bring her home instead of to jail. Then he would lecture her again and explain to us his love for her over rode anything she could do. We really admired their devotion to each other and to their family. Barb was ready to move on north toward her origin, but I was content to stay waiting to see what was next.

We wanted to see our friends from the encounter group, Mickey and Susan, at their plant boutique, *"Living Things for Loving People."* We found them there on Arthur Godfrey Boulevard and they were real busy making lots of money. But they told us about our dentist friend Carl Bauman who had developed cancer and had gone to New York as a guinea pig for the major cancer doctors of the world. He was a specimen of great health and they felt he would live through their tortuous chemotherapy. We saw Josie, his wife and she asked if we could go up to New York with her. We said we were heading that way and would come to New York's Sloan-Kettering Hospital and be with her as soon as we could. Mickie felt Dr Bauman should just stay home and die with dignity rather than go through the hell of Chemotherapy in its infancy stage. But being a Doctor, Carl felt he might help others through his battle even though it tore his family up. He was a real trooper. These two couples were of the Jewish faith, yet they had included us in their family celebrations and rites. We were the first non-Jewish people they had ever shared these intimate events with. They sure know how to eat.

Josie left her children in the care of parents and Mickey and Susan and flew up to New York to be with Carl. Barb and I spent a few more days going to old haunts here in Miami and even up to Ft Lauderdale to see who was at the marinas there. We saw many of our old boat 'rigger' friends and knew we were going to miss them. I had a feeling that in life's arcs I would probably see many of them again. But right now, my God, a buddy of our was dying. This gave life a whole different perspective. You think you might die, but not someone close to you, especially when they are so vibrantly healthy, wealthy and wise. I had to learn that none of that makes any difference. When the Creator calls, we come. It's how we do it that counts. I just knew I wasn't ready. And so did He.

Barb and I flew up to Kennedy Airport on Long Island and came into the big apple with our duffels bulging and her guitar case a bit tattered from its mileage over the past couple years. We took a cab directly to the Sloan Kettering Hospital. The cabbie asked if we knew anyone in there. We told him about Carl and he said, "That's sad. Sloan Kettering is for terminal cancer patients only." We said he was strong and might just make it. Our cabbie just shook his head.

We arrived and asked for Carl's room. He was to have no visitors. Freaky. But then we bumped into Josie who screamed delight at seeing us there. She said she was the guest of the head of the whole hospital and she was sure we could stay there at least overnight. We took our 'luggage' up to the penthouse on the top floor to Doctor Good's Apartment. There his assistant welcomed us and showed us a room we could stay in. Josie explained we couldn't see Carl right away because he was just suffering from a dose of Chemo and would feel rotten for a day or two.

Josie was still optimistic about his recovery. This was incredible. She had been having dinner up here with the leading cancer doctors in the world called together by Dr Good to hurry the cure of cancer.

That night Dr Good invited all of us to join he and some other doctors to go to dinner with them in China Town. This was one of the specialties he enjoyed and so we learned much that night. We went to an authentic Chinese restaurant where the whole fish is served, not just the filet. The good doctor then showed us his skills of surgery while he removed the eye and the this and the that. The piece de resistance is the jaw muscle, which all fish have. He cut it out and it actually was ok.

Back at the penthouse he gave Barb and I a tour of his long white hallway, which had a dozen or more large paintings. He had commissioned top artists around the world to put on canvas their inspired vision of the cure for cancer. It was here that a three-colored outline of three human forms caught his attention. One outline was red, the other green and the other yellow. He stood, he told us, for quite a long time meditating on this picture and it was then he came up with the new Chemo 'cure' that he was using on Carl. It seems the chemo is a two-stage process of injecting this rat poison in the patient, and then the antidote to stop the killing of cells. Hopefully it kills more cancer cells than good ones before the patient is dead. But this painting seemed to say to him there is a third phase and it was to take cells from the patients body and inject them into the serum and then back into the patient. This was Carl's hope. Doctor Good had come from a little farm town in Iowa to become the top of this cancer Mecca and this was real science at work. He was really upset when one of his lab doctors got caught painting black hair back on his rats to show a new successful cancer hope. This is done to help raise money. But that doctor went hiking that night.

We finally got to see Carl. He was better, but you could tell he was a hurting puppy. When we got up with him on his floor he was rubbing the feet of another patient who couldn't walk and never would again. This was Carl's life now, looking after other patients and giving hands on encouragement. He was their hero, the chosen one to overcome cancer for all of them. It was an amazing sight. Carl was just as amazed to see us there for him. We fed him all the love and encouragement we could in a quiet way.

Eventually we had to say goodbye and we headed for New Jersey and our respective homes. We were not on our usual high-on-life feeling. That experience at Sloan Kettering was very sobering. We had faced death out in the ravages of the Atlantic, but never had we been surrounded by hopelessness like this. I felt helpless to add anything here.

If we had only known what we had been put on earth to learn and been able to share that. But we were still on our own unknown journey toward that goal. If this makes no sense to you now, try to carry on to see where we were led from here.

Return To Reality

We had returned from Paradise. Believe me, New York and New Jersey are the ultimate cultural shock compared to life with nature. It was hard just to find a smile. I wanted to go to the marina across the Hudson River from my old apartment to see if that monkey is still running up and down the rigging to the joy of the boat people there. I just needed to see a smile. I also wanted to retrace some of my old haunts, including the apartment overlooking Manhattan on the Jersey Palisades. We had our cabbie swing by there, and I ran up to see if my old neighbor Irish John was still there. Sure enough, he was in his top floor apartment this sunny Sunday morning. He had been storing my telescope and plants as he wanted to enjoy them. He got divorced weeks after I did and was a mess. He didn't want to give me back my telescope and the plants were all dead. I took a quick look through it and focused in over at the marina. The boats were different and no monkey, no smiles. I told John goodbye and took my discouraged self back to the cab.

The first place we stopped when we got to Plainfield was Cotty's grandmother's big ole house. She had passed on at the age of 90 and now my old roommate Tom and his wife Carol were proud owners of the mansion. They invited us to stay there as they had two extra bedrooms. We could even pay rent if we wanted to stay long term. Wow, this was great. These were two of my favorite people. My parents lived just blocks away and Peter (my old skiing buddy) was just houses away. As reality set in, all sorts of people I knew were around, as this was still my hometown. There were many celebrations and even the local Courier newspaper came to the house to do a full-page article on our 'adventures'.

Within two weeks I had a job, selling cable TV door to door. It was brand new here and everyone wanted it. I had been to see my folks and they were really glad to see me. But once again all they saw was my beard and refused to let me into the house until it was shaved off. After a week or so, I was tired of it anyway, so I shaved half of it off and went to the house, rang the door bell and got a rousing welcome from my mom and invited into the living room to see dad. Then I did a 180, and there was the beard again. My mother screamed and so I got my point across and then went and shaved the rest off. I have to admit it felt much better, but it was still me with or without. I was the reality, not the beard. But not everyone can see that truth. And that is a reality too.

We had a big visit and I stayed for a cookout. The Prodigal son had arrived again and so we killed a steak. They never asked about my travels or where I was staying, I only heard about so and so, and how the market was doing and complaints about goings on at the country club and up the street. Oh well, some things never change.

I also pulled into my old insurance agency to see what it looked like. Everything was much the same with the same guys there, only they looked 40 years older and fatter and balder. What can I say, I've been in a time warp. Time goes by fast when you are having fun, so I guess I didn't age that much.

I figured I better get some health insurance now that I had a job, so I called Blue Cross and Blue Shield. I ordered the policy over the phone. They said I was covered and I could look at the policy for thirty days and pay the premium if I wanted to keep it. Before the policy arrived I thought it would be nice if I mowed Tom's lawn. His mower got clogged with grass and so I put it in neutral and started pulling the grass out of the side exit. Something was broken, and then I realized it was my right index finger was missing. Then the pain hit. I grabbed the finger end and went into the house. Carol, being a surgeons daughter, handled it well, got my hand wrapped in a towel and raised over my head, and drove me to Muhlenberg Hospital. This is the place where my parents had born me and where much money and time had been donated by my parents and all their friends. And where my surgeon, Carol's dad, worked. He wasn't around, and I waited and hour before I was seen, two hours soaking my short digit in peroxide, finally getting a shot for pain, and then a doctor did a very painful sewing job trying to put finger parts back together. I will spare the gory details, but it twernt fun. He had put a stitch right through...oh never mind. Just know I was in very severe pain for six to eight weeks, soaking and changing dressings for hours each day. This was reality at its rawest form.

After a week of suffering at Tom and Carols, Cotty came over and asked if we would like to share a house up in Essex Connecticut with him. It was too expensive just for him and his parents were renting the main house. I thought that sounded homey and a good place to recover. My Blue Cross Policy arrived that day, and I called the hospital to give them my policy number. All costs were covered. Wow. What timing. This is after no insurance for nine years.

Barb and I and Cotty drove up together and we had a great time catching up on who's where and why. We had not seen each other since St Thomas before I sailed out on Cotton Blossom to Newport and he saw Barb off on *Star Song* when she set sail for Bermuda. We sure had some great memories to look back upon.

We found out that of the old gang at Caneel Bay on St John, Bevy was still living on the 'rock.' She married some guy there and they were living happily ever after on the far deserted side of the island. Ivan, the red haired bursar, was doing some capers trying to get rich with one big drug deal. (The results later.) Of the St Thomas crowd, Brian and Cotty's sister Pam were moved north here and living on Martha's Vineyard. Cotts promised we'd go visit them when my hand got better.

Essex was where Cotts and I had gotten off the ill-fated charter sailboat we had brought down from Maine. We got off and Peter Van Ness decided to stay on and went down in a hurricane in November near Bermuda. So we had mixed memories of this neat little town on the Essex River.

A large charter boat was at the end of the small marina dock there. We found out later Frank (ole blue eyes) was hiding out on it. He used to hang out in the middle of the Hudson in front of my telescope too.

When we arrived at the house it was like old home week seeing the Barlow's. I had always liked Cotty's parents while growing up, and they were still sweet folks now. The arrangement of them having a house with us three in the adjoining guest house was very comfortable. I had a nook where I would take care of my soaking and watch TV. But the dang thing was sure taking its time healing and I was probably addicted by now to the pain pills. I wanted something stronger, and the doctor was threatening to cut off my prescription. Whoa.

One night, Cotty and I went to a doctor's grand opening of their new office. The whole town of Essex was invited, and there were 50-100 people that came by. Cotty and I were noticed dressed in doctors smocks, chasing Barb with a hypodermic and squirting water at her saying she better take her medicine. Then we were caught with someone in the stirrups, and many other such medical situations during the night.

Meanwhile we pretty well emptied the liquid refreshment stand there and on top of my codeine, I was blasted. We did notice that the doctor had two very cute nurses, and we certainly had their attention. One of them, Leslie must have thought she could save Cotty from me and himself. (She is still at it as his wife of 30 years now.) And we thought we could save them from this doctor. She won, obviously.

Barb and I started looking for some type of job situations. I still wasn't healed, but Barb's specialty was doing paste-ups and layouts for advertising. Mine was using my head for clever one-line copy. We discovered an agency of ad executives who had escaped NYC and lived in this small country setting of Essex. We went there by invitation and were asked to sit in on their morning session. Around a large round table about a dozen of us heard about different jobs to be bid on, one being the Mystic Seaquarium that was about to open. Then we found that everyone split to do their favorite thing on the property while they gave inspiration and thought a chance to evolve an ad campaign for these different jobs. Some went fishing, or horseback riding or golfing, all right there on the property. Barb and I went and sat under a tree by a babbling brook. Now this was the way to work. And these guys were getting rich doing it. We all met back at the big round table over a catered lunch of everything and reconstructed our thoughts on the different subjects over the morning. Some were outstanding and others dove tailed with others ideas. It was a very productive day. And Barb ended up doing the artwork and paste up storyboards for some of the accounts. I guess I was just there for the skills of the mind.

While Barb did her artwork, I soaked my still hurting finger and redressed the wound. I had refused to give the doctor that treated me at Muhlenberg Hospital my Blue Cross Policy number because he was such a louse. And besides, doctors had said that the stitch through my finger nail bed was quite unnecessary and of course would be very painful. So I let him sweat for a month or so as to whether I would pay him or sue him. Of course I would let Blue Cross pay him, but he would have to sweat as long as I have hurt. Then I would maybe give him my insurance number.

We had a great time up here in the New England Yankee territory. We visited old restaurants, went to the annual firemen's clambake picnic, with lobster and corn on the cob, and lots of beer. There were moments like these to make me forget the pain in my finger that seemed not to have subsided for over six weeks. So I had plenty of the beer. The medicine men had finally cut me off from all painkillers thinking I either was over the pain or I was addicted. Neither was the case. So I had a case of beer.

Cotty was good company for me through all this, but it was soon after when the influence of Leslie had my ole drinking buddy Cotts on the wagon. We had not only grown up together in High School getting smashed on the train to and from Lake Placid, New York, but at parties all the year round. Then down in the islands, of course, smashed all day long. There's a sad song there somewhere.

Before Leslie had total control, however, we four went to Martha's Vineyard for a long weekend to visit Brian and Pam, Cotty's sister. We had not seen them since sailing on Spartan down in St. Thomas. That was the yacht Brian was Captain of and that we would spend nude weekends on (excuse the hanging prepositions), anchored off some deserted island when he wasn't out chartering her. We had so many good times. And then Pam was always Cotty's little sister, who had grown all up. She was as able as any guy on a sailboat, and on land. Little was she, and little did I know how my life would depend on her one week in the future.

I was really in my element here as these people on beautiful Martha's Vineyard were also a part of the sea. Their whole lives revolved around their understanding and appreciation of the sea. During our visit with Pam and Brian we also got to see other families from the exclusive hippie hangout of Hassle Island off of St Thomas. There were sail makers here as well as yacht surveyors, both of which I have the ultimate respect. These people know more about the world than anyone I know. Doctors included. Or so it seemed at the time with my finger still bandaged after months of pain. All of our old friends were consulting each other on different designs they were secretly working on in old boat sheds. The shavings of wood and the intricate architectural designs were a sight for private eyes only. Were they building the next American Cup Yacht?? I was not that privy.

But what a pleasure to be with folks that appreciated a good sail, a meal from the sea, the smell of salt air, and the camaraderie that is only amongst us bilge bums. We ate lobster, clams, had some rum, showered outside, and many of the other pleasures of our company. We even rented some motorbikes and went the way of the tourist there, just to make sure we didn't miss anything. And it was then that we met Barbara's ex-boss, our friends Michael and Anne, who were dating when we met them in St Thomas. They were thinking of getting an apartment in Boston and wanted to know if we would be interested in sharing one. I'm easy and ready for anything, so we say let us know.

It was soon after our return to Essex that we heard from them. "You guys have got to come up an see this Bean Town. It would really be fun to experience it together." Michael had just landed a job as the Art Director at BBD&O, a large Madison Avenue advertising firm I remember from my New York days. Anne had been hired as an emergency room nurse at the famous Boston Memorial Hospital. Michael told us he could send all the artwork to Barbara at $60 dollars an hour that we needed. That didn't leave me much to do, but I was sure I could find something. I had a feeling I would be a fish out of water again. But, hey, what's to lose, ya know what I mean? (That's Jersey for those of you in Rio Linda)

We decided to tell Cotty that we were leaving the nest soon, and that made him even closer to Leslie. That was good. And we packed up our things and hitched to Boston the old fashioned way. We used our thumbs. After our first ride to the interstate we got a ride to right near the apartment by a guy that commutes daily from New York City to Boston at 120 miles per hour average. We were not in that big of a rush. But we kept a stiff upper lip and were there in the blink of an eye. He had a new fangled device called a radar detector and so he would slow down about sixty miles an hour when it started making weird noises.

When we arrived, our bodies were still moving faster than our legs. We took a cab from where he let us off to our new apartment site that was one and a half blocks away. Who's to know? We took the elevator up to the seventh floor, which was the top floor, and met Michael and Anne and the realtor in what was to become our new home: A seven-room apartment that had the roof and a view of the Charles River. I knew from experience that very soon our added view of all the rooftops with their black chimneys would be invisible. Overlookable. Not discernible. We would tune out the nastiness of living in a city and just see what we wanted to see. And so we signed the year lease and paid the enormously Harvard rich rent of over $750 per month. Well, this was going to be another culture shock, but that is exactly what I loved. And having survived New York and other big cities before, this was going to be a snap.

My traveling buddy Barbara and I hitched back to Essex after having made a commitment on this cool apartment penthouse overlooking the Charles River. Oh, I told you that already. But did I mention that the amphitheater was nearby on the banks of the river. And that Harvard and MIT were across there somewhere, and that the Prudential Building was within walking distance, as was Knob Hill, Commonwealth Avenue, sail boat rentals, and football in the park and on and on was right there? It looked like we were going to have a ball here.

Cotty was excited for us, as he was also going full circle on his culture shock since the islands and was getting very comfortable here in Essex. Especially with his folks living here now and with his new love of his life, Miss Leslie. He was ready for Barb and I to go to a new frontier, so he could more freely pursue his.

My finger was finally almost better after these six months of pain. Had God been trying to get my attention? Was this attention getter related to my six months in bed after breaking my ankle skiing, or when I had spent six months recovering from my fatal car accident while in the Army? Or related to any of the accidents incurred on the 26th of a month for seven years in a row? Will I ever know? Probably not, but the miracle remains. The search goes on almost as if the mystery of life is a piñata and I am swinging wildly while blindfolded to find the answer. If only I had been told how simple the answer really is, or had I been told, and yet I keep swinging wildly?

Occult or not to Occult

Barb and I went down to the ole Jersey warehouse where I had all my worldly possessions in storage. I had been faithfully paying storage each month so I wouldn't lose the few things I still had. I guess I didn't want to totally let go of the past and this was one of my links. We rented a U Haul and loaded couches, fridge, tables and mattresses and boxes of books along with other odds and ends. Michael and Anne were doing the same somewhere and we all met back at our apartment and it was amazing what all came together. We had about everything we needed to make our new abode the best sleeping, eating, working, partying environment ever.

This was incredible that the four of us just clicked so well after having only work experiences in St Thomas together. Michael, as art director for an ad agency in Charlotte Amalie, used to call Barbara in to do paste ups and layouts. She was very good at it as was Michael in his field. Now in Bean Town, his new position is as Art Director for BBD&O, a rather well known agency here and on Madison Avenue. And now Michael would contract out work to freelancers, and that meant all the paste up work for the whole agency could be sent to Barbara. Obviously we didn't want to be working all the time and so it was as mutually agreed on at the time whether work ($$) was desired at the time. A few hours a day kept the bill collectors away.

That left us with time to enjoy doing what people can do in Boston, everything. In the warm days we'd go sailing on the Charles River, in the fall we'd pick up a touch football game in the park, go to museums or just stroll the streets of history and see the buildings and statues that tell our country's story. In the winter we'd roll a snowball down Commonwealth Avenue until it was bigger than we were. And always we would just sit on the floor in our living room enjoying friends' conversations from all walks of life. Some of our friends were street musicians, doctors, stewardesses, nurses, old friends from sailing days and new friends we might meet in the park. And some were very heavy into the occult, but none of us except Anne recognized what they were. But she was always reserved and held much in about her Christian upbringing. She was the only one who had any knowledge of the truth amongst us. It wasn't until near the end of our one-year lease that she challenged the head occultist with some words from the Bible.

But until then we just enjoyed ourselves in many ways. Michael was a self-styled gourmet cook and would get Anne and Barb and I involved in many of his creations. And while I had had my own cooking experiences here and there already, I was probably the grunt of the gang. But I didn't mind as we all just helped each other with everything. We also enjoyed every bite from the appetizers right on through the incredible homemade desserts. And as one of us perched on the dead camel ottoman that arrived from our Moroccan shopping spree, and the rest sat on the floor in our spacious living room around a large glass topped table, we had plenty of time to share stories especially from our new guest friends.

One of Michael's guests was intriguing as I had encountered him by one of his accomplishments when skiing at Stowe the year after I broke my leg there. Remember the blind ex-ski patrol guy that I saw there? He was wearing the radar that Mike's friend invented. This friend, we called him Doc, had been blind since almost birth. But he could see better than we could. He came into our living room and by clicking his fingers and just being aware, he started asking if there was a couch over there and windows behind him and the hallway there and another room there? He didn't really have to ask, he was just being polite in describing how he 'saw' our apartment. When he went to the park with us he could click and tell us about the different trees and surroundings we weren't even aware of. Well I could go on about Doc's amazingness, but I later asked him how he dreamed if he had never seen anything. I realized our dreams are all visual. He told us his dreams were totally tactile, and so his dreams were not in color but in smell, taste, touch and hearing. Now that told me how unaware my senses had been. How intriguing. He also had his Masters degree in physiology and a Doctorate in electrical engineering, thus the 'Doc.' Much of the year he would go on a talking tour of the country, often by himself. I was truly humbled before this most humble man.

Anne was a nurse in the operating room at the famous Boston Memorial for most of the year. We met many of the doctors there as well as the nurses. Michael kept his business and home world pretty separate, and Barb and I met people from all over town that seemed to come back to our place. It wasn't long before we had a pretty steady group that made up the Dartmouth Street Players. We had more fun just carrying on with impromptu skits or stories or listening to Barbara sing her sweet songs, some from our sailing days and some she had just finished writing. But the camaraderie here was just incredible. We all became the best of friends.

And then there was the night when our friend Ivan came to B-town. This was a surprise after not hearing from him since our days in St John when he was the bursar at Caneel Bay Rockefeller Resort. We had heard rumors that Ivan was determined to make himself rich by doing one drug deal somewhere down in the Caribbean. I give you the briefest outline of his caper without guaranteeing the details.

First Ivan puts on the role of a wealthy businessman and charters a very large yacht. Then he has his yacht go to the Royal Yacht Club in Jamaica and starts talking about buying major Real Estate. So he gets the Governor and all his rich friends looking for real estate for him. They have the local police give him escorts around the island. Now that he had the white hats won over, he goes to the other side of the island and meets at night with the farmers that generate great fields of ganja. He then coordinates the two sides in an incredible climax of the two sides helping him get a monster load of ganja on board his yacht. He steams out of the harbor with both sides thinking he is going to win for them. Little did they know that ole Ivan dropped his 'treasure' off at a deserted island before his yacht had a great misfortune and sank at sea. With distress signals going out to the coast guard from his raft, he was rescued at sea. He was the object of newspaper articles from Jamaica to Newport. But being the hardy seaman he had become, he rented another smaller boat and revisited the deserted island and dug up his treasure and went to places of commerce where he traded it in for some big cash.

Now this is nothing I condone or would recommend for any reason. But we did not know all this when Ivan shows up outside our Dartmouth Street address in a stretch limousine, has the chauffer keep the engine running, and comes up and has a couple drinks etc with us, and then invites us to join him for dinner on the town. We all go on down the elevator of our deserted building and there by the cobblestone walkway is the limo he had casually mentioned. He has the driver take us on a seven stop progressive cocktail, hors d'oeurves, entrees and dessert orgy before going to a large book store and buying dozens of books for us and friends and then to other all night stores to get tuxedos and jewels and what ever. I was just happy with dinner, not being sure of the source of this wealth. The patient driver put all the goodies in his trunk and kept it all there until the next morning. The driver drove us all wherever we wanted, including to the park for our touch football game with the rest of the Dartmouth Street Players. Ivan became a Dartmouth Street Player at this point. He just loved all we were doing and decided this was to be his way of life too. But he also decided he just needed to do one more run, and then he could 'retire.' We never heard from Ivan again as long as we lived in Boston. But he stayed there for Christmas with us and we recorded a brand new version of the Night Before Christmas, where Santa had all us elves, and trucks, instead of a sleigh, which delivered toys to all those kids etc. It was very funny yet cynical, and one of the Players last skits before Jim came into the picture.

Barbara had stopped at a bar for some reason and Jim came up to her and starts telling her all about herself. She is amazed that he knows she is creative and sings and plays guitar. And as is typical with these people they feed off of what ever you say from what they have deducted. Of course she has grooves in her fingertips and it didn't take a rocket scientist to tell she probably plays guitar. Well it was this keen sense of observation that led Barb into being sucked into this guy's very strong personality and his vision to take over the earth. This was the original Pinky and the Brain combination. Barbara would play her 'cosmic' songs and he would teach her transcendental meditation.

This went on for some weeks after which Jim and his cult wanted Barb to get me into their lair. I finally went over there to his apartment, which he shared with some groupies, and did as I was told to learn to meditate. I was so good that I earned my own real honest to goodness mantra right then and there. From now on when I meditated I would have my own mantra and my own spiritual guide, and his name was, was, ahh yes, his name was Ishmael. Ole Ishmael became my guide in life, and I became very proficient at meditating and making contact with him.

I also started seeing 'miracles' again such as the ones I used to perform for my friends at Caneel Bay when I would zap people to get them to do things. But now with Ishmael on my side we could really do some incredible things together. One afternoon Barb and I were walking back from the Prudential Building where we picked up paychecks for the work Michael's office had given to her, when a very loud and obnoxious motorcycle seemed not to go away. I gave him the zap and told Ishmael he could take care of the matter. A block later we saw this guy going nuts because his bike had just quit. Barb was impressed with the powers of Ishmael and me. I was also a little impressed. What was this really all about? Had I really landed on the secrets of the universe? Was I now really in possession of powers beyond the human realm.

Well according to spiritual counseling by Jim, I was very very something or other. In other words I was so perceptive I could play a major part in saving the world. Jim, who had a full beard and looked much like artists renditions of Jesus, said that because of my sailing the seas I needed to learn how the sea could feed the world. I also had to learn how to farm at sea and create vast areas of seaweed and extract nutrients from my crops so the world would never hunger. Barbara was given her message from him that he received during his meditation from his spiritual guide. She and his groupie friend were to sing at the top of the musical range to give new vibrations to the supernatural world for them to come here to communicate with us.

Because of my mission I started to run into all sorts of other loonies that convinced me of the authenticity of this, this occult? I had a sales job where I would go from Boston south to Cape Cod, north to Newberry Port and west to Framingham to sell people music on the fantastic new cassette tapes. If they pledged to buy two tapes per week (for two years), they would also get a quadraphonic stereo system free. I sold a lot, but this was also during the oil scam when gas became a scarce commodity and went from $.39 per gallon to $1.90. Sales became an expensive occupation and made one want to sell really bad. Our sales boss even bought a whole tanker of fuel and made a deal with a gas station so we could all get gas whenever we wanted it. This was worth the job itself just to avoid the long lines for gas and the ensuing fights that were breaking out at gas stations all over the country.

One night I heard on the radio, as I traveled from town to town, a man who could make contact with many willing spirits, who had long died, but which told him that night on the radio many secrets never before told about themselves. And then this clairvoyant would confirm these mystical revelations with phone calls to descendants of Edgar Cayce and other 'willing spirits.' This was pretty convincing.

Then at my next appointment, the couple told me they were not interested in my music but did I know of a football player named Brian Piccolo? I said no, why? And they told me that they had been spiritually told to contact him and give him a message. I told them about Jim and they said to tell him to contact Brian, who had died, and give him this very important message. So, when I got home late that night I called Jim and gave him the message. He freaked and said I had to get back with these people and find out more information as they may be the missing link to some mystical puzzle. I could never find them again, but did Jim get that message to Brian whoever? The message was to 'move on, go on up. It is finished.' Now that meant nothing to me but it sure seemed important at the time.

Jim was so impressed with my progress as with Barb's, that he wanted to pay our way to take a train and have a car waiting in Greenwich, Connecticut to whisk us to a clairvoyant that would give us each a reading and even put it on cassette tape for us to have. They contacted the spiritual world and told us all about ourselves as well as who we were in three other previous lives and what our mission was to be here on this trip on earth. Wow, this is pretty heady stuff, no? I had no idea if this was all 100% BS or just 95%. But it was so convincing that we checked it out through our spiritual guides, and went to the library and looked up our previous personalities.

It turns out we were all interrelated in one or more of our previous lives. Barbara was a master musician named Frederick Chopin and I was an author named George Sands. Yikes, we changed sexes. And as we learned at the library, the two not only knew each other but they both secretly vacationed together in Valldemossa, Mallorca in the very same town Barbara and I went to when we first arrived there.

Now, no one knew about our visit to Valldemossa but us. And I remember getting a chill in an old castle like building there and so did Barb, and then we read that Chopin died there of consumption due to a chill. Consumption may have been the cause of his death, but I probably died from smoking cigars. Yet our love never died.

The clairvoyant also told me that I am a writer and that if I am not writing I need to be. How did she know? She also warned us about Jim, and that they were not sure about him. I have to admit, that this guy that looked like Jesus really had a super presence when we were around him. He seemed to always be on a higher level than any normal earthling, and he kind of made the hair on the back of my neck get all fritzy. He wanted me to grow to join him on this level he existed on so we could all be together to 'take over the world.'

I was assigned the job of feeding the world and my first task was to set up kelp farms in the oceans of the world. Barbara and Jim's groupie roommate were to communicate through beautiful high vocal vibrations conjuring visions of other worlds. Another follower was to develop laser lights to put holograms over the heads of audiences that would let them feel they were in Jim's world too. Then there was Michael and Anne. Well Jim just couldn't find a place for them in the grand scheme of things. They were just not spiritually developed yet. Maybe in their next life they will be more capable of communicating on a higher level.

All this was about to drive me wacky, but then Jim decided to put the serious make on Barbara. He already had two groupies and now he wanted Barbara Regina (Strange Queen of the Heavens) to be his also. I let it be to see where Barbara was, and I came up very disappointed. I had been loyal in every relationship I had ever had, but Barb failed me here. I had to hate Jim for taking advantage of her, but he just grinned and said I needed more growing.

And grow I did. I became more independent and aloof, to the point where I was out on the town alone, and met some really neat people. Sometimes I would just walk the few blocks through to the park to the Charles River and rent a sail boat and just sail around the waters for hours. I was longing for the open sea again. Yet Boston is such a unique town, and there is just no end of things I discovered to do. An old theater nearby opened again after being completely refurbished. The new owner showed me around and pointed out the huge pipe organ he had found buried in the walls and which he had put into perfect working order with some new technological tricks installed. Apparently the old movies before 'talkies' had the organ to be played along with the moving pictures. Well, could this be the theater of the New World Order? Jim wanted me to get all the details. I told him to shove it. My, I sure had a lot of growing to do, almost as much as Michael and Anne. They didn't buy his act at all either.

We, the Dartmouth Street Players, decided to get out of town together for a few days and refresh ourselves from his omnipresence. We drove up to the northern coastline where we meandered around the shorelines, sat under new spring leaves around Walden Pond, and just got back in touch with reality. Michael took many really neat pictures that captured the history of nature, which seems to never change. He has a keen eye for art. Maybe that is why he is the BBD&O art director. Duh!

Anne was just as sweet, but somehow she endured the grim of reality at Massachusetts General Hospital Emergency Room and Operating Rooms as a Nurse.

As we didn't have a car, she would ride her bike down and back the several miles to work, in all kinds of weather. This is all to say, she is not a wuss. So not by chance she became the head nurse for an OBGYN doctor. He is very special and would often come to our apartment and sit on the floor with us, and just chat and occasionally indulge in some fun if he didn't have to operate that night.

Some months later, he wanted us all to come to his very special open house that his wife put on annually for their special friends. We were first to arrive at their stately home in North Boston, and I had on my jalaba (*galabeyah)*, which I had picked up in Morocco. I could hear her inside panickly calling to her husband that "Someone was coming to the door and he has a dress on. Get rid of them!" Why, didn't she realize we were his very special guests of honor? And we really were an oddity that all their friends wanted to chat with and find out about this world of which they were not yet aware. They really admired the large circular medallion I had on a chain around my neck with an Egyptian Ankh in the circle. I told each of them a different story about it. Barbara sang and I think the wife went to bed early. Anne just grinned the whole evening. Doc's other three nurses were there also, so we got to meet Anne's working buddies. What fun. Too bad the Doctor's Mrs. got tired so early. Was she ill?

A few weeks later I had a call from the good Doctor asking me to come to his office. There, I was received by his three nurses I remembered from the 'party.' They all knew why I was there, but I didn't. They were almost giggling and I was thinking it was still my 'dress' that had them going. But the doctor was more interested in my helping one of his patients get pregnant. When he first told me, I said that it seemed a bit extreme to think that I would impregnate some woman I didn't even know. But then he explained that I had all the characteristics of her impotent husband and that she would be artificially inseminated if I would donate the semen. I was told to think about it and the $75 I would 'earn.'

I went home and meditated as usual and asked Ishmael whether I should do this dastardly deed. My spiritual guide said that it would be a great thing for me to do. And so I called the doctor to see if his nurses could give me a hand. The Doc intervened and said I would be an anonymous donor and that not even his nurses would know it was from me. I asked if the lady would ever know, and he assured me she would not know anything other than his assessment of me as far as physical features and mental facilities. If I was to donate I was to put the donation into a sealed bag and send it by cab to his office. Well, I rested my case and now leave the rest to your 'preverted' imagination. But, I had to do it several times over the next six months, as the donation was not received very well. I was never cloned, to my knowledge. Sorry, I tried. I just hope it wasn't the Doctor's wife we did this for.

Jim said he blocked it through his Spiritual Guide. That may be the only thing his guide did that was in my favor, as I was paid for each attempt, and now I would not have to look around for people that look like me.

As the warmer weather continued to come upon us, my longing for sailing the waters became stronger than a salmon's drive to go up stream to home. One of our Dartmouth Street guests, Douglas, who lived around the corner on Commonwealth Avenue, bought himself a small 24-foot sailboat, and he wanted me to sail with him from Boston to Cape Cod.

I was very apprehensive as we had sailed up to some northern points with him, and Douglas was not really made to be at sea. Once we arrived at the Pier restaurant he was ecstatic about sailing, and while we dined over a lobster diner, I looked out to see that there was more than a twenty foot tide and his little boat was about to be hung from the pilings. We could hardly cut her loose before she was completely out of the water. But she was saved. A few weeks later he decided if we (he and I) sailed her down to Cape Cod, he could have some more enjoyable sailing down there.

This would be a very long trip, and as he was not much help, I asked him to get another crew for the voyage. He did, had food packed and stored, and off we went. We were about an hour off shore when I realized our crew knew nothing about sailing and our owner was so seasick he wanted to give me the boat if I would just take him to shore. Any shore. I refused and he continued to chum for sharks off the stern. I really felt sorry for him but he had to get past this or he would never enjoy sailing, or the food he had bought.

We finally arrived at the entrance of the Cape Cod Canal where the charts showed that just on the inside would be calm waters. His hope only exceeded his impatience. We no sooner jammed our way into the canal and we looked astern and there was a gigantic tanker steaming into the canal at about seven times our speed. The channel was hardly wide enough for the tanker let alone both of us. I set sail as trim as I could for maximum headway and we were just at the opening of the far end of the canal when the giant's bow wake lifted us up and over the sunken rocks that we saw on the charts that could have wrecked us if we cut the corner. We made it with some kind of 'luck'. Was it from our guides? Somehow I didn't think so.

But the serenity of the waters inside there let us enjoy the final miles of our trek. Douglas actually did some sailing. It was a joyous sight that made it all worthwhile. Doug had arranged dock space in a very quiet cove, which was tree lined and had a cute walking bridge over a stream.

I later found out that this is my mom's parents' stomping grounds. Her grandfather was a preacher in Falmouth on Cape Cod, and would travel by horseback to three different churches every Sunday doing the Lord's work. And my grandmother was the social hostess at an old hotel here in Falmouth Heights for decades after his death. So I had reason to feel like the proverbial salmon, which had swum upstream back to its homeport of origin.

Weeks later, through the grapevine, I got a call from a doctor that had a sailboat at a marina down near Falmouth on Cape Cod. He was looking for someone to live on board and have his yacht ship-shape and ready to sail when he could get loose from the hospital duties. I told him that I was the man. Now you may think that with all my experience sailing that I knew everything I needed to know to pull this job off. But I am here to tell you that most of the boat 'people' knew ten times more than I did. But when I said I was his man, he hired me. Now this meant I would have to leave the Dartmouth Street Nest and pack my duds and get a car and drive down there to this isolated marina where nothing ever happened.

Get a car! I would just have to scrape enough money together to get a junker and fill it up with gas that cost more than gold. I headed out of town toward Salem to try to get a lower deal than big city prices. I finally found the ultimate used car dealer who had an old rusted out station wagon. Perfect. Three hundred dollars later I was on my way back toward Dartmouth Street past the House of Seven Gables in Salem where there were a dozen witches on the porch. Spooky.

I really wondered if the old crate would make it, but it did. It may have loosened a few cobblestones as it wobbled down the roads, but other than using up almost all the gas I put in it, success!

The next morning I went out and noticed the 'woody' was leaning awkwardly on three flat tires. After I got them fixed with a borrowed pump and some patches, I was ready to head down to Falmouth, my duds and a day's snacks packed in my duffle. I made it to the Boston

Freeway southbound just before rush hour early in the am. Not many were heading my way, they were all heading into the city to go to their 9 to 5 jobs. I went to celebrate my good fortune with a snack the girls had made for me to take. Reaching back into the rear of the wagon, I suddenly realized my snacks and duds were all sitting on the cobblestones outside the apartment baking in the sun because I had forgotten to load them again after fixing the tires. I said, 'Darn', and got off at the next exit to do a U-turn. Unfortunately it was at one of those exits with overpasses and you know what else, I'm sure.

Finally I get back on the freeway with the rush hour traffic and in the stop and go I notice the car is overheating. Then a motorist pulls up to me and gets my attention to tell me that my car is on fire. OH no! I get out and look under the car and it is just dripping fire all over the pavement. My whole engine is on fire! I run back to a truck two cars behind me while noticing traffic backed up for miles to get around me. I asked if he had a fire extinguisher and he said yep as he jumped out of his truck and ran up to my bar-b-q car. He popped the hood and gave everything a big spray. After it was out it looked very grim with wires melted and black char everywhere. He asked if he could push me to the next exit, and I said no, it would start one more time. He said, "No way." I got in and after a short prayer to no one in particular other than maybe Ishmael, I turned the key and it started better than ever. The trucker was dumbfounded and after thanking him I was able to drive the 1/4 mile to the next exit and then it died as I coasted down the ramp to a street just at the bottom where I parked, took off the license plate and started walking toward the big city some ten miles away.

I couldn't help thinking a miracle had just happened and it was for a reason. I just had to find out what it was. I came upon a subway station and had just enough change to get up to Commonwealth Avenue near home. I walked the few blocks to our penthouse and saw my duffle bag there where I had parked just hours earlier. Cussing and moaning about my misfortune and that I couldn't get to my boat job, I went up to the apartment to eat my humble pie. But instead I was fed the typical gourmet meal that Barbara and Michael always seemed to produce. We were all happy to be together again, and we celebrated for the rest of the night.

The next day arrangements were made for Douglas to drive me down to 'my boat,' as he wanted to go see his little sailboat and maybe do some sailing as well. We had a neat trip and finally found the marina where the *Jacqueline_* was docked. I couldn't believe the coincidence that I was to be living with a Jacqueline again for the third time. I just hoped this time would be better, or was I still to learn another lesson? Doug helped me get settled and did a grocery stock up before leaving me there alone with no wheels. The first night I cooked a steak out over the stern on the charcoal grill. Then I bundled up against the evening cold and was thankful for the little coal heater the owners had on board. I kind of had nightmares that night about dying, but I lived to realize the coal fumes were just about to really kill me. I managed to open the hatch and get a breath of fresh air before it was too late. Never knew that coal was so dangerous.

I spent a few days getting the rigging set and de-winterizing her before the owner came down for a shakedown cruise. I was looking forward to that as they had sounded neat over the phone and it would be great to finally get back out to sea in a 'real sailboat' with real people. But they were also going to bring down my paycheck, and that is the part that hurt the most, as I was really quite broke. Especially since they had cancelled their arrival twice, and so it was at least ten days before they finally arrived.

Somehow, I had a mysterious visitor during this downtime. Her name was Naomi, and she finally admitted that Jim had sent her to service me any way I needed. She wore a turban and was a young Jewish American girl that must have been Jim's other groupie. She was as far out as he, and read my aura with great perception. She could actually see the colors emanating from me. She was surprised I couldn't see her aura as Jim said it was really strong. I thought I was really going to get away from all this phony baloney, but I was grappling with it again. I played the game as long as she wanted, and then she finally realized I was not as serious as Jim about 'taking over the world.'

She finally left and I was again without the use of a car and gratefully alone. A dock man was at the marina and we became buddies. He knew just about everything about boats that I didn't. It was a pleasure to pick his brains and put my new info immediately to practical use. And he enjoyed my 'home' cooking that I would put together for lunch, and a cold one after work before he went home. We ran tests on the rigging and on the motor and checked the bilge for problems, pulled out the sails and checked them for rips or tears. He even went under the hull in his wet suit and scraped the barnacles while checking the rudder and keel.

When the doctors finally arrived I knew my stuff. They were impressed with all that I had done. Every time they asked about some concern of theirs, I had already checked it out and corrected any problems. Boy, was I smart._

So out of the harbor we putt putted with the kicker just a humming. Once clear of traffic around the docks, we decided to hoist the sails. They flew up the mast as I cranked the winch on the main mast, but then when I locked the winch and let go of the winch handle, the brake didn't work and the handle spun around with so much force that when it hit me in the head it threw me from the starboard to port side of the boat. Fortunately, I didn't go overboard. They knew the brake didn't work and were very sorry for forgetting to tell me. But being doctors, they made me lay in the shade and just relax and enjoy the sail. They waited on me as if I was the owner. I guess the blood scared them. We all enjoyed finally getting back to sailing that day, and they gave me the back pay and left me a car to get supplies for them for the next cruise in a week or two. I was now ready to enjoy this job.

It was about week later that they gave me a call and said that they would be coming down for a weeks cruise, but that they had decided they no longer needed my services. I could use their car to return to Boston and they would pick it up. I found out later one of their sons wanted to live on board, now that all the work had been done. I wrote it off to 'experience'. An experience I seemed to have encountered before with another Jacqueline?

It was great to be back home with Barb, Michael and Anne, sleeping in my cozy mattress on the floor, and having gourmet meals around our glass coffee table while having fun. Many of our friends came over for my homecoming and one was especially glad to see me home. She was also a very attractive nurse with flaming red hair and I will never forget her, because I said no. She couldn't believe it, and neither could I. But I think we each will remember that night back at her apartment because of it. We called radio stations and had tunes played for us to dance to, romped all over her apartment, and yet I said no. Jennifer, I'll never forget you.

Our lease was going to be ending soon and we were going to have to make decisions as to what we would do next. Anne was thinking of moving to California, Michael was proposing to her to stay and marry him. Barbara was still confused by Jim, and I was ready to go back to Florida and do some sailing. Barb couldn't decide whether to stay and become the third groupie, or go with me for the fun of it to see what life would deal us next. I told her to make the decision, occult or not to occult, that is the question. But I was getting out of Dodge.

Jim and his weird dreams had caused me enough grief. He was at our apartment for a going away lunch, before our big going away dinner party. Anne asked him what he thought of Jesus. He admitted Jesus was real, but just a prophet and maybe one of the best. Anne asked if Jesus was God? "No" he reiterated "he was a man, a prophet." All I could do was listen to my inner self and know that he gave me the willies, made my skin crawl and my rage engage. It was all I could do to do nothing to him. I just figured he would do himself in someday, so why bother. I was relieved at our going away party that I would never see him again and that I was ready to move on. Michael and Anne would be missed and Barb too. But she did decide to go with me. All Dartmouth Street Players were here for our grand finale and we did it up big time. We had all our favorite people, foods, wines and songs. It was awesome.

Shortly after, as autumn appeared around the corner, I arranged a car delivery to Fort Lauderdale. Barb and I had done two or three of these already to travel up and down the east coast. I put all my furniture I had accumulated, mostly antiques from my parents. They were going to trash it when they moved from their home in Plainfield to retire permanently down at the smaller Jersey shore home.

I found a warehouse that was quite friendly, clean and convenient. I packed a Hertz truck to the hilt and they put it into a huge crate and filed it away. I would have to pay the storage fee every month as I had been doing before Boston: paying from Florida, St John, St Thomas and Spain and wherever. My price for freedom is a whole lot cheaper than rent, phone, electric, insurance etc. Of course if I stopped payments, I would lose everything.

The end of our lease arrived and Anne had decided to fly out to California to a new life on her own. Michael was devastated and decided to buy a place out on the North Shore and commute to the city. This was a real bait job to keep Anne here with him, which didn't work either, at least not yet. But for now, the four of us hugged and Barb and I in our 'new car' headed south leaving our cult behind.

Just a Bilge Bum

I didn't realize it, but Barb was thinking that I was not serious enough about us as an item to even mention marriage. I thought that we were friends, and that would not survive being married. We only survived together as a non-entity. We were best of friends, so why wreck a good thing. Barbara had read this in me without ever bringing it up for conversation. But I believed she would have said, "Yes" had I popped the question. These were days when that is not a popular choice.

I hadn't realized that our friend Jose Baumann[25] up at the NYC Sloan Kettering Hospital had told Barbara that she ought to leave me, because after all we had been through, if I had not 'popped the question' I was not serious. No one asked me, and as far as I was concerned, all was just fine. I didn't want to sweat the 'small stuff'.

Before we turned in our 'old car' in Miami to it's expectant owner for whom we anonymously delivered it, we drove down Arthur Godfrey Blvd to see if we could find our old encounter group friends, Mickey and Susan at their plant boutique, "Living Things for Loving People." And there they were, and so glad to see us. We loved their creative shop, and so did their clientele. While Susan planted exotic plants in hand made pottery, she told us about our friend Carl Baumann and how he finally died at Sloan Kettering, not due to the cancer or chemo, but due to a hospital infection. Whew, I always thought that it was more dangerous at the hospital without cancer than at home with it. Mickey had tried to talk Carl out of becoming a medical guinea pig and stay home with his family and die with dignity. Carl, being a doctor, was an easy catch for the cancer experimenters. And so goes another friend. I am trying to sound callous, but it never helps. Mickey and Susan said Jose was still at the old house and that she would love to see us, so we went there to try and comfort her.

---

[25] Another Baumann was to become a name in my future again. I knew so little.

275

Jose, being still strong, and ready for some company and recollections of Carl, she begged us to stay with her and her children until we got settled. It was very strange to just move into the lifestyle and home that Carl had created for himself and his family. He had shared much of it while he was with us: his music, his food and his fun. But now we were enjoying it with him not here. Is it fair? Or was he in a better place and wanted us here to look after Josie for a while. We had to believe the latter.

I didn't realize it, but Jose and Barbara had another tete-tete about our relationship. She suggested that Barbara might want to leave me in order to either instigate my being aggressive and making a proposal to marry, or get on with her life. I did feel all was well as was, and Barbara has always been free to go whenever she wanted. I had not forgotten the disloyalty I had experienced in my first marriage by Jackie, and I was not ready for any commitments at this time. Being totally unaware of this situation, I began to look for a place for us to live.

A neat couple had just purchased a choice corner lot with two of Florida's typical motel-looking efficiencies. It was on SE 13th Street in Fort Lauderdale. We decided it was perfect and took leave of Josie and children with hugs and tears. We got a ride up to Fort Lauderdale and moved into our new digs. It was beautiful to us. Upon exiting our apartment, if you went straight after leaving the front door, you would have five steps before dropping into a kidney shaped pool. Almost overhanging the far side of the pool were an orange and a grapefruit tree. It became my morning ritual to stumble out of bed and into the pool, pluck the fruits of the day, and while floating alone, enjoy them. Then I would prep a breakfast for us in our kitchen. I thought all was well, when Barb said she was going to go to Washington State to see her ex-husband. I had never even given my ex a thought let alone hers. She never mentioned him. But I was not one to hold people back from what they felt they had to do. Who was I to interfere with 'destiny'?

I didn't realize how hard this was for Barbara, but Mrs. Jose Baumann's advice was what influenced our demise. Or was it really destiny? We had barely lived in our new home before I was taking Barbara to the airport to fly her across to the other side of the country.

We were leaving so much behind, but neither of us thought it was the end of an incredible friendship. We would write to each other and other promises. We didn't know much about prayer. We hugged at the airport and a million memories welled up in me. All I could say was, "See ya later, Boo".

My long tear streaked drive back to my apartment reminded me of my goodbyes with others: such as my exit from Las Vegas when I had to leave my lovely Jackie, and when I left New York after my last goodbye after ten years with my friend and wife Jacqueline, my internationally renowned model wife. And then Sherry, after many summers together on the Jersey shore and our cruising south on *Jill's Mermaid*. But Barb and I had shared more in a few years than most friends have experienced together in a lifetime. The tears were just as real each time. Is life just a bowl of tears? I knew better, but it still hurt. It hurt a lot.

After a good afternoons nap, I walked down the 17th street causeway to the Marina del Rey across from the luxurious Pier 66. The marina was dockside for some incredible yachts, but usually not the 100+ footers that seemed to hang all around the Pier 66 docks on the east side of the Intracoastal Waterway. I preferred the more casual business of yachting on the west side of the Intracoastal Waterway than the formal Yachting of starched uniforms on the crews of the super yachts.

And there at the marina watering hole I saw many old friends that proved to me that we do live on a small planet. Now living down here in Fort Lauderdale I found Cotty's sister Pam and her main man, Brian. Do you remember them from when he was captain on *Spartan* down in St Thomas. They knew Barb and I as one for a long time, even up in Martha's Vineyard when we visited them from Essex. Was I ever glad to see them. They invited me over to their apartment for a dinner party that night and I met many new and old friends. It was great to be free and to see. Several of the bilge bums I hadn't seen since St Thomas, and some were to become very close friends. I was even within staggering range of home. It had been a long day, both bad and good, but definitely long. Pam had mentioned that she may have a job on a cruising yacht for some maintenance and maybe she could get me on also. I needed the work, and the money. As it turned out, we got that job and several others on which she actually taught me a bunch.

I had known Pam since she was Cotty's little sister and maybe ten years old. We had a common reality of our past,[26] and now our present. But there was never anything but a brother sister type of relationship. It was just amazing how many times our paths crossed. She was also of the same era as Bevy, my temporary love in St John. We all had grown up together in New Jersey. Now the party was here in Florida. Pam and Brian, her POME boyfriend and a great boat captain, were an item as much as peanut butter and jelly. We had often played tennis together, when not working on a boat, at Chris Everett's dad's tennis courts. We were really quite good and had some fantastic matches, but fortunately Chris never offered to play with us. We did see her socially sometimes, and out for dinner at Chuck's Steak House on the 17th Street Causeway. But poor Chris had to live the life of fame surrounded by bodyguards whenever she went out in public. The price she paid for being the best women's player in the world.

Speaking of social life, our world of boat people had the best. We partied on a different yacht at least twice a week. We would just take it over as the owners were out of town. We were like the spoiled kids that party at their parents' house when they are away on vacation. But we were much smarter now and either had permission or covered our tracks. With this way of unwinding after a hard day or weeks work, we have some close friends we would see often. And of course there are always a new bevy of very pretty girls that would have sailed into the harbor as well.

One of the girls, a German beauty named Ingrid, was between jobs when I first met her. We would gab it up when ever we got to see each other. I finally heard that she had landed a job on a certain formal yacht across the Intracoastal at Pier 66 that usually took out the Hollywood type. I was standing on the dock when I spotted her on board the fancy ship, which was waiting for the Causeway Bridge to

---

[26] Cotty and Pam were neighbors to Peter Lynch, my street football team mate who quarterbacked the Denver Broncos to many a win.

open and let it escape to the open seas. I called to her, but she ducked below. I yelled again to the guest, "Sammy, get Ingrid." He finally caught on and retrieved her. We waved and I blew her a kiss. The guest asked her who is that? and she replied, "Oh, just a boat nig...I mean just a bilge bum friend of mine that works on boats."

She told me all this later, and we had a good laugh as the guest was Sammy Davis Jr. She also told me how she got off the boat at their first port of call. Ingrid had been exposed to the vilest actions on board. The Hollywood bunch had drugs of all kinds just laying around. Lines of Cocaine lay ready and waiting on the salon tables. Porn movies were constantly running. Booze constantly and sex everywhere. It was one of their wives that had her dike girl friends making it where ever and with whomever. Ingrid, as a cook, wanted to poison the food to put them all out of their misery, but decided getting off without pay and hitching a ride back to Fort Lauderdale instead. I told her that I had seen Sammy and the Rat Pack in action back in Las Vegas years ago. They were all pretty rancid then too. It is 'National Icons' like these whom the media idolizes which makes one lose faith in the human race. People like Ingrid however, made one proud to be just a 'bilge bum'.

Sometimes I would wonder, was all this grunt work worth the price of the freedom I've had from the rut of commuting to Wall Street and selling stocks, or to Newark and selling insurance, or to Plainfield selling cable TV subscriptions? Sometimes I would be down in the hold, the bowls of the Yacht *America*, chipping away at rust with a hammer to the tune of six other 'bilge bums' doing the same thing, and then the smell of acid being painted on every spot of metal, and the fumes from acetylene torches cutting through the hull. This could have been considered hell for most folks, but to me it was all worth the price. I wouldn't trade places with anyone. I considered it a privilege just to be working on such a yacht, and also to be associated with Captain Peter from England and his wife, George, as she would qualify as the best cook on the seas, next to Barbara of course. After slaving away we would all mount up in the yacht's vans and head for the skipper's house and George would have a major dinner and beer awaiting us. We had many good times together and I respected every one of my crewmates. I sometimes wondered, chipping away in the hold, why anyone doing menial work who came from Africa, Mexico or wherever would not consider what ever they were doing a privilege just to be in America instead of as a slave to some tribe back on the dark continent. That is why people from all over the world want to come to America, to be free and have a chance to *be* themselves, *do* what they are, and *have* so much. Even if it is little one has, it is so much compared to what was. I was touched that Ingrid[27] would consider me a fellow bilge bum. But Sammy D would not understand that now, would he.

---

[27] Remember my model friend Ingrid in New York.. The Jackies, and Ingrids and Franks and Peters and Barbaras seem to be swirling around my life line as it spirals ever upward and onward.

Almost Heaven

One typically sunny Fort Lauderdale day I was walking the docks around the marina when I saw a familiar looking guy bringing up the teak on the deck of a sailboat. As a lark I said, "Hey, y'all want to go sailing?" And this unmistakable smile turned around and yelled, "Peter! I was just thinking about you!" Sure enough it was Frank, who I hadn't seen since I had left him in Grenada. We had a great old reunion, but Frank had changed. He no longer had his beard and long hair, but was slim and trim. He told me he was going to school. "Naugh", I said. "What for? You already have your Captain's license."

He told me the story of how he and his old buddy that he used to sail and smoke with, had sold their sailboat and that his old car had taken him down this road toward the beach in Hollywood toward a very pretty hotel. "Well" he said to himself, "What ever you want Lord". The hotel it turned out, had been given to the Lord by the previous owners and was now a fully accredited Bible College. Frank had no money, but he talked with some people there and before he could say 'ready about' he was offered an almost full scholarship. He was doing some bilge bum work to pay his way through. He said school was really hard, not exactly what he had been used to. But he told me the Lord is seeing him through. I said "Sure Frank, sure. Just like the Lord used to bring you flying fish onboard during your watches, right?"

"Sort of,' he said. "Come on down with me and see. My room's not fancy, but you may just want to go to school too." "No way," I promised him. But I did promise to come visit him. He still had something, and I wanted to know what it was.

I thought about visiting him at a 'Bible College' and it filled me with some kind of fear. I was just not excited about that anymore than going to some church. But I had been through so much that only a God could have brought me through, that I was curious. But what was really stopping me? Was it pride? I hoped not, after all, I had come from being Wall Street management meat with all the trimmings to a bilge bum with nothing. Where did I have pride. But I did. I had my dignity within me even if it didn't show to the outside world. I was still me inside, what ever I was. And I had pride. Because I also didn't want to become some namby pamby wishy washy holier than God good guy either. But Frank wasn't like that at all. He did have something, and I was curious enough to finally accept an invitation to let him pick me up and take me the 15 miles south for a Sunday service at the Florida Bible College.

When Frank arrived he had some friends in the car, other students and they all seemed cool. Not wanting to be out of the religious conversation I offered a joke about Jesus and Mary. It was not too well received and I wanted to crawl under the car seat. But they just changed the subject and we chatted about sailing or some such thing.

When we got to the college I was really impressed. It was right on the ocean with a broad boardwalk running up and down the beach. His room wasn't fancy as he said, but there was a spirit here I had never felt before. Everyone was smiling from within, not just on the surface. A peace and joy that I had been searching for was surrounding me, but I knew it was not within me. I felt very inadequate and rather detached from all the wonderfulness. Of course I didn't let on and carried on a cool and guarded conversation with his friends. My eyes would keep checking out people as we chatted in the 'hotel's' lobby. The girls and women all had a different demeanor than I had ever experienced. Not only was everyone smiling, but also they were glowing and just beautiful somehow. Of course I started thinking how lucky Frank was to be surrounded by so many sharp girls, but I still didn't want to go back to school.

It was finally time to head to the auditorium for church. I felt as if an anchor was sitting on my chest. I carried it in front of me into this huge converted ballroom where there were barely two seats available together. I told Frank that I could wait in the car, but then a guy got up and offered us two seats. People were looking at me as if they could see my anchor, smiled and nodded and just seemed to relate to my situation. I had never, in all my church days experienced anything like this service. It was not boring, but exciting. It was not ritualistic, but spontaneous. It was not drudgery, but joy. It was not fear, but praise and worship of a loving God, and His Son and the Holy Spirit.

It was a personal relationship they each had with God, not with some mediating priest or human leader. I listened to words that rang of truth within me, and to hymns that rang my bells when I sang them. But not to fear, I kept cool.

After the service, Frank, Andy and a guy from India went out on the boardwalk and just strolled, and stopped to look at the ocean rolling in. Frank said they do baptisms right there in the surf. I told him I had already been baptized. Then an older guy pulled up to us on his bicycle, and Andy asked him what he thought about eternal life? He looked of Jewish decent and he just got back on his bike and drove away. Fifteen minutes later he came cruising by and pulled up to us and said he had been thinking about what Andy asked, and that he would like to talk about it. [28] Andy went down the boardwalk sharing the Good News with him.

Frank took me home and left me some tracts and he gave me a Bible in which he signed it over to me from him, with a prayer inside. That Sunday afternoon I sat around the little pool in front of my room and some of the other neighbors were there too. One of them was my next-door neighbor who I had never met. She was a cute young blonde named Debbie. She saw the tracts on the table and asked if she could read them. I said, "Sure, if you want. I got them at the Florida Bible College this morning." She was very impressed. She was very sweet and conversive and she really liked the tracts. She told me she had accepted the Lord just a year ago. That was cool. I didn't know what exactly that meant, but she was surely on higher ground. I think she may have had a very rough life and that is why she 'accepted the Lord.'

I was feeling some very strange pulling on my strings. Some of the tunes were saying that I am on the verge of something wonderful, and other tunes were singing forget all that nonsense before I lose all the fun in my life. I had been just enjoying the bar scene until recently when I was out at a bar with Frank's old sailing partner, Richard. He still had his long black hair and beard, and being Jewish he had some real overcoming to do too. He was cynical when he was sober, but when he had a few drinks you would think he was not only drunk, but

---

[28] Andy not only led him to the Lord, but has a wonderful prison Ministry in New York to this day.

that he was trying to get himself killed along with anyone else around him. This night we went to a bar of his choice. It was a big nothing except for a pool table. We played as partners against some ok guys when all of a sudden Richard wanted to fight them both. Then he breaks his pool cue and threatens to stab them. It was as ugly as the Devil could make him, but this was life around Richard. I was 'lucky' to have escaped some serious injury this night. How did Frank ever survive years of sailing the oceans alone with this guy. But it was influences like this that was making me take a look at myself and wonder. I had been hitting the nightlife looking for 'trouble' and I was finding it. But something seemed to protect me ever since my first 'accident' when I was 15. Or was it since I was born?

I was protected growing up, and into high school with the fast life of drinking and smoking cigs and even driving illegally. I had survived having an ever-worsening accident every year for 7 years in a row on the same date. Why? I had heard of Grace at the Bible College, but does Grace have anything to do with me?

I was actually ashamed of my life so far. But I covered it up real well with the happy go lucky persona and by not even thinking about all the unspeakable stupid actions of a mislead kid. Sure, I had been to church every Christmas time and even Easter. My parents even dropped me off at church for Sunday school and then Scouts on Tuesday nights. I knew my manners and proper etiquette, but I also went along with the flow of friends and society. I was going down stream fast.

Frank stopped by my apartment to see if I wanted to visit FBC this Sunday again. I really didn't, and I really did. I flipped a coin and it said no. So being a contrarian, I went! I was greeted by many guys and girls I had just seen here before as an old friend. And they were just nice and sincere about it. I felt no put ons here at all. I found out that the headmaster, or president of the college, who gave the sermon as well, was an ex-highway patrolman when he 'came to the Lord.' Everyone was so down to earth real that it was truly refreshing. The sermon that day was about an extraordinary gift that is offered to us, and that it is up to us to accept or reject that gift. If we accepted the gift we were guaranteed it could never be taken away from us. We were guaranteed we would live forever in peace and love and in harmony with God. These were my kind of words. He had me listening.

If we rejected the gift we would continue living separated from all of the blessings in that gift including being forgiven of all our past, present and future sins, things that God could not tolerate, for He Is perfect and without stain or blemish. If we rejected the gift we would continue on our downward spiral toward destruction and a permanent state of agony forever. Whoa, I had never thought of it in these ways before. Sure sounded like I was on the wrong road, but this is the first time I had actually been offered the gift, known what it was and what it would do. Now it was up to me to accept the gift. The preacher asked that anyone who had not already accepted this Gift and would like to have this gift, to come on forward now and they would show us how we could know for sure that we would have eternal life with Jesus Christ, be relieved of the burden of any and all our sins forever, and be in fellowship with Him now and forever. "God loves you," he said, "He always has and always will."

Then a little voice kept me in my chair and said, 'See, He has always loved you, so why do I want to change anything now. You better just stay in that chair and not get involved in something you know nothing about.' My heart was pounding and I felt as if my body and mind and soul were being tugged apart. Then I started feeling self-conscious and that everyone was looking at me. I started coughing and got up and slipped out the door to the hallway and into the men's room. Wow, that was close. I almost had to make a decision. Now I have time to think about it. If God loves me He will give me a little more time.

Frank came out to see if I was ok. I told him that the water fountain took care of it. I don't know what happened. Frank said, "No problem, it's ok, don't worry about it. God has a very special time for you and He has been very patient with us before, so He will surely be patient with us now." I told Frank about the tearing at my heart in there, and he explained "There must be a war between the spirit of God and the spirit of the devil going on in there." He said it smiling, and yet I knew he was telling the truth.

I asked a lot of stupid questions as Andy, Frank and a guy from India drove me home. I told them of the 'miracles' that seemed to happen when I was meditating and conversing with my spiritual guide Ishmael. The Indian explained that if someone has enough faith in a garbage can, one could perform miracles. But he still does not have eternal life! Only by being washed clear and clean by believing on the cleansing blood of Jesus, and accepting that Gift from God, His Son's sacrifice for us, do we have eternal life. And the blessings begin immediately, for as soon as we admitted we needed and accepted the Gift, and gave our lives to Jesus, the Comforter or Holy Spirit comes into every believer. So that is what the song means: "And He walks with us and He talks with us". It is the Holy Spirit within us, the one third of the Trinity of God. So Jesus and God the Father know everything about me. How embarrassing!

But, the Indian explained how by accepting the Gift, the slate is wiped clean, erased and poof, gone. How could that be? He admitted there was some great supernatural miracle here, but God said it, we believe it and that's it, period! "For by Grace you have been saved through faith, and that not of yourselves, it is the gift of God, not of works lest anyone should boast." I could tell he was quoting the Bible so I asked him where it says that. Every religion I had experienced taught that to get to heaven you had to be good, and to be good you had to do this and that. And the other thing too. Frank verified that that is the Gospel truth; we can't earn our salvation, as it is a free Gift accepted by faith alone in God's Word. And in the beginning was the Word, which was and is Jesus. Frank opened his Bible, which he keeps with him like a cowboy carries a six-shooter. He opened in the New Testament to Ephesians Chapter 2, versus 8 and 9. Sure enough that's what it says. And they also said that the Bible is the inerrant word of God. "What did that mean?" I queried. There are no conflicts, just truth. God cannot lie or make mistakes. Wow, I thought, finally someone I can trust all the time?

Pieces of the truth were starting to fit together and make incredible sense. I wasn't ready to jump into the ocean to get baptized or anything, but I was quietly anxious to learn more. I wrote and told Barbara about it all. She's out in Washington State romancing her ex-husband, an artist named Sam. She was very interested as well, and she was really glad that our sailing mate Frank was back in our lives. She also wrote to tell me that Sam lived on a

40-acre ranch and had his own cottage to live and work in. He was doing five-foot square canvasses with oil paints. She said he was really good, but was not interested in her moving in with him. She could stay there, but in the big house. So she wished I was there. She described how beautiful it was there in Maple Falls, and that a Mount Baker was so incredible when you could see it on a non rainy day. The peak looked like a woman's breast with a white glacier topping all year. She went on and on about the fields of flowers, and the ferns growing in the virgin forests. She made it sound really neat, almost like Heaven, and I hoped I could see it some day.

Trashman's Trash

But then Pam came over to my place and asked if I wanted to do a delivery with her and her neighbor Bob. I said sure, what, when and where? She explained it was a 40-foot Hinckley designed yawl and we would leave in three days and we would fly to Houston and sail her across the Gulf of Mexico to Marathon in the Florida Keys. Now this sounded really good, and the pay was very attractive to my broke status as well. So with that much thought I signed on. Lil Debbie said she would pray for me, as did Frank when I told him about my new great fortune. He told me that a Hinckley is a top of the line sailboat with all the latest gadgets on a classic shaped wooden hull.

Pam, Bob, & I were invited to several parties before our departure. Usually there is no big deal, but for some reason, this one seemed special. Then we flew to Texas and were met by the owner at the airport. He sported a black beard like Frank used to have, and he was very humble. Later I found out that he was one of the rich of Houston and owned the contracts for the entire garbage pick up in the city. I discovered all that when I saw that the boat was named *Trashman*. Usually yachts are named after women, not trash men. But she was the best looking *Trashman* I ever saw. Hunter green hull and perfect teak deck, new sails and all the amenities. She even had a centerboard, which is raised and lowered with an electric button so we could adjust it depending how much wind we had and how shallow it might be out there.

We spent a few days shopping in the rain and eating at all the western restaurants, all paid for by the *Trashman*. We were living high on the steer. I even charged a carton of Pall Mall cigs on the account to get me through the 5 days it would take us to make the crossing. They say if you don't like the weather here in Houston, wait a couple hours as it can change that fast. And so it did.

Instead of the rain we had for days, the day of our sailing was beautiful. We still didn't get out of the harbor until just a few hours before nightfall. I did notice that the horizon out in the gulf looked like a mountain range as the sun set over our right shoulder. We had a perfect night of sailing and getting used to how she felt under sail. There were a few problems getting some of the fancy gear to work, but we could figure that out tomorrow in the daylight. We set up watches so each of us would have four hours on and eight hours off. I picked the short straw and got the twelve to four watches. Not my favorite, but for just a few days it shouldn't matter. I stayed awake after my first watch with Pam to get her started.

She also noticed that the Gulf seemed to give our ship a different rock and roll than the ocean. The waves must have been mixed or shorter together, for the ride was noticeably strange. I brewed some coffee for us, and put some brandy in mine so I would get some sleep. But I wanted to enjoy the sunrise in just another hour.

As dawn broke I could see that the sea was a bit choppy and waves seemed to be coming from different directions. The horizon still looked like mountains, and then we saw the most beautiful clear sunrise. The sun looked like a harvest moon except it was red. Red!? What does the sailor's bible say about red sun in the morning, sailors take warning? Aww, couldn't be, it was too clear and pretty out here.

But like they said in Houston, if you wait a few hours the weather will change, and as noon approached I was awakened with shouts and wind and clouds and rain screaming sideways across our decks. We all worked to reef down the sails in case we were in for a really bad blow. And then as quick as a tornado, we were into a super storm. We had reached the mountain range at the Gulf's horizon and all hell was breaking loose. It became dark as night and even with the sails reefed we were healing way over. Bob went below to make sure the centerboard was all the way down when lightning hit something and all our electric was gone. Nothing worked on this boat from hell. There was no manual override for anything except for the sails and the helm. Thank God it didn't have power steering. Or did it, as it was very difficult to steer too. And we couldn't even tell if the centerboard was up or down or half way. We had just assumed it was in sailing order. So we reefed again so our main sail was the smallest it could be without taking it down completely.

Now we also have no engine, which means no radio, no refrigeration, and no water. Fortunately we had bought some bottled water, beer and sodas. The stove was alcohol, so we could cook, but not in these seas. We took a quick assessment of what foods we had that didn't need cooking. Then we rationed out loud what our plan was for food and water. We had to shout at each other to hear ourselves over the wind. The wind direction had changed and instead of a nice reach to our destination in Marathon, we would have to be beating right into the wind on a close tack. That meant a very close watch on the compass so we wouldn't lose our momentum and get caught standing still luffing into the wind. Otherwise if a wave or gust came, that could knock us down in a heartbeat if the centerboard isn't making headway in the water under us. That is if we have a centerboard down. We could not tell where it was, nor could we change that.

The seas were definitely building, and this was not just a passing storm. We were into something big. These days there were no satellites giving us weather reports and aerial maps. But even if we had that, with no electric, no weather reports. There was not even battery power to run a radio. We were no better off than Christopher Columbus, or the Vikings for that matter. But we had a blind confidence that we would be fine.

I had a hard time getting even a cigarette lit. If I was so lucky, it would be soaked and out within two waves. Pam said I should quit. What an idle thought. Here was a sea that could kill us and she is thinking I should quit smoking, my main purpose in life. No way.

The seas were so high that we came upon a freighter just abeam of us and less than a half mile away. We only saw it once as we both happened to be on top of waves at the same time. By the middle of the third day we were wet and cold and hungry. We had been doubling up on the watches so we were eight hours on and four off. It was starting to take its toll on us. While Pam and I were on, waves were breaking over our heads into the cockpit. We just looked at each other and smiled a wet grin and continued gritting our teeth. We also had to watch that not even matches fell to the well of the cockpit, as they could block the scuttles where water escaped. Often waves breaking over us would fill the cockpit and if another one hit us before the water had a chance to drain back out into the sea, we could be goners. We were literally pillars of salt as the seawater had more than permeated our foul weather gear. We didn't even take off our gear for our four-hour break, but rather just collapsed on the floor of the salon as we were.

Again the seas seemed to be getting higher as did the wind, maybe because the night accentuates everything. Then I thought I saw lights just off our bow. Then they disappeared. But suddenly we were upon a giant oil rig, one of those cities on stilts. The stilts, or legs of the rigs were wider than our boat was long. And the waves of the Gulf seemed to want to crash us into them. We actually had to fight our way past them through the howling winds and rain and down from the peaks of crashing waves. The giant of the Gulf disappeared behind us, but there were others to dodge throughout the night. It was as dawn approached that we were about to come right under a rig that had no lights on it. It was a derelict oil platform, but they were supposed to at least have some lights on them. This had none visible at all. We were about to get sucked under a skyscraper of twisted metal. Bob went about and we changed course for the first time on a different tack. This is the stuff nightmares are made of.

I really started wondering, are we going to make it? And what if we don't. What about all that stuff I had been hearing and learning about being saved. Was I saved? I had the natural feeling to think I might have been, but I wasn't. I did call out to God to be with us and protect us, and to bring us home safely in case He could hear me anyway. I had hoped that because by His Grace I had been saved so many times from destruction, that He would save me one more time. The hope that He wasn't finished with me yet, and that I wasn't finished with Him yet, gave me some sense of security. But in actuality, I deserved to die and then I would have spent eternity in Hell, and in permanent separation from God. I remembered hearing that at the Bible College. After searching for the truth for so long, I certainly didn't want that. I thought about just giving myself to the Lord then and there, at this place where He had brought me to scare the hell out of me, but I still didn't. What was wrong with me? Am I stupid? Or was I really confident we would be ok and I could do that later. I can't tell you the answer.

"Peter, go on below and get some rest. The wind is letting up some. I can handle it for now," Pammy shouted over the wind. I nodded and told her not to hesitate shouting at me if she needed me. I was asleep in seconds as my body laid on the salon floor squeezed between the centerboard and a chest type seat. Two hours of solid sleep and a giant wave awoke me as I was thrown up the side of the chest. I felt my way toward the hatch in the dark and finally pulled it back just in time to get a big wave in the face. I saw little Pam up there just gritting and grinning and we had a mutual smile. She said all was well and to get some more rest, but I had done that and the quarters became kind of close what with the hatches all closed up so as to not take on water and with no lights at all. I decided I would rather be up on deck and maybe even do something important. Sleep was not my immediate necessity. Survival was numero uno. There seemed no end to this hellacious night, and this vicious storm. But we were still here, and that meant we were going to make it.

Bob had been up on deck with Pam as he had gotten so wet even down below that he figured his best chances were on deck also. So the three of us were finally all together on the watch and had an evaluation meeting. We were in deep doo doo was the grand summary. It was nice to have a sense of humor at this time but I wish we had known how to pray and believe. It would have been so much more comforting.

I had sailed many different waters, and they had their own rhythm. But this was not a beat I remember in any ocean, or even in Vegas or New Orleans. The Gulf was dealing us a beating not a beat. And then two opposing waves seemed to collide just to our starboard causing nothing but white water to come pouring over all of us and filling the cockpit waist high. It was as if some one had just smacked the side of my head, and left me dizzy and wondering 'whaps happen'. *Trashman* seemed to up end us like trashcans and then throw us back up on the curb, but again we landed right side up and survived another moment of terror. I just hoped we wouldn't end up side down and rolling down the street like my favorite trash men in West New York that awoke me every Tuesday dawn outside my apartment with metal cans rolling down the street after bouncing them off a few cars. I would shout at them in a few languages, but to a big "no comprende!"

Or they would say "yo mama". That's what I felt like saying about now. But another wave would cover me up and bury my deteriorating thoughts. I was afraid that my life was beginning to pass in front of me, and that could mean the living end.

Time for a double brandy and a long awaited cigarette. I looked in my compartment below for my carton and the cigs were no place to be found. I asked Bob and Pam if they saw them and they both said they hoped they never see them again. I about tore the boat apart, but still no cigs. I tried not to have a nicotine fit, but not with much success. If I had found them surely they would have been soaking wet, for there was nothing dry on this boat anywhere.

I needed something to calm my fears. Then I remembered how Frank used to whistle and sing hymns, even during storms, when crossing the Atlantic. I decided with no brandy, no cigarettes, no hope for relief, I would try to remember some song and noticed I started whistling a familiar tune. The words, "He walks with me He talks with me", came to mind to the tune. I liked the thought and kept whistling to myself. Somehow I felt calm, at ease and at one with the storm. I remembered about Jesus Who calmed the seas and I prayed that Jesus would calm these seas. Miraculously I now had the hope that I could out last whatever came over the bow next. I never thought of cigarettes again during this sail.

The seas raged on, however, and I had to go forward and release some jammed rigging. I had my harness on and clicked it on and off the lifeline as I moved low and slow up forward. The rain is still blinding as it whips sideways into my eyes and yet I could still feel the bow raise up high like a bucking horse and then shake everyway but loose. I missed my re-snap, and as the wave came over the bow and crashed at my feet spilling tons of water over me I was raised up and miraculously set back down on the deck instead of into the vast waters around us. I said a quick thank you and resnapped onto the lifeline. I finally got to the snag in the sheet and jerked it loose and made my way back to the cockpit. Pam hadn't been able to see what happened to me, but I knew that I had been spared, and I think I knew why. I didn't want to explain to her now, for she probably would have said, "Sure Pete, sure."

During my watch I noticed that I seemed to be in rhythm with the seas and the ship. Bob and Pam said they slept real well and were refreshed to continue the stormy night. We had no idea of where we were but if we were where we guessed, we had two more days till we reached the Florida Keys. During the cloudy windy day the seas became calmer. Could it be? We didn't celebrate yet. We had a long way to go before we did that. Then the stinging rain slowed and finally ended. At about 1600 we spotted a patch of blue. Were we finally going to get a clearing, was it going to be possible to get a sun or star reading with our sextant? This would be really important. Like life, it is hard to know where we are going unless we know where we are. But the patch of blue was not near the sun, and yet the sky at night exploded with stars, which it seemed, I had never seen like this before. The heavens had opened up and so did something inside of me.

We were able to get a good triangulation of stars and plot them on our charts. Dang, we were still on earth! It surely seemed we were elsewhere. The sailing was perfect and we actually had a course to sail that was close to our original course. We had done well, and by nightfall the next day we should be within sight of land, and lights and the Keys.

And so it went, and without my ever thinking of a cigarette. We each slept during our off watch for the first time in four days, or was it five? We had a glorious day of sailing and just about at sundown we saw land, and even some other boats' lights. But we couldn't navigate between all the islands and shoals at night without an engine, and so we decided to get in close enough where we could drop an anchor and spend a safe night in a protected haven. We all three snored that night.

The next morning we cooked a humongous breakfast with everything we could find, and then we started cleaning up the boat as we did our anchors aweigh. We were able to sail exactly where we needed to go to get around channels, and under bridges and into a cove due to a complete wind change from yesterday. But then the wind died some and we would have to go directly into the light wind into a dangerously narrow inlet to our dockage at Marathon.

It was incredulous that we were even here, but we were ecstatic that we would have made a good delivery of *Trashman* and be calling friends at home that night. They had been calling Coast Guard and other ships to be watching out for us, as we were over two days late. The emergency searches were not implemented yet as no distress signals had been reported and we still had two days before we would have been regarded as lost at sea. This was terribly frustrating to Brian and to Bob's girlfriend as well. Was it only me that had only the Lord looking after me? After me!

But before we could call friends back at Fort Lauderdale, we had to get into that harbor. We all agreed on my idea of let's just run aground and we will have plenty of boats wanting to tow us into our harbor. Bob agreed and so with less than two miles to go we aimed for a sand bar on our chart. Beautifully we just came upon the edge of the sand and stopped, at an angle that made no sense unless we were aground. Immediately boats came to us like moths to the flame, and one was big enough to tow us off and carry our burden to the shore. I got up on the bow and while expressing my thanks, threw the skipper a coil of our rope. We were towed right up to the dock and next to a phone booth. We thanked our benefactor and he said he would bring us dinner. Did we like rock shrimp? And beer? I held it back, but there was an expression I had heard around the Bible College, "Praise the Lord!" that I said out loud to myself. With all the phone calls made, and with a boat with electricity, we all showered and did the things that real people do. We sure looked fancy at the dock in our 40' Hinckley, but they never knew how hopeless we had been.

Our new friend had brought us fresh rock shrimp and we cooked them over our grill hanging over the stern while we toasted each other's friendship with champagne. What a night. It was like a wedding it was so special. This was Marathon at its best, to this point. Little did I know what more this Harbor had ahead in God's plans. [29]

But right now I was as happy, yet somber as a groom. I was so glad to finally be enjoying the little niceties of life, but I had come to see death closer than I had ever seen it before. If God was still trying to get my attention, He had it. How does one express thanks to someone he doesn't know who has saved his life in more ways than

---

[29] The Lord had plans in the future for Marathon, using the Gospel Ship painting Frank and I received from the old man at the Seamen's Mission in Gibraltor. See *"Second Arc of the Great Circle."*

one? Who has loved me before I loved them. "Why so pensive?" queried the vivacious Pammy. "I don't know" I replied. "I don't know."

Every Knee Shall Bow

The reunion was jubilant as our friends arrived in Marathon to give us a ride back to Fort Lauderdale, our home. But it didn't seem like my home any more. No place did. I was homeless it seemed. I was here, but that seemed to be nowhere. 'What's happening to me', I wondered. When Bob and Pam and gang dropped me off at my modest motel apartment, I walked in and it felt cold, not warm and cozy.

I sat on the couch even until the sun set and I was immersed in the darkness. I believe hours went by when I heard a kind caring Voice ask me "Are you ready, Peter?" I didn't move. I just started sobbing. I fell down on my knees and managed to say, "I'm sorry, oh Jesus I'm sorry. I have made such a mess of my life, I have just made a big mess. Forgive me Jesus, I'm sorry." After sobbing for a time, I asked God, that if He would take over this mess of a life I would give it to Him, if He would take it, mess that it is. I heard that Voice again saying, "Come Peter, I have been waiting for you. You are one stubborn man, but if you will give yourself to me, and accept the gift of which you know, you will have a home with me. Forever." "Yes Father, yes. I am yours. Thank You Father, oh thank You. I know You have been looking out for me forever. And I have been looking for You, and now I have really found You. I know what Your Son has done for me, He died for me. I should have died, but He died. Oh thank You Father God." My sobbing finally subsided as a peace came over me.

Still, I stayed on my knees for over an hour, I'm sure, as He talked to me and I to Him. It was like the ultimate encounter group session. I had had an unbelievable burden weighing on me, heaviness on my chest, and now it was gone. I was cut free from that anchor, and my sails are full with the breath of the Lord, driving me in the direction He chose as the new Captain of my life. Never again would I be led to run aground, as I had asked Him to "Lead me not into temptation, but deliver me from evil." I released every burden I had upon Him and knew He would handle all of them. How do you spell relief? I remember when I confronted my bio father in the encounter group and the relief that gave me. Now here I was, on the deck with my eternal Father. I have never experienced such relief. My searching was over, but not in vain, rather in fulfillment.

My life seemed to pass in front of me as I saw the times He had saved me from myself. Then I would hear that voice, "I have better plans for you, Peter." My sobbing subsided, I just sat in total peace, totally relieved, cleansed as it were, listening and seeing what He wanted me to see. It seemed to begin with the fire I was saved from as a child. Then the Grace I was given in the desert and in the air and the water. I saw that hippie Frank in St Thomas, whom God had saved and who had found me over and over again to bring me the Word. Frank was the flying fish the Lord brought me during my watch. No one else has ever told me the 'Good News' of God's Son Who came down for the unlovely like me and paid the ransom for me to go to heaven. Only God can do that, and that was in the embodiment of Jesus, One of the three persons in the Deity of God.

I thanked Him for His patience with me. We had circled the stormy Atlantic, following the currents and the winds known as the northern and southern arcs of the great circle. I saw the accidents seven years in a row, and remembered the promise I made to God at that time. He was here to collect. I thought of all the diversions that Satan had jammed in front of me to hinder any spiritual vision I could have had, and which Satan didn't want me to see. And I marveled about the Halloween on which Barb and I were possessed by a demon in Mallorca and saved by the name of Jesus. And I had just been given one more proof of Grace by protecting Pam and Bob and I in that nightmare on the Gulf. That could have been the end of it all.

I saw my life as in an arc going in a time line from my left hand on the floor over to my right hand. Now my soul did a 180-degree turn, and I didn't see an end, but a new beginning. The beginning of the *Second Arc of the Great Circle*.

The
excitement
has
just begun!
Praise Be to God!!!

298

Epilogue

Just when I thought I had learned all my lessons, the Good Lord showed me otherwise. The biggest lesson I was to learn was that He was to change me, not me change me, or Him! Because the victory is the Lord's.

There were still disciplinary lessons I was yet to learn. I thought I would never run aground in my life again. I never wanted to be stranded on a sand bar or a reef and look like a shipwreck again. But until I learned to stand properly on the Rock, which I am still gladly learning, I stubbed my keel more than once on hidden disasters. I was now a pawn of the Devil, and he knew it. I was a threat to his reputation because I was saved by the Blood shed by Jesus. That made me a target rather than just a player. I still have much to learn about the Grace of God, yet I am here to tell anyone who wants to go through the excitement with me that life has just begun! This is just the beginning of eternal life with the Lord, and an end to death with Satan.

Let me be encouraging rather than otherwise. God will permit what we allow to open our self to by not obeying Him or just being ignorant. But He will also give us the Grace, the provision, to get through the lesson to be learned. And this is the real beginning of a new life for us. Do we live in the will of God, or keep messing up due to ego or pride or just plain stupidity? The important truth is that once we have accepted God's plan of salvation and given Him our self, no one can pluck us from His promise to us of eternal life with Him. No One!

Can we count the times of Grace and Mercy we see behind us in the rear view mirror of life? Not really, because every time we look back, we see more. But even more important is what we see ahead and the perspective of our lives held up to the light of eternal life. [30]

---

[30] Amazing Grace: A wretch like me now has a wonderful family including a daughter named Mercy and a granddaughter by son Aaron and Kelly, named Grace Kelly Cannon. All by coincidence? Don't think so.

Thank you for hearing the first verse of my song, and God Bless you as you go and grow. And now I hope you will voyage with me on the ***Second Arc of the Great Circle*** of life.

About the Author

The First Arc of the Great Circle is about the author. But as Peter has written, this book is neither about him, nor about you, but about Grace. Without giving too much away in *The Second Arc of the Great Circle,* Peter Cannon is currently touring the country visiting people, (maybe you) who have emailed him about their story of similar wonders in their lives and want to tell their story.

Once you have finished the *First Arc of the Great Circle* he would like to hear from you. You don't have to write him, but it is rare when an Author gives this opportunity: *petergun1210@yahoo.com* or his web site at www.1starc.com

Presently, Peter is married to his wife of over two decades, Susan. They are the very proud parents of three great children: Mercy, finishing her PhD at the University of Tennessee with husband Paul who is cloning cows to help rid them of diseases; Aaron, in food management in MN, married to Kelly and have the spoiled first grandchild Grace Kelly Cannon; and Stephen who is finishing plans to attend college in MN to be near big brother. The whole family hope to be together there to watch Stephen play soccer each fall.

Printed in the United States
997800003B